中国绿色金融发展报告
China Green Finance Progress Report

2020

中国人民银行研究局 编著

中国金融出版社

责任编辑：马海敏
责任校对：潘　洁
责任印制：张也男

图书在版编目（CIP）数据

中国绿色金融发展报告. 2020=China Green Finance Progress Report（2020）/中国人民银行研究局编著. —北京：中国金融出版社，2021.11

ISBN 978-7-5220-1368-8

Ⅰ. ①中… Ⅱ. ①中… Ⅲ. ①金融业—经济发展—研究报告—中国—2020 Ⅳ. ①F832

中国版本图书馆CIP数据核字（2021）第215669号

中国绿色金融发展报告（2020）
ZHONGGUO LÜSE JINRONG FAZHAN BAOGAO（2020）

出版
发行　中国金融出版社

社址　北京市丰台区益泽路2号
市场开发部　（010）66024766，63805472，63439533（传真）
网上书店　www.cfph.cn
　　　　　（010）66024766，63372837（传真）
读者服务部　（010）66070833，62568380
邮编　100071
经销　新华书店
印刷　北京侨友印刷有限公司
尺寸　210毫米×285毫米
印张　14.5
字数　258千
版次　2021年11月第1版
印次　2021年11月第1次印刷
定价　168.00元
ISBN 978-7-5220-1368-8
如出现印装错误本社负责调换　联系电话（010）63263947

《中国绿色金融发展报告（2020）》编写组

主　　编： 王　信
副 主 编： 雷　曜
统　　稿： 杨　娉
编写人员： 李妍妮　王　琰　韩鑫韬　余剑科　管晓明　张薇薇　续　猛
邢秉昆　杨鸿森　郭黎萱　程艳芬　蔡春春　车士义　张炎涛
毛奇正　贺　坤　葛志苏　王湃涵　滕　锐　戚雅林　高　明
刘维特　许　欢　曲维民　郭　苑　程翠云　林岚岚　刘宁琳
殷　帅　艾　攀　杨　鑫　倪政琴　许哲萍　韩　宁　李秋菊
董彦萌　史佳乐　王　炫　杜　健　肖　侃　刘嘉龙　程　琳
袁　萍　张宣传　蔡恒培　刘　弘　李海平　朱　缀　刘利红
徐振鑫　温亚桓　吴逾峰　郁志坚　陈思梦　巍　川　杨文博
褚　丽　姚　敏　徐世龙　唐方琦　徐韶华　盛　未　史祎红
商　瑾　李荣丽　郭正江　任秋潇　李卫娥　兰　陈　殷晨辰
张静文　崔艳梅　高惟凌　龙　欢　段　炼　王文　彭建良
陈亚芹　沈忠泉　彭　然　田　波　董善宁　李　博　周宗天华
华　楠　陈　荃　周　殷　陈　倪　张向飞　盼　刘景允
綦久竑　杨捷汉　林　殷　郭沛源　沈双波　李　悦　郭思彤
王顺利　金子盛　陆文钦　关　睿　袁　田
安国俊　廖　原

提供材料： 中国人民银行货政司、市场司、调统司、科技司、国际司、征信局，发展改革委环资司、财金司，财政部金融司，生态环境部综合司、气候司，住房和城乡建设部标准定额司、科技与产业化发展中心，银保监会政策研究局、财险部，证监会债券部、中证金融研究院，银行间市场交易商协会，中国证券投资基金业协会，中国保险资产管理业协会，中国金融学会绿色金融专业委员会，中国人民银行广州分行、营业管理部、重庆营管部、南昌中支、贵阳中支、兰州中支、乌鲁木齐中支、深圳市中支、太原中支、湖州市中支、衢州市中支，中央国债登记结算有限责任公司，中国进出口银行，中国农业发展银行，中国工商银行，中国农业银行，中国银行，中国建设银行，兴业银行，华夏银行，江苏银行，湖州银行，丝路基金，中国再保险集团，中国人保财险股份有限公司，北京绿色交易所，深圳排放权交易所，中诚信绿金科技（北京）有限公司，联合赤道环境评价有限公司，中节能咨询有限公司，北京商道融绿咨询有限公司，中航信托股份有限公司，联合国环境规划署，中国社科院金融研究所

目 录

第一章　概要 ·· 1

第二章　绿色金融制度安排不断完善 ································· 8
　　第一节　积极响应国家战略 ·· 8
　　第二节　持续完善制度机制 ·· 10
　　第三节　试点先行　以点带面 ·· 14
　　第四节　鼓励绿色金融产品和服务创新 ························ 15

第三章　绿色金融市场稳步发展 ·· 17
　　第一节　绿色信贷市场保持高速增长 ···························· 17
　　第二节　绿色证券市场稳步发展 ···································· 22
　　第三节　绿色保险的风险保障作用继续扩大 ················ 34
　　第四节　绿色基金与绿色PPP创新发展 ························ 38
　　第五节　环境权益市场发展进入快车道 ························ 40
　　第六节　绿色信托项目环境效益进一步显现 ················ 42

第四章　绿色金融基层实践成效显著 ···································· 45
　　第一节　绿色金融改革创新试验区建设深入推进 ········ 46
　　第二节　其他地区绿色金融改革创新广泛开展 ············ 55
　　第三节　绿色金融支持污染防治和民生重点领域 ········ 58

目 录

第五章 绿色金融国际合作深入开展…………………………… **67**

    第一节 "一带一路"绿色金融合作取得积极进展………… 67

    第二节 参与和引领绿色金融多边国际合作……………… 71

    第三节 绿色金融双边合作取得新进展…………………… 79

    第四节 市场机构的国际合作实践更加丰富……………… 81

第六章 绿色金融任重道远………………………………………… **84**

附录一 2020年绿色金融大事记………………………………… **87**

附录二 2020年绿色金融主要政策文件………………………… **91**

附录三 2020年绿色金融标准体系建设成果一览……………… **93**

目 录

专栏

专栏1-1	全球绿色复苏共识	3
专栏3-1	2020年绿色贷款结构分析	19
专栏3-2	绿色信贷产品和服务创新案例	20
专栏3-3	2020年绿色债务融资工具概览	24
专栏3-4	疫情防控债	29
专栏3-5	绿色保险创新	36
专栏3-6	核能保险创新实践	37
专栏3-7	绿色基金创新案例	39
专栏3-8	绿色信托创新案例	44
专栏4-1	湖州发布全国首个区域性环境信息披露报告	51
专栏4-2	绿色金融与绿色建筑协同发展案例	60
专栏4-3	绿色金融支持黑臭水体整治的广东实践	65
专栏5-1	气候和环境风险评估工具箱简介	69
专栏5-2	《金融机构环境风险分析综述》简介	72
专栏5-3	绿色金融标准中外一致性研究取得积极进展	74
专栏5-4	可持续蓝色经济金融原则	77
专栏5-5	积极发挥转贷优势，推动国际可持续发展	81

第一章 概要

科学构建绿色金融体系，是深入贯彻落实习近平新时代中国特色社会主义思想的重要举措，是生态文明体制改革的重要任务，是金融供给侧结构性改革的重要内容，也是推动我国经济社会绿色低碳高质量发展的强大内生动力。2020年，面临新冠肺炎疫情全球蔓延带来的严峻挑战，以及提出碳达峰、碳中和目标愿景这一巨大历史机遇，中国绿色金融以聚焦绿色低碳高质量发展为首要任务和根本遵循，着力完善政策框架和标准体系，不断丰富产品工具和服务模式，持续深化绿色金融区域改革和国际合作，成绩斐然。在推动实现"绿水青山"与"金山银山"相互转化的同时，为提升我国金融业的适应性、竞争力和普惠性，构建中国特色现代金融体系作出重要贡献，谱写了绿色金融发展的新篇章。

一、全球绿色发展面临新挑战和新机遇

2020年，新冠肺炎疫情全面暴发、迅速蔓延，全球经济陷入第二次世界大战以来最严重的衰退，国际金融市场剧烈震荡。受此影响，全球绿色发展和气候风险防范面临一系列新挑战和新问题，发展路径遭受多维冲击。

一是国际碳排放进程被扭曲。疫情导致国际交往和经济活动停滞，全球碳排放水平显著下降。国际能源署（IEA）预测，2020年全球与能源相关的二氧化碳排放量减少近20亿吨，同比下降5.8%，为第二次世界大战以来最大年度降幅。由此导致碳配额供过于求、碳排放权市场价格下跌、碳价格形成机制失灵。

二是疫情冲击累及绿色发展政策出台。从国际层面看，第二十六届联合国气候变化大会（COP26）、《生物多样性公约》第十五次缔约方大会、第二届联合国可持续交通

大会等重要会议延期，全球绿色治理机制的作用被弱化。首个全球性行业减排计划——国际航空碳抵消和减排计划（CORSIA）被打乱[1]，航空业减排不确定性上升。从国家层面看，疫情导致各国公共债务大幅攀升，财力不足问题延缓绿色低碳转型进程。

三是经济刺激政策或利好高碳行业，强化高碳锁定。大部分国家推出的经济复苏计划以抗击疫情、保障民生和降低经济危机风险为重点，绿色元素不足。牛津经济复苏项目与联合国环境规划署（UNEP）牵头发布的报告《我们是否正在"更好地重建"？》[2]显示，2020年全球50个主要经济体已公布的用于应对新冠肺炎疫情的支出共14.6万亿美元，其中用于绿色复苏的支出仅3 410亿美元。究其原因，一方面，煤炭、钢铁等高碳行业多为重资产行业，企业规模较大、行业份额占比较高、信用评级较好，在大规模量化宽松和资产购买计划中更容易得到资金支持。另一方面，为防止经济持续快速衰退，部分国家放松了对高碳行业的环保要求，进一步强化了经济发展路径对高碳行业和高碳项目的依赖。

四是疫情冲击增加了气候变化相关金融风险隐患。全球大多数经济体采取了大规模货币刺激政策，在短期内为抗击疫情提供有力支持的同时，也面临退出难题。未来，低利率、负利率环境可能长期存在，气候变化相关金融风险的应对将面临更加复杂的局面。保险公司资产负债表承压、能源企业资产贬值和转型风险加剧、货币政策当局政策空间不足、欠发达国家和地区更容易受到冲击等问题尤其值得关注。

福祸相依、危中有机。面对一系列问题和挑战，绿色复苏逐步成为全球共识和提振经济的重要发力点，绿色金融也迎来新的发展机遇和空间。从全球看，国际能源署（IEA）在《2050净零排放：全球能源行业路线图》中指出，到2030年，年度能源投资在净零情景下将增至5万亿美元，比每年全球GDP增长率还高0.4个百分点。根据政府间气候变化专门委员会的估计，若2050年将温升幅度控制在2℃以内，每年需投资3万亿美元，对低碳能源技术和能源效率的年度投资需在2015年的基础上增加约5倍。从国内

---

[1] 国际航空碳抵消和减排计划（CORSIA）是首个全球性行业减排计划。截至2020年初，已有82个国家和地区自愿加入第一个控制期，覆盖全球民用航空业77%的碳排放量。国际民用航空组织（ICAO）原计划，以2019年和2020年为基准年，即航空公司以2019年和2020年的平均排放水平为基准线，并为该基准线以上的增量支付费用。受疫情影响，许多航空公司大幅削减航班，2020年全球航空业的碳排放量预计将减少37%。2020年6月30日，针对基准年排放量的非正常下降，国际民用航空组织36个成员国的理事会决定，至少在国际航空碳抵消和减排计划实施的前三年，将基准线调整为2019年的排放水平。国际航空运输协会（IATA）对这一调整方案表示支持。2022年，国际民用航空组织大会将审议是否需要进一步修正基准线，这增加了航空业减排的不确定性。

[2] Are we Building Back Better? Evidence from 2020 and Pathways to Inclusive Green Recovery Spending.

看，对于实现碳达峰和碳中和的资金需求，各方面有不少测算，规模级别都是百万亿元人民币。这样巨大的资金需求，政府资金只能覆盖很小一部分，缺口要靠市场资金弥补。这就需要建立、完善绿色金融政策体系，引导和激励金融体系以市场化的方式支持绿色投融资活动。

专栏1-1

全球绿色复苏共识

2020年以来，为应对新冠肺炎疫情冲击，国际社会强调疫情后世界复苏需"重建更好的世界"（Build Back Better），"绿色复苏"受到全球各国高度重视。

国际组织积极督促各国实行"绿色复苏"。联合国秘书长古特雷斯表示，当前的危机以前所未有的方式给我们敲响了警钟，正是经济"由灰变绿"的契机，各国政府应推动"绿色复苏"，并提出"通过清洁生产和绿色转型提供新的就业和商机""拯救企业必须与实现绿色就业和可持续增长挂钩"等六点行动建议。世界银行提出"可持续性要素核查表"，包括气候适应和去碳两大类要素，指导各国政府考量其经济复苏计划。国际货币基金组织、国际能源署等机构均督促各国政府利用经济重启之机向净零排放目标迈进。非洲开发银行行长阿德西纳表示，新冠肺炎疫情和沙漠蝗虫侵袭是非洲的双重危机，须将更多资源用于健康、环境保护和气候适应。

多国力推"绿色复苏"计划。继2019年12月《绿色新政》中明确提出到2050年率先在全球实现"碳中和"目标后，欧盟27国领导人于2020年7月21日就疫后经济复苏基金和未来7年预算达成历史性协议，将总额高达1.8243万亿欧元的资金用于疫后重建，突出绿色发展和数字转型，其中30%将用于资助与气候相关的政策和项目，为欧盟"绿色复苏"提供资金保障。德国宣布了总规模1 300亿欧元的一揽子经济复苏计划，包括拨款500亿欧元用于推动电动汽车发展及设立更多充电桩、支持德国铁路和公共交通企业等内容。韩国是世界第七大温室气体排放国，燃煤发电约占全国能源的40%。7月14日，韩国总统文在寅表示，未来5年在"绿色新政"上投入946亿美元，大力发展以数字技术为动力的环境友好产业，包括电动和氢动力汽车、智能电网和远程医疗等，并摆脱对化石燃料的依赖。美国总统拜登上任首日即宣布美国重返《巴黎协定》，提出"清洁能源革命和绿色正义"计划，承诺美国不迟于2050年实现净零排放。非洲国家普遍感到深陷"新冠—气候双危机"，5月25日发布了一份由加蓬共和国总统牵头撰写、非洲各国领导人支持的报告，建议各国刺激计划聚焦有韧性的基础设施、食品和水安全。法国、英国、丹麦等经济体也推出了"绿色复苏"计划或更高减排目标。

绿色金融正日益成为疫后绿色发展的重要动力。绿色投资、可持续投资等理念在国际资本市场日益主流化。据德意志银行测算，全球环境、社会和治理（ESG）投资规模到2030年将达到135万亿美元，占总资产规模的95%。欧美金融机构对疫后低碳发展表现出更大决心，也在积极主导绿色金融规则标准制定。英国能源部长在7月15日表示英国政府计划打造"绿色投资银行2.0"，以确保实现2050碳中和目标。7月20日，摩根士丹利表示将正式加入碳会计财务伙伴关系（PCAF）[①]组织，成为首家公开披露其贷款和投资业务碳排放的美国大型银行，并将帮助PCAF制定全球碳会计标准，供所有金融机构使用。

绿色生产生活方式日益成为新常态。远程办公、视频会议、在线教育、互联网医疗等低碳生产生活方式在疫情期间迅速普及。产业界积极推进这一转型过程。5月4日，法国92位工业企业领袖联名刊文承诺，"以社会正义之名将环境置于经济复苏的核心"。5月11日，世界经济论坛成立欧洲绿色政纲首席执行官行动小组，旨在带动、支持和鼓励欧洲企业界专注绿色复苏。7月21日，苹果公司宣布计划到2030年，在整个业务、生产供应链及产品生命周期实现碳中和。马士基、微软等9家跨国企业也发起成立了净零碳排放联盟。

二、中国绿色金融发展开启新篇章

作为全球经济的重要引擎，中国高度重视绿色复苏、加速推动低碳转型。无论是

[①] PCAF于2019年启动，其66个正式成员包括来自世界各地的金融机构，资产超过5.3万亿美元。该机构将计算并标准化由资产管理公司、银行和其他机构资助的项目所产生的温室气体排放。

2020年《政府工作报告》提出的"两新一重"[①]建设任务，还是国家"六稳"工作和"六保"任务[②]，都对绿色复苏、绿色产业升级和资源优化配置提出新的更高的要求，也给绿色金融发展提供了新的空间和机遇。尤其是在2020年9月召开的第75届联合国大会上，国家主席习近平郑重承诺"力争于2030年前实现碳达峰、努力争取2060年前实现碳中和"目标愿景，我国气候和环境约束进一步增强，绿色金融迎来新的发展机遇，取得一系列新成绩和新突破。对内，我们撸起袖子加油干，认真办好自己的事。绿色金融在全社会范围内逐步实现从蓝图和理念到选择和行动的跨越，日益成为地方政府和市场主体的自发选择。对外，我们秉持大国责任感，积极以绿色金融发展助推人类命运共同体建设。目前，中国绿色金融体系的五大支柱基本形成。

一是绿色金融标准体系加快构建。绿色金融的关键不是事后"统计绿"，而是规则"引导绿"。2018年人民银行牵头成立全国金融标准化技术委员会绿色金融标准工作组后，重点聚焦气候变化、污染治理和节能减排三大领域，遵循"国内统一、国际接轨"的原则推动建立和完善跨领域、市场化、具有权威性且内嵌于金融机构全业务流程的绿色金融标准体系。截至2020年末，已有1项国际标准获国际标准化组织可持续金融技术委员会（ISO/TC322）投票通过并提交发布，有1项国家标准经国家标准化管理委员会批准正式立项，有5项行业标准已完成送审稿，有4项标准草案在绿色金融改革创新试验区先行先试。

二是信息披露要求和金融机构监管不断强化。监管部门不断推动金融机构、证券发行人、公共部门分类提升环境信息披露的强制性和规范性，着力提升绿色金融市场透明度。中英金融机构环境信息披露试点工作不断推进，中方参与机构扩展至15家，试点经验已初步具备复制推广价值。组织金融机构和部分地区试点开展环境风险压力测试，探索将气候和环境相关风险纳入监管框架。

三是激励约束机制逐步完善。在绿色信贷业绩评价基础上进一步完善绿色金融评价机制，引导金融机构增加绿色资产配置，为中央银行应对气候变化预留政策空间。环境执法信息主动采集机制逐步完善，"褒扬诚信、惩戒失信"的社会信用体系建设加快推进。绿色金融改革创新试验区积极创新财政支持和监管政策，加大绿色项目投入和精准

---

① "两新"指新型基础设施和新型城镇化，"一重"指交通、水利等重大工程。
② "六稳"指稳就业、稳金融、稳外贸、稳外资、稳投资、稳预期，"六保"指保居民就业、保基本民生、保市场主体、保粮食能源安全、保产业链供应链稳定、保基层运转。

施策力度，出台一系列政策推动绿色金融改革创新。截至2020年末，试验区绿色贷款余额2368.33亿元，在全部贷款中占比15.14%，比全国平均水平高8.22个百分点。

四是绿色金融产品和市场体系不断丰富。绿色金融产品和服务是直达实体经济、传递政策意图的最直接途径。通过鼓励产品创新、完善发行制度、规范交易流程、提升透明度，中国已形成包括绿色贷款、绿色债券、绿色保险、绿色基金、绿色信托、碳金融产品等在内的多层次绿色金融产品和市场体系，为绿色项目提供了多元化的融资渠道，识别和服务绿色低碳发展的效率不断提升。截至2020年末，中国本外币绿色贷款余额11.95万亿元，存量规模居全球第一；绿色债券存量规模8 132亿元，居世界第二。绿色金融资产质量整体良好，截至2020年末，绿色贷款不良率为0.33%，比同期企业贷款不良率低1.65个百分点，绿色债券无违约案例。

五是绿色金融国际合作日益深化。中国积极利用各类多双边平台及合作机制推动绿色金融国际交往，提升国际社会对中国绿色金融政策、标准、产品、市场的认可和参与程度，在讲好中国故事中提升绿色金融国际话语权，有效引领绿色金融国际主流化进程。人民银行参与发起的央行与监管机构绿色金融网络（NGFS）已扩展至84家正式成员和13家观察机构。银保监会参与发起的可持续银行网络（SBN），在促进发展中国家加强绿色金融合作交流中发挥着日益重要的作用。中欧等经济体共同发起可持续金融国际平台（IPSF），重点推动全球绿色金融标准趋同等工作。绿色金融持续成为中英、中法高级别财金对话和"一带一路"建设的重点议题。

三、绿色金融发展空间广阔

生态文明建设任重道远，绿色金融发展空间广阔。当前，中国正处于经济社会加快恢复发展、全面建成小康社会的关键时期，又是"十四五"和全面建设社会主义现代化国家新征程的开局之年，贯彻新发展理念，主动探索新的绿色复苏道路，引领后疫情时代世界经济健康发展方向，具有重大现实意义。从国内看，短期内，这是做好"六稳"工作、落实"六保"任务、有效抗击疫情的有效途径；中长期，这是培育中国经济新增长点、增强经济发展韧性和可持续性、走向高质量现代化发展的内在要求，也是提高金融体系自身适应性、竞争力和普惠性，建设金融强国的必然选择。从世界范围看，绿色复苏有助于推动中国在可持续发展领域的国际合作，彰显负责任大国形象。从重点任务看，2021年要着力推动强制性气候和环境信息披露制度、继续完善绿色金融评价体系、创新推出碳减排支持工具、以碳达峰和碳中和为约束条件进一步完善绿色金融标准体系、持续推进地方绿色金融试点和国际合作等。

展望未来，金融业必将不辱使命，不断提高政治站位，聚焦碳达峰、碳中和目标愿景，大力推动绿色金融改革创新，为绿色低碳发展国家战略和人类命运共同体建设持续贡献力量。

第二章 绿色金融制度安排不断完善

2020年,绿色金融政策体系进一步完善,绿色金融标准体系加快建设,激励约束机制进一步优化,成为中国绿色金融快速发展和市场规模持续扩大的重要基石。

第一节 积极响应国家战略

一、构建现代环境治理体系

2020年2月,中共中央办公厅、国务院办公厅印发《关于构建现代环境治理体系的指导意见》,提出"设立国家绿色发展基金。推动环境污染责任保险发展,在环境高风险领域研究建立环境污染强制责任保险制度。开展排污权交易,研究探索对排污权交易进行抵质押融资。鼓励发展重大环保装备融资租赁。加快建立省级土壤污染防治基金。统一国内绿色债券标准。"

二、建立健全绿色低碳循环发展经济体系

12月,中央经济工作会议在北京举行,将做好碳达峰、碳中和工作确定为2021年要抓好的八大重点任务之一。会议要求,抓紧制定2030年前碳排放达峰行动方案,支持有条件的地方率先达峰;加快调整优化产业结构、能源结构,推动煤炭消费尽早达峰,大

力发展新能源，加快建设全国用能权、碳排放权交易市场，完善能源消费双控制度；继续打好污染防治攻坚战，实现减污降碳协同效应；开展大规模国土绿化行动，提升生态系统碳汇能力。

12月30日，中央全面深化改革委员会第十七次会议审议通过《关于加快建立健全绿色低碳循环发展经济体系的指导意见》，提出大力发展绿色金融。发展绿色信贷和绿色直接融资，加大对金融机构绿色金融评价考核力度。统一绿色债券标准，建立绿色债券评级标准。发展绿色保险，发挥保险费率调节机制作用。支持符合条件的绿色产业企业上市融资。支持金融机构和相关企业在国际市场开展绿色融资。推动国际绿色金融标准趋同，有序推进绿色金融市场双向开放。推动气候投融资工作。

三、设立国家绿色发展基金，推广PPP模式

7月，财政部会同生态环境部、上海市政府正式发起设立国家绿色发展基金。基金落户上海，首期规模885亿元，由中央财政和长江经济带沿线11省（市）地方财政共同出资，同时也吸引社会资本参与，以公司制形式进行市场化运作。基金在首期存续期间以长江经济带为重点投资区域，聚焦生态环境保护修复和相关绿色产业发展，推动经济结构调整和绿色转型。

此外，财政部会同有关方面坚持规范推广运用政府和社会资本合作（PPP）模式，引导社会资本参与绿色低碳项目投资建设运营，在缓解绿色发展资金压力、改善城乡生态环境等方面发挥了积极作用。

四、强化绿色金融支持应对气候变化

10月，生态环境部、发展改革委、人民银行、银保监会等五部委联合印发《关于促进应对气候变化的投融资的指导意见》（环气候〔2020〕57号），以助力碳达峰、碳中和为目标，大力推动应对气候变化投融资发展，鼓励银行保险机构在风险可控、商业可持续的前提下，开发气候友好的绿色金融产品，对重大气候项目提供有效的金融支持，促进经济社会低碳绿色转型。

五、完善金融支持绿色环保产业发展政策

5月，发展改革委、科技部、工业和信息化部等六部门联合印发《关于营造更好发展环境 支持民营节能环保企业健康发展的实施意见》（发改环资〔2020〕790号），鼓励金融机构将环境、社会、治理要求纳入业务流程，提升对民营节能环保企业的绿色金融专业服务水平，大力发展绿色融资。积极发展绿色信贷，加强国家重大节能环保项目的信息沟通，对符合条件的项目加大融资支持力度。支持符合条件的民营节能环保企业发行绿色债券，统一国内绿色债券界定标准，发布与《绿色产业指导目录（2019年版）》相一致的绿色债券支持项目目录。拓宽节能环保产业增信方式，积极探索将用能权、碳排放权、排污权、合同能源管理未来收益权、特许经营收费权等纳入融资质押担保范围。7月和12月，发展改革委会同有关部门，先后印发《关于组织开展绿色产业示范基地建设的通知》（发改办环资〔2020〕519号）、《关于印发绿色产业示范基地名单的通知》（发改办环资〔2020〕979号），要求强化政策支持，加大绿色信贷、绿色债券的支持力度，支持绿色产业示范基地开展绿色金融创新。

第二节 持续完善制度机制

一、夯实绿色金融标准体系

绿色金融标准是更好发挥市场服务功能、增强金融服务实体经济能力的重要保障。2020年，中国绿色金融标准研制工作按照"国内统一、国际接轨、清晰可执行"的原则持续推进，初步形成政府引导、市场驱动、社会参与、协同推进的工作格局，多项工作取得显著进展。

（一）国内绿色金融标准的制定与实施稳步推进

人民银行依托全国金融标准化技术委员会绿色金融标准工作组、会同有关部门和市场机构，按照"需求导向，急用先行"原则，有效推动一批重要绿色金融标准编制。截至2020年末，《绿色金融术语》国家标准已正式立项，将成为界定绿色金融内涵与外延

的基础通用标准。《绿色债券信用评级规范》《金融机构环境信息披露指南》《环境权益融资工具》《绿色私募股权投资基金基本要求》《碳金融产品》5项行业标准已完成送审稿，《上市公司环境信息披露》行业标准正在申请立项，将为绿色金融产品和服务的规范发展提供有力支撑。

2月，人民银行办公厅印发《关于在绿色金融改革创新试验区试行部分绿色金融标准的通知》（银办发〔2020〕15号），《绿色金融术语》等4项标准的草案在绿色金融改革创新试验区率先试用。

（二）金融标准创新建设试点完成总结验收

2020年末，人民银行联合银保监会、证监会和国家标准委在重庆市、浙江省开展的金融标准创新建设试点完成总结验收，绿色金融标准创新和实施作为试点重要内容之一成效显著。其中，重庆市依托重庆市金融学会，成立绿色金融专业委员会和金融标准化委员会，制定《绿色信贷基础数据元》团体标准，在"长江绿融通"绿色金融大数据综合服务系统实施；推动重庆银行制定《绿色信贷业务流程规范》《绿色债券信息披露规范》等企业标准，约束金融机构合规有序开展绿色金融服务。

（三）绿色金融标准国际接轨取得积极成果

中国和欧盟积极推动绿色分类标准趋同。2020年10月，人民银行与欧盟相关部门在可持续金融国际平台（IPSF）下成立专项工作组，研究对比中欧绿色分类标准异同，提出中欧标准趋同路径，研究构建中欧双方认可的绿色金融/可持续金融共同分类标准，为推动中欧绿色金融市场协同发展奠定基础。

人民银行持续参与国际标准化组织可持续金融技术委员会（ISO/TC 322）的工作。中国专家牵头编制的《可持续金融 基本概念和关键倡议》即将发布，将为可持续金融活动提供国际通用的基础参考。12月，ISO/TC 322第三次全体会议召开。会上，中国专家提出制定《可持续私募股权投资基金基本要求》等2项国际标准，技术委员会将其确立为预备工作项目（PWI）。中国专家还参与了《可持续金融框架：原则和指南》等国际标准研制。此外，为更好统筹国内外绿色可持续金融标准化工作，国内相关机构共同派出专家，组建了ISO/TC 322对口工作组，为参与可持续金融国际标准制定提供支持与保障。

二、完善绿色融资统计制度

2020年6月，银保监会办公厅印发《关于绿色融资统计制度有关工作的通知》（银保监办便函〔2020〕739号），结合发展改革委、人民银行等部门联合印发的《绿色产业指导目录（2019年版）》，重新界定了绿色融资的范畴和统计口径。根据该通知，绿色融资不仅包括表内贷款和表内绿色债券投资，还包括绿色银行承兑汇票、绿色信用证余额等表外融资。该通知为全面反映银行机构绿色金融实施成效奠定了数据基础，为银行机构更好支持绿色产业发展提供了制度保障。

三、优化绿色债券发行相关业务规则

5月，发展改革委办公厅发布《关于开展2020年度企业债券主承销商和信用评级机构信用评价工作的通知》（发改办财金〔2021〕409号），并委托第三方机构发布评价方案，将证券公司参与绿色债券等企业债券创新品种情况作为重要的业务能力指标进行评分。

11月，上海证券交易所修订注册制配套规则，发布《上海证券交易所公司债券发行上市审核规则适用指引第2号——特定品种公司债券》，设置"绿色公司债券"专章，规范绿色债券募集资金用途、信息披露要求及评估认证安排。

11月，深圳证券交易所发布《深圳证券交易所公司债券创新品种业务指引第1号——绿色公司债券》，对原涉及绿色公司债券业务的通知、指南、问答等业务规则和文件进行优化整合，将具有长期指导规范意义且有条件成熟的内容上升为交易所业务规则，打造简明清晰的公司债券创新产品序列规则体系。该指引对绿色公司债券定义、绿色产业认定标准、第三方评估认证、发行绿色公司债券申报材料和信息披露要求、中介机构核查标准等事项作了明确规定。

四、继续完善信息披露和共享政策

（一）建立环境信息依法披露制度

12月，中央全面深化改革委员会第十七次会议审议通过了《环境信息依法披露制度改革方案》。会议指出，环境信息依法披露是重要的企业环境管理制度，是生态文明制度体系的基础性内容。要针对存在的突出问题，聚焦对生态环境、公众健康和公民利益有重大影响，市场和社会关注度高的企业环境行为，落实企业法定义务，健全披露规范要求，建立协同管理机制，健全监督机制，加强法治化建设，形成企业自律、管理有效、监督严格、支撑有力的环境信息强制性披露制度。

（二）强化上市公司和发债企业环境信息披露监管

3月和6月，深交所先后发布《深圳证券交易所上市公司规范运作指引（2020年修订）》（深证上〔2020〕125号，主板、中小板企业适用）和《深圳证券交易所创业板上市公司规范运作指引（2020年修订）》（深证上〔2020〕499号，创业板企业适用），对社会责任及环境信息披露要求进行了优化，强调上市公司应根据其对环境的影响程度制定整体环境保护政策，指派具体人员负责公司环保体系的建立、实施、保持和跟进，并为环保工作提供必要的人力、物力、技术和财力支持。创业板还新增上市公司在生态环境等领域的技术研发行为规范。

9月，深交所修订《深圳证券交易所上市公司信息披露工作考核办法》，将上市公司履行社会责任的情况纳入考核。重点关注上市公司是否主动披露社会责任报告，是否主动披露环境、社会和治理（ESG）情况，是否主动披露公司积极参与符合国家重大战略方针，报告内容是否充实、完整等信息。

9月，为贯彻落实修订后的《中华人民共和国证券法》，鼓励和规范科创板上市公司自愿开展信息披露，提高自愿信息披露的有效性，防范自愿信息披露中的不当行为，上交所发布了《上海证券交易所科创板上市公司自律监管规则适用指引第2号——自愿信息披露》（上证发〔2020〕70号）。其中第十四条"环境、社会责任和公司治理"规定，科创公司可在根据法律规定，披露环境、社会和治理等一般信息的基础上，根据所在行业、业务特点、治理结构，进一步披露个性化信息。

（三）将环境执法信息纳入金融信用信息基础数据库

人民银行征信中心定期将省级环保部门通过互联网公示的环保执法信息纳入金融信用信息基础数据库，并在信用报告中展示，为金融机构提供参考。截至2020年末，征信系统共采集环保处罚信息12.72万条，涉及9.67万户企业；采集环保许可信息20.88万条，涉及13.44万户企业。2020年，全国共有8 947户企业的环保处罚信息被1 484家金融机构查询190万次，协助金融机构预防企业信贷风险合同4.3万份，涉及金额约合5.6亿元；向金融机构提示有信贷风险的企业1 565户，涉及融资金额171亿元。

第三节 试点先行 以点带面

一、绿色金融改革创新试验区建设制度持续完善

2020年，全国六省（区）九地绿色金融改革创新试验区积极加强政策制定，完善标准，强化激励，推广经验，推动试验区建设再上新台阶。例如，江西出台《江西省绿色票据认定和管理指引（试行）》，在全国率先落地绿色票据标准。广州出台《广州市黄埔区、广州开发区促进绿色金融发展政策措施实施细则》（穗埔府规〔2020〕11号），逐步将花都区绿色金融改革创新经验向全辖推广。浙江湖州印发实施《湖州市重大项目专项贷款和财政绿色专项贴息资金实施办法》，进一步加大财政激励措施，推动辖内经济绿色复苏。

二、部分地区对环境信用失信企业开展跨区域联合惩戒

10月，长三角三省一市（江苏省、浙江省、安徽省和上海市）有关部门共同制定《长三角区域生态环境领域实施信用联合奖惩合作备忘录（2020年版）》，要求根据国家和三省一市已确定的联合奖惩措施，将企业环保信用情况作为长三角区域内企业享受优惠政策和制度便利的重要依据，在行政审批、综合监管、金融服务、行业自律、市场合作等方面，实施全过程信用管理和联合奖惩。

三、绿色金融为区域经济发展提供支撑

2月，人民银行、银保监会、证监会、外汇局、上海市人民政府联合发布《关于进一步加快推进上海国际金融中心建设和金融支持长三角一体化发展的意见》（银发〔2020〕46号），从积极推进临港新片区金融先行先试、在更高水平加快上海金融业对外开放和金融支持长三角一体化发展等方面提出30条具体措施。其中第25条规定，要推

动长三角绿色金融服务平台一体化建设。在长三角推广应用绿色金融信息管理系统，推动区域环境权益交易市场互联互通，加快建立长三角绿色项目库。

5月，人民银行、银保监会、证监会、外汇局联合发布《关于金融支持粤港澳大湾区建设的意见》（银发〔2020〕95号），提出开展碳排放交易外汇试点，研究设立广州期货交易所，构建统一的绿色金融相关标准，鼓励更多大湾区企业利用港澳平台为绿色项目融资及认证，支持广东金融机构在港澳发行绿色金融债券等。这一政策的出台有利于进一步提升粤港澳大湾区在国家经济发展和对外开放中的支持引领作用，为建设富有活力和国际竞争力的一流湾区和世界级城市群提供有力的金融支撑。

第四节　鼓励绿色金融产品和服务创新

一、支持绿色企业利用资本市场直接融资

3月，为落实证监会《关于在上海证券交易所设立科创板并试点注册制的实施意见》中对包括新能源与节能环保在内的产业进行重点支持的要求，上交所发布《上海证券交易所科创板企业发行上市申报及推荐暂行规定》，支持节能环保与新能源行业的发行人申报科创板并在上交所上市融资。

6月，深交所发布《创业板企业发行上市申报及推荐暂行规定》，明确规定支持新能源等符合高新技术产业和战略性新兴产业发展方向的创新创业企业在创业板上市融资。

二、建立健全环境污染责任保险制度

2月，中共中央办公厅、国务院办公厅印发《关于构建现代环境治理体系的指导意见》，明确规定"推动环境污染责任保险发展，在环境高风险领域研究建立环境污染强制责任保险制度"。

9月，《中华人民共和国固体废物污染环境防治法》正式实施，其中第九十九条明确规定，"收集、贮存、运输、利用、处置危险废物的单位，应当按照国家有关规定，

投保环境污染责任保险"。

三、引导基金积极支持绿色发展

3月，证监会修订发布《上市公司创业投资基金股东减持股份的特别规定》，完善反向挂钩政策[①]，引导创业投资基金投早、投小、投长，放宽享受差异化减持政策的标准，简化有关申报程序，促进创业投资基金更便捷退出，实现"投资—退出—再投资"良性循环，推动创业投资基金扶持具有发展潜力的中小型绿色企业，支持绿色金融发展。

四、加快开发环境权益类金融产品

党的十八大报告提出了开展碳排放权交易试点、建立碳排放交易市场的要求。党的十九大报告指出，要加快生态文明体制改革，建立健全绿色、低碳、循环发展的经济体系，启动全国碳排放权交易体系，稳步推进全国碳排放权交易市场建设。2020年10月，生态环境部等五部委共同发布的《关于促进应对气候变化投融资的指导意见》，提出在风险可控的前提下，支持机构及资本积极开发与碳排放权相关的金融产品和服务，有序探索运营碳期货等衍生产品和业务。同年10月9日，经国务院批准成立了广州期货交易所筹备组，筹备组也积极探索碳期货产品的开发与运用。

根据国务院办公厅《关于进一步推进排污权有偿使用和交易试点工作的指导意见》要求，2015年，财政部会同有关部门印发《排污权出让收入管理暂行办法》。在上述政策背景下，财政部积极推进建立排污权有偿使用和交易制度，规范排污权出让收入征收、使用和管理，并引导浙江、江苏等28省（区、市）开展试点工作，发挥市场机制作用促进污染减排。各试点地区稳步推进排污权有偿使用和交易工作，在制度建设、平台搭建、政策创新等方面开展了大量实践，还探索出刷卡排污、排污权抵押贷款等创新做法，产生积极示范效应。

[①] 反向挂钩政策，指的是创投基金所投股份的锁定期与IPO之前的投资期限成反比，即前期投资的时间越长，锁定期越短。

第三章　绿色金融市场稳步发展

2020年，中国充分发挥市场机制在金融资源配置中的基础性作用，支持市场主体创新绿色金融产品、工具和业务模式，推动将环境与气候变化风险纳入金融定价体系，环境风险管理水平不断提升。绿色金融市场保持高速增长，环境效益逐步显现，绿色金融产品和服务更加多元。

第一节　绿色信贷市场保持高速增长

我国金融体系以间接金融为主，绿色贷款在绿色金融体系中占据举足轻重的地位，是实体经济绿色低碳发展的重要资金来源。大力发展绿色信贷，着力完善绿色贷款标准、统计、评价等基础性工作，始终是我国绿色金融体系建设的重要任务。2020年，面对突如其来的严重疫情，我国准确把握疫情形势变化，统筹兼顾、协调推进，成为疫情发生以来第一个恢复增长的主要经济体。绿色贷款持续增长，显示了强大的修复能力和旺盛的生机活力。

一、绿色贷款业务开展情况

（一）全国绿色贷款总体情况

2020年，绿色贷款持续增长。据人民银行统计，截至2020年末，全国绿色贷款余额

11.95万亿元①，在本外币各项贷款余额中占比6.7%；余额比年初增长20.3%，全年增加2.02万亿元。其中，单位绿色贷款余额11.91万亿元，占同期企事业单位贷款余额的10.8%；全年增加2万亿元，占同期企事业单位贷款增量的16.5%。

绿色贷款资产质量总体较高。截至2020年末，绿色不良贷款余额390亿元，不良率为0.33%，比同期企业贷款不良率低1.65个百分点，比年初下降0.24个百分点。其中，基础设施绿色升级领域绿色贷款不良率0.16%；东部地区不良率0.2%。大中型银行绿色贷款不良率分别为0.19%和0.39%，比年初下降0.37个和0.14个百分点。

（二）24家主要银行机构②绿色贷款情况

截至2020年末，24家主要银行机构绿色贷款余额10.33万亿元，比年初增长21.89%，占24家银行各项贷款余额的7.79%。绿色不良贷款余额253.16亿元，不良率0.25%。

从贷款余额看，24家银行2020年末绿色贷款余额最高为22 682亿元，最低为106亿元，均值为4 302.53亿元，中位数为1 845.68亿元。

从贷款余额占各项贷款比例看，24家银行绿色贷款余额占比最高为18.79%，最低为0.84%，均值为5.77%，中位数为5.72%。24家银行中仅两家绿色贷款余额占比超过10%，整体看绿色贷款业务存在较大提升空间。

从贷款余额增速看，24家银行绿色贷款余额比年初增速最高为60.84%，最低为-5.12%，均值为22.62%，中位数为19.99%。

从不良率看，24家银行绿色贷款不良率最高为1.82%，最低为0.07%，均值为0.57%，中位数为0.405%。

---

① 因统计口径和对象范围不完全相同，人民银行绿色贷款统计数据与银保监会绿色信贷统计数据存在一定差异。银保监会对全国21家主要银行机构进行了统计，包括国家开发银行、中国进出口银行、中国农业发展银行、中国工商银行、中国农业银行、中国银行、中国建设银行、交通银行、中国邮政储蓄银行、招商银行、上海浦东发展银行、中信银行、兴业银行、民生银行、光大银行、华夏银行、广发银行、平安银行、恒丰银行、浙商银行和渤海银行。截至2020年末，21家主要银行绿色信贷余额为11.5万亿元。

② 数据来源：人民银行。24家主要银行机构包括国家开发银行、中国进出口银行、中国农业发展银行、中国工商银行、中国农业银行、中国银行、中国建设银行、交通银行、中国邮政储蓄银行、招商银行、上海浦东发展银行、中信银行、兴业银行、民生银行、光大银行、华夏银行、广发银行、平安银行、恒丰银行、浙商银行、渤海银行、北京银行、上海银行和江苏银行。

专栏3-1

2020年绿色贷款结构分析

据人民银行统计，截至2020年末，全国绿色贷款余额11.95万亿元。分用途来看，基础设施绿色升级产业[①]和清洁能源产业贷款余额分别为5.76万亿元和3.2万亿元，分别比年初增长21.3%和13.4%，合计占绿色贷款余额的74.9%。分行业来看，基础设施行业[②]绿色贷款余额为8.86万亿元，比年初增长15.9%，余额占绿色贷款的74.1%。

分地区看，东部、中部地区绿色贷款增长较快，西部和东北地区增速较低。截至2020年末，东部地区[③]绿色贷款余额为5.91万亿元，比年初增长23.5%，增速比全国平均水平高3.2个百分点，全年增加1.12万亿元。中部地区绿色贷款余额为1.97万亿元，比年初增长26.6%，增速比全国平均水平高6.3个百分点，全年增加4 144亿元。西部地区绿色贷款余额为3万亿元，比年初增长14.5%，全年增加3 802亿元。东北地区绿色贷款余额为5 335亿元，比年初增长12.4%，全年增加589亿元。

分机构看，中小型银行绿色贷款增长较快，大型银行绿色贷款用途相对集中。截至2020年末，中资大型银行绿色贷款余额为7.75万亿元，比年初增长20.6%，全年增加1.33万亿元。中资中型银行绿色贷款余额为2.46万亿元，比年初增长25.5%，全年增加5 005亿元。中资小型银行绿色贷款余额为9 421亿元，比年初增长22.4%，全年增加1 723亿元。

[①] 依据《绿色产业指导目录（2019年版）》（发改环资〔2019〕293号文印发），基础设施绿色升级产业包括建筑节能与绿色建筑、绿色交通、环境基础设施、城镇能源基础设施、海绵城市和园林绿化；清洁能源产业包括新能源与清洁能源装备制造、清洁能源设施建设和运营、传统能源清洁高效利用和能源系统高效运行。

[②] 本报告中的基础设施行业指交通运输、仓储和邮政业，电力、热力、燃气及水生产供应业和水利、环境和公共设施管理业。

[③] 东部地区包括北京、天津、河北、上海、江苏、浙江、福建、山东、广东和海南10个省（市）；中部地区包括山西、安徽、江西、河南、湖北和湖南6个省；西部地区包括内蒙古、广西、重庆、四川、贵州、云南、西藏、陕西、甘肃、青海、宁夏和新疆12个省（区、市）；东北地区包括黑龙江、吉林和辽宁3个省。

绿色信贷环境效益逐步显现。据银保监会统计，按照信贷资金占相关绿色项目总投资的比例计算，截至2020年末，国内21家主要银行绿色信贷预计每年可支持节约标准煤3.2亿吨，减排二氧化碳当量7.3亿吨，为实现碳达峰、碳中和目标作出了重要贡献。

专栏3-2

绿色信贷产品和服务创新案例

"碳汇贷"。杭州市余杭区中泰街道以使用当地苦竹生产竹笛著称，拥有全国独一无二的万亩苦竹种质资源基地。邮储银行创新推出"碳汇贷"，面向余杭区中泰街道竹笛产业链经营主体定向发放经营性贷款，贷款用途不局限于竹林抚育，可用于包括种竹、养竹、制笛、售笛及文化推广在内的竹笛产业链内各环节的生产经营。根据项目年固碳量给予专项优惠利率，年利率最低可至3.95%，低于当地市场经营性贷款利率（5%+）105个基点以上。截至2020年末，邮储银行成功发放1笔金额30万元的"碳汇贷"，用于企业日常经营资金周转。

"节水贷"。2020年5月，江苏省财政厅、水利厅与兴业银行合作推出"节水贷"，设立10亿元专项贷款额度，为长江经济带沿线节水型企业复工复产和高质量发展提供专项融资服务。江苏省政府搭建"节水贷"项目平台，筛选合格企业推送给合作银行，重点支持节水技术改造、供水管网改造、非常规水源利用等项目。兴业银行在抵质押率、审批通道、融资成本等方面为符合"节水贷"准入的企业提供便利。2020年，兴业银行共落地"节水贷"项目4笔，融资金额4 300万元。

生态环境导向的开发（Ecology-Oriented Development，EOD）模式融资服务。江苏银行针对沿江生态保护修复等公益性项目融资痛点，探索生态环境治理和产业协同发展的EOD模式，为长江大保护、采煤塌陷地整治等重大项目提供针对性的融资方案。EOD模式下，江苏银行的收益主要来自土地溢价及土地出让收入和产业反哺分成收益。前者最容易实现但缺乏可持续性，后者由于产业培育周期长、不确定性大等因素成功案例较少。江苏银行创造性地将有现金流的经营性项目和无现金流的类公益性项目进行有机结合，妥善解决了南京市某岸线搬迁复绿工程的融资难问题。

二、绿色金融评价情况

2018年7月《关于开展银行业存款类金融机构绿色信贷业绩评价的通知》印发后，人民银行率先对24家主要银行开展了绿色信贷业绩评价。2019年第一季度，业绩评价工作推广至全国银行机构。2020年，24家主要银行业绩评价情况如下。

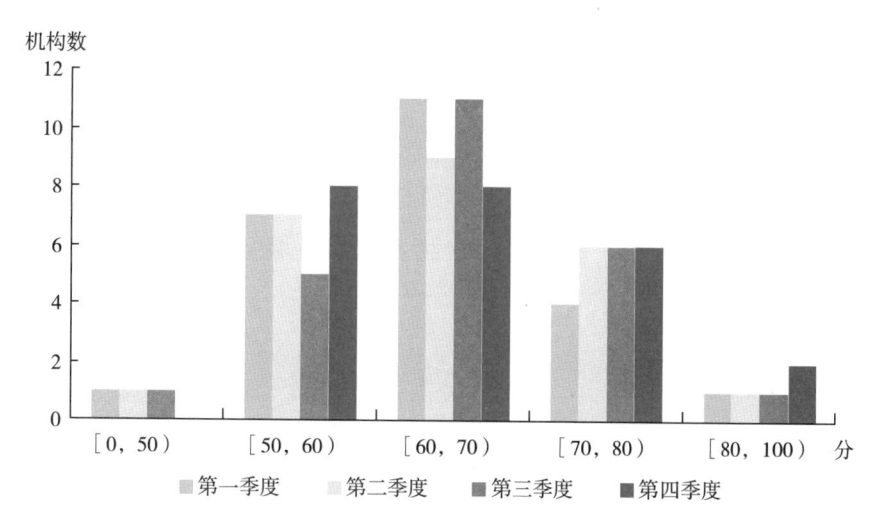

图3-1 2020年24家主要银行绿色信贷业绩评价情况

从结果看，24家银行绿色信贷业绩评价结果总体呈上升趋势，结果集中度不断提高。这表明业绩评价有力提升了银行机构对绿色贷款业务的重视程度，为推动绿色贷款发展创造了良好的激励约束机制。但是，在大型银行（如国家开发银行、中国农业发展银行、中国工商银行、中国建设银行等）、绿色金融特色银行（如兴业银行、华夏银行等）评价结果优势突出的同时，部分城市商业银行得分持续较低的情况仍在延续，还需进一步提高对绿色贷款等绿色金融业务的重视程度。

碳达峰、碳中和目标提出后，我国经济绿色低碳转型的要求更加迫切，绿色低碳领域的投资需求巨大。可以预见，未来实体经济对绿色贷款的需求将进一步增长。下一步，要继续破除绿色贷款发展面临的制约因素，完善绿色贷款业务激励约束机制，为绿色贷款发展创造更加有利的制度和市场环境。

第二节 绿色证券市场稳步发展

一、绿色债券市场对绿色融资需求的适应性提高

2020年，中国绿色债券呈现新特点。市场参与主体日益多元，发行期限进一步丰富，创新型产品不断涌现，绿色债券市场对实体经济绿色融资需求的适应性不断提高；碳达峰、碳中和目标为绿色债券创新发展注入强劲新动力，绿色债券政策支持力度进一步强化。绿色债券债项评级继续维持较高水平，成本优势逐渐凸显，对绿色企业融资持续形成利好，募集资金继续聚焦绿色服务、基础设施绿色升级等绿色产业。

（一）总体发行情况

2020年，境内主体共发行绿色债券约2 580亿元。其中，155个发行主体在境内市场发行各类绿色债券220只，规模合计2 165.82亿元；10个发行主体离岸发行绿色债券17只，规模合计414.2亿元。截至2020年末，境内绿色债券累计发行14 134亿元，存量规模为8 132亿元。全年，中国债券市场共发行各类债券57.3万亿元，同比增长26.5%。其中，绿色债券占比0.3%，较2019年0.6%的水平下降一半。

（二）绿色债券对实体经济的适应性不断提高

1. 市场参与主体日益多元化

2020年，境内绿色债券市场参与主体更加多元，发行、承销、交易等方面均保持活跃。

从发行主体行业分布看，工业部门成为绿色债券发行的重要力量。全年工业部门发行绿色债券1 087.08亿元，占比50.19%，比2019年增加18.47个百分点。公用事业发行占比24.38%，居第二位，同比增加2.19个百分点。金融业发行规模占比居第三位，为17.84%，同比下降17.91个百分点。从2016年金融债在绿色债券中占比超过90%回落至今，绿色债券发行主体不断丰富，实体企业对绿色债券的需求进一步增加。

表3-1　　2020年境内绿色债券按Wind行业一级分类统计

行业分类	债券规模（亿元）	发行规模占比（%）	债券数（只）	发行数量占比（%）
工业	1 087.08	50.19	119	54.09
公用事业	527.98	24.38	55	25.00
金融	386.36	17.84	26	11.82
材料	51.9	2.40	8	3.64
可选消费	46	2.12	7	3.18
能源	30	1.39	1	0.45
房地产	27	1.25	3	1.36
信息技术	9.5	0.44	1	0.45
合计	2 165.82	100	220	100

从发行主体企业性质来看，绿色债券发行主体以地方国企、国有控股企业和央企为主，金融机构发行人占比明显下降。2020年，绿色公司债是发行规模最大的绿债品种，共发行91只，规模732.1亿元，同比减少13.85%。绿色企业债共发行47只，规模485.4亿元，重点支持了绿色交通、污水处理、海绵城市建设、清洁能源、能源生态园建设等领域。绿色中期票据共发行30只，规模338.5亿元，总体保持稳定。绿色金融债发行规模继续下降。全年9家金融机构发行绿色金融债券11只，规模272亿元，同比下降67.3%。绿色资产支持证券共发行30只，规模246.32亿元，有效降低了企业融资门槛和成本，一定程度上缓解了民企融资难、融资贵现象。

表3-2　　2020年绿色债券境内发行情况

债券分类	债券数量（只）	债券规模（亿元）
公司债	91	732.1
企业债	47	485.4
中期票据	30	338.5
金融债	11	272
资产支持证券	30	246.32
短期融资券	6	36.5
地方政府债	1	27
定向工具	3	16
项目收益票据	1	12
总计	220	2 165.82

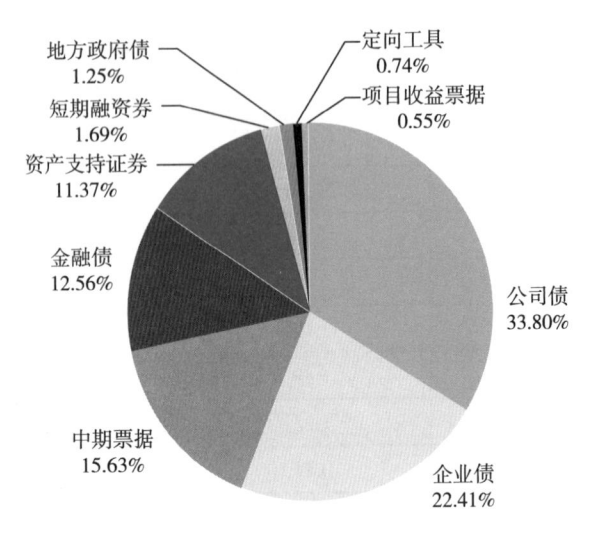

图3-2 2020年绿色债券境内发行情况

（数据来源：中央国债登记结算有限责任公司、Wind）

专栏3-3

2020年绿色债务融资工具概览

2020年，绿色债务融资工具热度提升，环境效益显著。2020年，绿色债务融资工具（含绿色资产支持票据）发行53只543.7亿元，同比增长19.0%。绿色债务融资工具在国内绿色债券市场中的占比由2019年的19.8%增长至2020年的23.8%，市场份额持续增长。截至2020年末，累计发行绿色债务融资工具1 498.2亿元，节能减排效果明显。根据绿色评估认证报告披露的数据，预计支持的绿色项目每年节能量超过1.8亿吨标准煤，相当于2019年全年能源消费总量的3.7%，减排二氧化碳4.5亿吨。

产品种类不断拓宽，产品结构日益丰富。2020年以来，蓝色债券、绿色资产支持商业票据（ABCP）、绿色并购票据等创新产品纷纷落地，持续满足发行人多元化的绿色融资需求。2020年共有13只绿色资产支持票据（ABN）完成发行，发行141.2亿元，持续盘活绿色存量资产。

市场主体覆盖区域广泛，行业类型多样。一是重点省份及区域发行规模不断增长。截至2020年末，长江经济带企业发行绿色债务融资工具615亿元；京津冀地区企业发行绿色债务融资工具490亿元；粤港澳大湾区企业发行绿色债务融资工具167亿元。二是区域分布与地方政府重视程度及出台的激励措施直接相关。浙江、广东等绿色金融改革创新试验区所在省份合计发行绿债290亿元，占市场规模的20%。江苏出台鼓励政策，对全省发行绿色债券的企业按30%进行贴息，当地企业发行绿色债券162亿元，占比11%。

发行人信用资质较高，产品期限以中长期为主。信用资质方面，绿色债务融资工具发行人信用水平相对较高，截至2020年末，AAA级绿色债务融资工具发行主体占比61%，AA+级占比19%。产品期限方面，鉴于绿色债务融资工具募集资金用途需匹配绿色项目，产品期限以中长期为主。全年新发行的131只绿色债券中，119只项目期限在3年及以上，占比达91%。

市场主体积极性持续提升，参与程度逐步加深。一是发行主体参与积极性不断增强。2020年，累计42家发行主体参与绿色债务融资工具发行工作，发行主体区域分布、信用分层及企业类型均不断丰富。其中，已有10家发行人全年多次发行绿色债务融资工具；此外，2020年通过绿色债务融资工具引入11家首次注册债务融资工具的企业，包括福建海峡环保、鲁能新能源、国开新能源、武汉碧水、杭州优行、徐州公交、南京公交、广州公交、上海深能融资租赁、大唐商业保理、宜春国资。

表3-3　　　　　　　　2020年绿色债务融资工具多次发行情况

序号	发行人名称	累计发行数量（只）	累计发行规模（亿元）	募集资金用途	主承销商
1	重庆市轨道交通（集团）有限公司	2	30	清洁交通	中国银行
2	宁波市轨道交通集团有限公司	2	30	清洁交通	国家开发银行、中国建设银行
3	南京金融城建设发展股份有限公司	2	24	绿色建筑	交通银行、南京银行、海通证券、宁波银行
4	华能天成融资租赁有限公司	3	20	风力发电	中国银行、北京银行、东方证券、华夏银行
5	成都轨道交通集团有限公司	2	20	清洁交通	中信银行
6	大唐商业保理有限公司	2	11	光伏、风电（基础资产）	兴业银行

续表

序号	发行人名称	累计发行数量（只）	累计发行规模（亿元）	募集资金用途	主承销商
7	中电投融和融资租赁有限公司	2	19.9	新能源汽车、光伏、风电等（基础资产）	兴业银行、恒丰银行
8	国电电力发展股份有限公司	2	17.68	风力发电	华泰证券、浙商银行、交通银行、中国工商银行
9	华能澜沧江水电股份有限公司	2	15	水力发电	国家开发银行、中国工商银行
10	沈阳地铁集团有限公司	2	15	清洁交通	招商银行

资料来源：中国银行间市场交易商协会。

二是投资人参与度持续提升。从绿色债券持仓面额来看，截至2020年末，兴业银行、中国农业银行、中国银行在全国性商业银行及政策性银行中名列前茅，广州农商行、江苏银行、长沙银行在城商行及农村金融机构中表现突出，中信证券、易方达基金、全国社保基金在证券基金类投资机构中较为活跃，泰康资管、长江养老保险、大家资产在保险类金融机构位列前三，香港金融管理局、中国银行（香港）有限公司等境外投资机构也积极参与到国内绿色债券市场之中。

三是主承销商参与热情不断提升。2020年，累计25家金融机构参与了绿色债务融资工具的承销。从承销金额来看，中国银行承销绿色债务融资工具总金额为79.4亿元，市场占有率为15.7%；兴业银行、招商银行紧随其后，承销金额为61.4亿元和54亿元；中信银行、中国农业银行、国家开发银行、中国工商银行、中国建设银行、上海浦东发展银行、中信证券在绿色债务融资工具承销中表现也较为突出。

2020年，82家金融机构参与了境内绿色债券（首单绿色类REITs除外）承销。其中，24家为银行，累计承销582.68亿元。银行机构承销量前三名为中国银行、兴业银行、招商银行，分别为87.51亿元、75.05亿元和56亿元。58家为证券公司，同比增加7家，累计承销1 573.9亿元。证券公司承销量前三位为中信建投、中信证券和国泰君安，分别为168.52亿元、121.04亿元和98.36亿元。

绿色债券二级市场交易量持续增长。2020年共480只绿色债券发生交易，规模7 250.89亿元，同比增长19.86%。其中，绿色金融债交投活跃，占总交易量的60%左右。

2. 发行期限进一步丰富

2020年，绿色债券发行期限仍以3年、5年和7年为主，长期限债券占比增加。其中，3年期绿色债券规模占比37.23%，同比下降9.24%；5年期规模占比23.97%，同比下降9.51%；7年期规模占比12.83%，同比上升9.33%。此外，2020年首次发行了21天、60天、90天、180天等短期限绿色债券品种，较好地满足了疫情影响下发行人的短期流动性需求。

表3-4　　　　　　　　　2020年境内绿色债券期限分布情况

期限	债券发行总额（亿元）	发行规模占比（%）	发行数量（只）
1年	147.28	6.80	23
2年	60.23	2.78	7
3年	806.33	37.23	71
4年	40.89	1.89	4
5年	519.23	23.97	55
6年	47	2.17	3
7年	277.8	12.83	33
8年	8.7	0.40	1
9年	27.06	1.25	2
10年	132	6.09	15
15年	20.5	0.95	2
18年	6.8	0.31	1
20年	72	3.32	3
合计	2 165.82	100	220

3. 创新型产品不断涌现

2020年，各类创新型绿色债券产品不断涌现。在品种方面，资产支持证券创新活跃；在主题方面，疫情防控是发行较多的新增主题。

1月，龙源电力在深交所发行设立公司可再生能源电价附加补助绿色资产支持专项计划7.13亿元，这是全市场央企首单可再生能源补贴绿色ABS。

2月，大唐融资租赁有限公司在上交所成功发行全国首单绿色疫情防控债，募集资金主要用于保障重点地区电力供应。华电国际电力股份有限公司成功发行全国首单绿色疫情防控债券和绿色防疫资产证券化产品——绿色定向资产支持票据（疫情防控债），基础资产为可再生能源电价附加补贴款，期限2.5年，募集资金15.51亿元，优先用于保障湖北、宁夏、山东、内蒙古等疫情防控地区的绿色基础设施建设电力供应及疫情防控供电系统的抢修。

3月，首单绿色创新创业疫情防控公司债券——凯伦股份5 000万元1年期绿色双创防疫债券在深交所发行。

4月，首单支持防疫创新品种公司债——武汉车都四水共治项目管理有限公司绿色项目收益公司债在深交所发行，这是新冠肺炎疫情发生后，湖北省首单获批的创新品种公司债券项目。

4月，农业发展银行首次面向全球投资者成功发行20亿元3年期"两山"生态环保主题金融债券，利率1.649%，募集资金主要用于支持生态文明建设重点领域，包括生态保护和修复、水资源节约与利用、重点流域水环境治理、城乡环境治理与污染防治等。

7月，国家开发银行面向全球投资人、多市场同步发行首单"应对气候变化"专题"债券通"绿色金融债券，合计规模100亿元，发行利率2.4984%，募集资金用于低碳运输等绿色项目，有效减缓和抑制气候变化，降低污染物排放。

10月，首单新能源发电基础设施类REITs产品、绿色类REITs产品——"工银瑞投—中能建投风电绿色资产支持专项计划"发行，中国能建为原始权益人，发行规模7.25亿元。

11月，中电投融和融资租赁有限公司发行10.5亿元绿色资产支持商业票据，系银行间市场首单绿色资产支持商业票据（ABCP）。本次绿色资产支持商业票据将ABCP与绿色债券相融合，发行期限30天，主体评级AAA，项目为16家小微企业提供融资支持，基础资产涉及集中供热、污染防治、新能源汽车和光伏风电等17个项目，在节能减排、资源回收利用、能源可持续发展等方面发挥良好的效应。

11月，中债金融估值中心发布全球首只中债—ESG优选信用债指数。该指数成分券由待偿期不短于1个月、中债市场隐含评级不低于AA级、在境内公开发行且上市流通的中债ESG评价排名靠前的发行人所发行的信用债组成。该指数是依据中债ESG评价体系编制的全球首只宽基人民币信用债ESG因子指数。

11月，青岛水务集团发行2020年度第一期绿色中期票据，规模3亿元，期限3年，募集资金用于海水淡化项目建设。该笔债券不仅符合绿色债券标准，同时符合蓝色债券属性，是全球非金融企业发行的首单蓝色债券。蓝色债券作为绿色债券的一种，募集资金专项用于可持续型海洋经济，在推动海洋保护和海洋资源的可持续利用中可发挥重要作用。

专栏3-4

疫情防控债

2020年2月1日，人民银行、财政部、银保监会、证监会、外汇局共同发布《关于进一步强化金融支持防控新型冠状病毒感染肺炎疫情的通知》（银发〔2020〕29号），强调提高债券发行等服务效率，对募集资金主要用于疫情防控及疫情较重地区金融机构和企业发行的金融债券、资产支持证券、公司信用类债券建立注册发行"绿色通道"。各债券监管机构陆续发布疫情防控期间债券业务"绿色通道"的具体安排，提出"发行人募集资金全部或部分用于防控疫情有关用途的，在申报或发行阶段可以在债券全称后添加'（疫情防控债）'标识"。

2020年，共发行10只投向疫情防控方面的绿色债券，规模共计64.06亿元，募集资金投向包括武汉经济技术开发区（汉南区）"四水共治"项目、高分子防水材料项目建设、偿还精准扶贫项目借款、支持精准扶贫项目、建设高标准绿色蔬菜大棚及补充发行人流动资金、偿还有息负债等。

表3-5　　　　　　　　　2020年部分疫情防控债发行情况

债券名称	发行主体	主体性质	规模（亿元）
华电国际电力股份有限公司2020年度第一期绿色定向资产支持票据（疫情防控债）	华电国际电力股份有限公司	央企	15.51
杭州优行科技有限公司2020年度第一期绿色定向资产支持票据（疫情防控债）	杭州优行科技有限公司	其他	10
20寿光G1（疫情防控债）	寿光市惠农新农村建设投资开发有限公司	国有控股	5
G20唐租1（疫情防控债）	大唐融资租赁有限公司	国有控股	10
20凯伦SG（疫情防控债）	江苏凯伦建材股份有限公司	民营企业	0.5

续表

债券名称	发行主体	主体性质	规模（亿元）
长江楚越—光谷环保烟气脱硫服务收费权绿色资产支持专项计划（疫情防控债）	武汉光谷环保科技股份有限公司	国有控股	4.4
G20永荣（疫情防控债）	福建永荣控股集团有限公司	民营企业	3
20四水G1（疫情防控债）	武汉车都四水共治项目管理有限公司	国有控股	10
G20金枪（疫情防控债）	苏州金枪新材料股份有限公司	民营企业	0.2
20华润租赁（疫情防控债）	华润融资租赁有限公司	央企	5.45

（三）绿色债券评级维持高水平，成本优势明显

绿色债券发行主体信用级别以AA级为主。因为审批机构对绿色债券开设绿色通道，级别相对较低的发行人更有意愿选择发行绿色债券。但绿色债券债项评级维持较高水平，AAA级占比最多，占总发行量的72.93%。债项评级高于主体评级，意味着投资者对绿色项目偿债能力较有信心。

表3-6　　　　　　　　2020年境内绿色债券评级情况[①]

债券评级	债券规模（亿元）	发行规模占比（%）	发行数量（只）
AAA	1 246.81	72.93	97
AA+	354.68	20.75	45
AA	95.2	5.57	17
AA-	3	0.18	1
A-1	10	0.58	1
合计	1 709.69	100	161

境内绿色债券发行利率继续下行，绿色项目融资成本进一步降低。2020年，AAA级1年到3年期平均发行利率3.27%，比2019年下行95个基点；3年到5年期平均发行利率

---

① 2020年发行的境内绿色债券中，有59只债券没有债项评级，规模合计约456.13亿元，本表仅对有债项评级的债券进行了统计。

3.93%，比2019年下行49个基点。

表3-7　　　　　　　　　　2020年境内绿色债券发行利率统计

单位：%

评级	1年及以内	1年到3年（含3年）	3年到5年（含5年）	5年到10年（含10年）	10年及以上
AAA	3.63	3.27	3.93	4.54	3.55
AA+	4.91	4.18	4.70	5.30	5.45
AA	—	3.82	6.96	6.66	6.09
AA-	—	4.50	—	—	—
A-1	2.54	—	—	—	—

2020年境内发行的190只绿色债券（不包括绿色资产支持证券）中，可比较发行成本[1]的绿色债券106只[2]。与同类债券（当月发行的同种类同期限同债券等级）相比，68.87%的绿色债券票面利率更低，具有一定发行成本优势。据统计，2016年至2020年，绿色债券发行成本研究样本共389只，按券种进行对比发现，近3年公开发行的绿色公司债、绿色中期票据具有发行成本优势的比例在70%以上，绿色企业债的优势比例也基本稳定在60%以上，绿色债券融资成本相对较低。

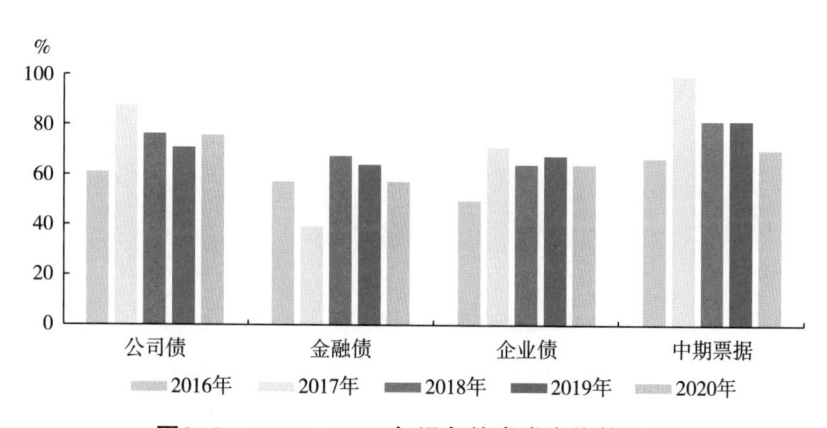

图3-3　2016—2020年绿色债券成本优势比例

（数据来源：中诚信评级公司）

---

[1] 发行成本分析旨在将绿色债券的发行成本与当月发行的同期限、同券种、同信用等级债券的平均发行利率进行比较分析，判断绿色债券是否具有发行成本优势。部分债券由于发行当月无同类债券，故未纳入发行成本分析样本中。

[2] 2020年发行的190只绿色债券（不含绿色资产支持证券）中，剔除私募发行的绿色债券、绿色政策银行债券、绿色超短期融资券，形成绿色债券样本共计106只。

（四）募集资金主要投向绿色服务等三大领域

2020年绿色债券募集资金主要投向绿色服务、节能环保和基础设施绿色升级三大领域，占比分别为30.13%、28.07%和19.98%。

表3-8　　　　　　　　2020年境内绿色债券募集资金投向统计

投向分类	债券规模（亿元）	发行数量（只）
绿色服务	652.64	59
节能环保	607.92	72
基础设施绿色升级	432.83	37
清洁能源	349.53	37
生态环境	67.4	10
清洁生产	55.5	5
合计	2 165.82	220

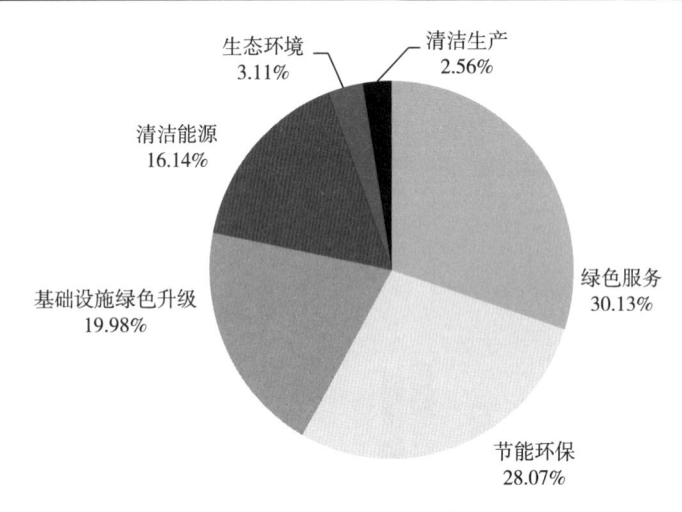

图3-4　2020年境内绿色债券投向占比

（数据来源：中央国债登记结算有限责任公司、Wind）

二、资本市场对绿色发展的支持力度持续加大

（一）积极支持绿色企业通过境内外股票市场上市融资

2020年，创业板申报"生态保护和环境治理业"企业20家，总拟募资金额为179.78

亿元（其中首发129.97亿元，再融资49.81亿元）。科创板申报节能环保企业26家，新能源企业14家，拟募资金额分别为377亿元、161亿元。截至2020年末，科创板申报的329家企业中，节能环保与新能源企业共40家，占比12%，绿色企业融资绝对及相对规模较2019年分别增加155.0%、1.2%。

2020年，溢丰环保H股IPO及"全流通"、辽宁清洁H股IPO、蓝深环保H股IPO、天保能源H股"全流通"等5家绿色企业的境外发行上市申请通过证监会核准；彩虹新能源的发行上市申请通过证监会核准，融资约15亿港元；天保能源H股"全流通"已完成。

（二）绿色指数编制应用研究取得新进展

中证指数有限公司于2020年12月3日正式发布中证ESG评价方法，评价方法综合考虑上市公司行业特点与信息质量，由环境、社会和治理（ESG）3个维度、14个主题、22个单元和180余个底层指标构成。该评价方法立足于市场实际，客观反映企业在ESG维度的基本面信息，是完善企业运营和投资管理的有力工具。

2020年，中证指数有限公司发布绿色指数12条。其中，股票指数9条，债券指数3条。截至2020年末，中证指数公司累计发布ESG、可持续发展、环保产业、新能源、社会责任、治理等可持续发展相关指数58条。其中，股票指数46条，债券指数12条。

绿色治理指数研究取得新进展。2020年，深圳证券交易所全资子公司深圳证券信息有限公司创新推出公司治理研究院绿色治理指数，为国内首只绿色治理指数；研发完成国证香蜜湖绿色金融指数。截至2020年末，深交所及下属信息公司累计推出绿色指数24只，涵盖环境、社会、治理等ESG主题，形成了覆盖面广、代表性强的绿色指数体系，对市场投资绿色产业发挥了积极引导作用。

表3-9　　　　　　　　　　深交所绿色指数明细

指数代码	指数名称	ESG领域	覆盖市场
399378	国证ESG300指数	E+S+G	深市+沪市
980058	公司治理研究院绿色治理指数	E+S+G	深市
399358	国证环保指数	E环境	深市+沪市
399412	国证新能源指数	E环境	深市+沪市
399417	国证新能源汽车指数	E环境	深市+沪市

续表

指数代码	指数名称	ESG领域	覆盖市场
399556	央视生态产业指数	E环境	深市+沪市
399638	深证环保指数	E环境	深市
399695	深证节能环保指数	E环境	深市
980032	国证新能源车电池指数	E环境	深市+沪市
CNB00013	中财—国证高等级绿色债券指数	E环境	境内债券
CNB00014	中财—国证高等级非贴标绿色债券指数	E环境	境内债券
CNB00015	中财—国证高等级贴标绿色债券指数	E环境	境内债券
G10013	中财—国证深港通绿色优选指数	E环境	深市+港股
G10165	国证深港通节能指数	E环境	深市+港股
G10169	国证深港通新能源车指数	E环境	深市+港股
399322	国证治理指数	G治理	深市+沪市
399328	深证治理指数	G治理	深市
399554	央视财经50治理领先指数	G治理	深市+沪市
399550	央视财经50指数	S+G	深市+沪市
399341	深证责任指数	S社会	深市
399369	国证社会责任指数	S社会	深市+沪市
399555	央视财经50责任领先指数	S社会	深市+沪市
399651	中小板企业社会责任指数	S社会	深市
399650	中小板治理指数	G治理	深市

第三节 绿色保险的风险保障作用继续扩大

一、环境污染责任保险取得积极进展

2020年，环境污染责任保险在全国31个省（区、市）开展，涉及冶金、制药、造纸、火电等多个高风险行业，提供风险保障646.61亿元，同比增长21.75%。

二、巨灾保险为绿色发展提供有效保障

2020年，中国巨灾保险产品和服务进一步丰富。中再集团为广东多个地市和湖北武汉等地推出强降雨巨灾指数保险等产品提供支持，提供风险保障60多亿元。在此基础上，在浙江、福建等地孵化各级巨灾保险，顺利推动宁波市突发公共卫生事件指数保险、宁波市堤防灾害创新保险项目及宁德市海上塑胶渔排升级改造保险项目落地。

巨灾风险管理平台是巨灾保险创新发展的重要数字化基础设施。2020年11月11日，中再集团研发的国际巨灾组合风险管理平台（一期）上线试运行，平台采用云原生架构技术，各项资源及服务可进行横向动态扩展，保证了平台的高性能和高稳定性，实现了中国再保险行业在巨灾风险实时累积、单笔及组合业务风险评估管理平台化从无到有的突破。

三、涉农绿色保险创新继续深化

继续推进适合各地特色农产品的指数保险创新。2020年，中国大地保险在江西省成功落地杂交水稻制种气象指数保险，为参保农户提供489.98万元风险保障，有效避免了异常降雨、高温及低温等异常气候变化导致的产量或者种子品质的下降，助力制种产业健康发展。中再产险开展多项地方优势特色农产品保险创新工作，创新推出重庆柑橘低温气象指数保险、山东临沂金银花干旱指数保险、浙江温岭甘蔗台风指数保险等10多款产品，有效促进了地方特色农业产业和农业经济发展。

青海省启动"化肥农药减量增效"项目试点。为提高农户对参与"化肥农药减量增效"项目试点的农作物减产风险的抵御能力，中国大地保险创新推出青海省农作物化肥农药减量增效产量保险产品，为青海省海南藏族自治州的1 514户次参保农户的32.59万亩次青稞、小麦、油菜等农作物提供4 881万元风险保障。

四、绿色建筑保险助力绿色建筑市场健康发展

各地积极推动开展绿色建筑性能保险、超低能耗建筑性能保险等绿色保险应用试

点，打造"保险+服务+科技+信贷"模式，为绿色建筑项目提供事前信用增进、事中风控服务、事后损失补偿。

专栏3-5

绿色保险创新

青岛在中德生态园被动房住宅推广示范小区项目（二期）开出全国首张建筑绿色保单，业主单位作为投保人、被保险人，向保险公司就超低能耗建筑进行投保。保险公司负责组织第三方风控服务机构，全过程监督超低能耗建筑的建造过程，若投保的超低能耗建筑项目在供暖年耗热量、供冷年耗热量、气密性三项指标方面未达到超低能耗建筑的相关性能指标要求，保险公司将根据保险合同的约定赔偿项目节能整改费用，或对能耗超标进行经济补偿，并承担由此产生的鉴定费用、法律费用。

此外，青岛市探索发展建筑节能保险，如若改造项目未达到保险合同中载明的节能指标（公共建筑综合节能率要达到20%）要求，由保险人承担对节能项目整改或经济补偿责任，保险人将按照保险合同的约定负责赔偿。

五、清洁能源保险助力能源产业发展

海上风电保险快速发展。2020年，中再产险承接了国电投滨海、大丰海上风电、舟山普陀6号海上风电、中广核如东海上风电等16个海上风电项目，保费收入约567万元；中国大地保险承接了34个海上风电工程项目和9个海上风电运营项目，保障额度分别为142亿元和27亿元。

核能保险稳步发展。2020年，中国核保险共同体（以下简称中国核共体）共计为价值约9 000亿元的境内涉核财产提供保障、2万多名一线工作人员提供累计高达130亿元保额的保险保障。在境外核保险业务方面，核共体共计参与全球27个国家或地区400余座核设施的分入再保险业务，承保核电机组数量约占世界总量的90%。

专栏3-6

核能保险创新实践

"华龙一号"全球首堆运营期核保险。核保险是具有低频高损特征的典型巨灾险种，也是最具代表性的全球化专业再保险险种。2020年9月，中国核共体为"华龙一号"全球首堆签发的运营期核保险保单正式生效，该保单是目前全球核保险市场保障范围最全面的保单条款之一。在承保过程中，中国核共体与福建福清核电有限公司密切合作，成功制定和实施了最佳的保险保障方案，得到境内外保险再保险主体的广泛支持和参与。

核损害赔偿应急响应平台2.0版。2020年，中国核共体推出核损害赔偿应急响应平台2.0版。在1.0版的基础上，2.0版全面迭代升级平台功能，实现对国内现有45台运行核电机组在不同事故情境下的影响范围和赔偿金额的模拟评估和可视化展示，可为核事故提供事前预案制定、事发应急响应和事后赔偿管理等全流程保障，填补了国家核事故应急机制中商业保险核损害赔偿的空白。

核保险智能风控管理平台。2020年，中国核共体启动开发核保险智能风控管理平台，借助大数据分析和数据挖掘技术实现核保险风险管理的数字化转型，进一步提升专业能力和风险管理水平，强化事前风险防范和防灾减损服务能力。

"核·星"核保险区块链运营服务平台。中国核共体核保险区块链运营服务平台"核·星"，系全球首创。平台利用区块链可追溯、不可篡改等特性实现可信存证，极大加强了数据的安全性；还以服务化方式进行灵活构建，以优化服务流程和功能，有效提高了运营服务的效率和水平。2020年，中国核共体推出"核·星"区块链平台3.0，上线境外分入业务等新功能模块，一站式解决核共体业务运营，可为成员公司提供永久、透明、可追溯服务。

六、保险资金绿色投资助推绿色产业发展

各保险公司积极创新保险债权投资、股权投资基金等产品，投向风力发电、清洁

能源、绿色交通等绿色项目，产生良好的环境效益与经济效益。截至2020年末，保险资金实体投资项目中涉及绿色产业的债权投资计划登记（注册）规模达10 277.62亿元。其中，投向交通行业3 113.22亿元、能源行业3 145.05亿元、水利行业688.04亿元。

2020年，中国人寿以永续债权的方式为中国能源建设集团锡林郭勒盟阿旗225兆瓦风电项目提供资金保障，同时为中国能建提供营运资金支持，投资金额共20亿元。该项目将促进当地建材、交通等产业发展，并有助于扩大就业和发展第三产业。该项目建成后，每年可提供5.8亿千瓦时清洁电能，节约标煤18.8万吨，减排二氧化硫1 598吨、氮氧化物约1 391.2吨、二氧化碳50.85万吨，具有良好的环境效益。

2020年，华泰保险以债权投资计划的方式为中节能原平长梁沟风电项目、中节能尉氏风力发电项目、博白云飞嶂风电场工程等7个风电项目提供30亿元资金支持。7个项目合计装机容量将达469.6兆瓦，年上网电量预估超100万兆瓦时，相应节约煤炭资源储备约20亿吨，并有助于促进就业和增加地方财政收入。项目建成后，每年可节约标煤约40万吨，相应可减少二氧化碳、二氧化硫、一氧化碳及氮氧化物的排放，同时还可减少灰渣排放及节约大量淡水资源。

第四节　绿色基金与绿色PPP创新发展

基金行业绿色投资理念不断扎根。截至2020年末，市场共有80只绿色主题公募基金，规模1 694.11亿元。其中，社会责任投资基金[①]6只，管理规模为106.14亿元；ESG投资基金[②]7只，管理规模为37.88亿元[③]；以生态、低碳、环保、绿色、环境治理、新能源、美丽中国为投资方向的基金[④]67只，管理规模为1 550.09亿元[⑤]。

[①] 基金名称中含"社会责任"。
[②] 基金名称中含"ESG"。
[③] 其中1只基金为2020年12月末新成立，暂无规模。
[④] 基金名称中含有"生态、低碳、环保、绿色、环境治理、新能源、美丽中国"等关键词的基金。
[⑤] 其中3只基金为2020年12月新成立，暂无规模。

专栏3-7

绿色基金创新案例

一、华夏基金绿色投资实践

华夏基金是中国第一家签署联合国负责任投资原则（PRI）的公募基金公司。在国内基金公司中，华夏基金率先在公司层面建立了CEO领导的ESG业务委员会，并在公司内实行了《华夏基金责任投资政策》和三层级ESG整合战略。PRI在2020年PRI签署方评价报告"策略与治理"模块中，将该做法评定为A+，系全球最高等级。华夏基金将ESG考量嵌入国际投资组合投资全流程，包括投资政策制定、基本面研究、组合管理、风险管理、上市公司治理参与、投后监督与报告。

2020年3月，华夏基金与荷兰合作伙伴NNIP共同发行全球首只投资中国权益市场的跨境责任投资产品NN（L）International China A-Share Equity Fund，这是全球首只由中国基金公司管理的欧盟可转让证券集合投资计划（Undertakings for Collective Investment in Transferable Securities，UCITS）产品。截至2020年末，该基金成立以来收益为87.92%，超越基准指数收益为31.87%，同时基金组合MSCI ESG评级为BB，超越基准指数一个等级。

二、禹阁资本绿色投资实践

2020年，上海禹阁投资管理有限公司以联合国17个可持续发展目标为指导，推出国内首份影响力投资主题图谱，在绿色投资领域，明确了清洁能源、废弃物管理与循环经济等8个一级主题及27个二级主题。

三、上交所深化绿色金融产品创新

上交所积极推动绿色指数产品挂牌上市，推动北信瑞丰中证ESG 120 ETF、工银瑞信中证180 ESG ETF、浦银安盛中证120 ESG ETF、兴业MSCI中国A股ESG ETF、嘉实中证沪深300 ESG ETF、富国沪深300 ESG ETF、招商基金沪深300 ESG ETF、富国中证ESG 120 ETF共8只产品上报证监会，ESG产品上报数量创历史新高。

四、中证指数公司发布多条绿色指数

截至2020年末，中证指数公司累计发布ESG、可持续发展、环保产业、新能源、社会责任、治理等可持续发展相关指数58条，其中股票指数46条，债券指数12条，为引导资金支持绿色产业发展，促进资本市场服务实体经济提供了多样化工具。

五、深交所致力于打造特色鲜明的绿色基金市场

在国家节能减排、能源革新、环保低碳、绿色发展的总体规划下，深交所拟全方位布局绿色、低碳、碳中和、新能源、环保产业、环境治理，以及ESG等绿色主题基金。截至2020年末，已有20余只基金拟发行上市，争取在深交所多层次资本市场实现绿色基金的示范效应和集群效应。下一步，深交所将继续秉承坚持绿色发展理念，持续开发更加丰富的绿色主题基金，更好地服务绿色金融发展战略。

绿色低碳领域PPP项目成效显著。绿色低碳领域PPP项目在缓解绿色发展领域投入不足、改善城乡生态环境、促进绿色低碳市场发展等方面，发挥了积极作用。截至2020年末，全国PPP综合信息平台项目管理库中累计污染防治与绿色低碳领域项目5 826个、投资额5.6万亿元，覆盖31个省（自治区、直辖市）及新疆生产建设兵团，涉及公共交通、供排水、生态建设和环境保护、水利建设、可再生能源、教育、科技、文化、养老、医疗卫生、林业、旅游等行业领域。其中，签约落地项目3 954个、投资额3.8万亿元，开工建设项目2 396个、投资额2.2万亿元。

第五节　环境权益市场发展进入快车道

一、碳排放权交易市场迎来重大机遇

截至2020年末，北京、天津、上海、重庆、湖北、广东、深圳7省市试点碳市场，共覆盖电力、钢铁、水泥等20余个行业近3 000家重点排放单位，配额累计成交量4.45亿吨，累计成交额102.79亿元，对试点地区控碳减排作出积极贡献。国家核证自愿减排量（CCER）在试点碳市场履约抵消中扮演重要角色。截至2020年12月31日，CCER累计成交量约2.69亿吨，累计成交额为23.14亿元。

2020年12月，中央经济工作会议要求加快建设全国碳排放权交易市场。12月30日，生态环境部印发《关于印发〈2019—2020年全国碳排放权交易配额总量设定与分配实施方案（发电行业）》〈纳入2019—2020年全国碳排放权交易配额管理的重点排放单位名单〉并做好发电行业配额预分配工作的通知》（国环规气候〔2020〕3号）；12月31日，《全国碳排放权交易管理办法（试行）》正式印发，标志着全国碳排放权交易市场建设取得突破性进展。

二、全国用能权交易市场即将启动

2017年起，浙江省、河南省、福建省、四川省4省相继开展用能权交易试点。2020年1月，福建发布《福建省用能权交易管理暂行办法》（福建省人民政府令第212号）。至此，4个试点地区的用能权交易制度建设初步完成，其中，河南、福建、四川为企业间总量配额制交易模式，浙江为政府与企业间增量交易模式。除试点地区外，其他地方也自主开展了用能权交易试点。"十三五"以来，湖北省用能权交易累计成交190多万吨标煤，成交金额超过1亿元。2020年12月，中央经济工作会议要求，加快建设全国用能权交易市场。

三、排污权交易抵质押融资在多地开展

全国共有近30个省、自治区、直辖市开展了排污权交易试点，其中江苏省、浙江省、天津市、湖北省、湖南省、内蒙古自治区、山西省、重庆市、陕西省、河北省和河南省及青岛市12个省（区、市）为国家级试点，另有部分省（区、市）自行开展了排污权交易。2020年，中国实现固定污染源排污许可全覆盖。截至2020年末，全国共核发排污许可证33.77万张，登记排污企业236.52万家。2020年，浙江省排污权成交量为1.15万吨，成交额约3亿元。9月21日，陕西省启动排污权二级市场交易，二氧化硫、氮氧化物两项排污权指标总成交量为1 746.81吨，成交额为1 673.84万元。

2020年2月，中共中央办公厅、国务院办公厅印发《关于构建现代环境治理体系的指导意见》，提出要研究探索针对排污权交易开展抵质押融资。3月末，山西省首单排污权抵质押贷款落地，提供融资2 000万元；6月，广东省首批排污权抵质押融资业务落地，为2家企业提供贷款资金4 000万元；8月，江苏省生态环境厅、江苏银行总行、江苏省财政厅、中国人民银行南京分行等共同发起排污权抵质押贷款启动仪式，为1家企业综合授信2 000万元。

四、其他环境权益交易市场持续稳定发展

截至2020年末，全国水权交易市场累计成交水量约31.88亿立方米。其中，区域水权/取水权交易成交31.67亿立方米，灌溉用水户水权交易成交0.21亿立方米。相比而言，区域水权/取水权交易单次成交水量较大，每单位成交价格较高，交易期限较长。灌溉用水户水权交易单次成交量、成交价相对较低，交易期限目前主要为1年，交易主体类型更多。2020年12月，全国首宗雨水资源使用权交易成交，市场主体将其收储的雨水使用权转让给环卫公司，雨水代替自来水用于绿化和清扫作业，中国非常规水资源实现生态价值市场化进入实践阶段。

自2017年7月1日起，中国实行可再生能源绿色电力证书自愿认购交易（简称绿证交易）。截至2020年末，风电类绿证交易量累计达41 618兆瓦时结算电量，每日成交平均价格174元/个；光伏类绿证交易量累计达166兆瓦时结算电量，每日成交平均价格668元/个。

第六节 绿色信托项目环境效益进一步显现

2020年，在《绿色信托指引》的指导下，信托公司积极践行绿色发展理念。在绿色信托资产规模方面，存续资产规模3 592.82亿元，同比增长7.1%，新增资产规模1 199.93亿元；存续项目数量为888个，同比增长6.73%，新增项目数量360个。

图3-5 2013—2020年绿色信托资产规模及项目数量

（数据来源：中国信托业协会发布的《中国信托业协会责任报告》）

信托公司结合绿色节能环保行业特点，积极创新产品和服务方式，在拓宽绿色产业

投融资渠道、填补传统银行服务等方面开展了有益探索。其中，绿色信托贷款仍为信托公司主要使用的绿色金融工具，存续规模为1 909.12亿元。创新业务中，绿色资产证券化业务表现尤为突出。

表3-10　　　　　　　　　2020年信托公司绿色金融工具统计

绿色金融工具	存续规模（亿元）
绿色信托贷款	1 909.12
绿色股权投资	184.44
绿色债券投资	44.82
绿色资产证券化	641.84
绿色产业基金	217.51
绿色供应链	17.30
碳金融	24.05
公益慈善绿色信托	15.88
其他	537.86

绿色信托项目环境效益进一步显现。2020年，累计节约标准煤256.12万吨、节水26 573.81万吨，减少温室气体排放798.89万吨二氧化碳当量、化学需氧量8.7万吨、氨氮37.78万吨、二氧化硫5.15万吨、氨氮化合物2.09万吨。

绿色信托支持绿色产业发展越发精准。2020年，绿色信托资金主要投向清洁能源生产产业和基础设施绿色升级产业，占比分别为33.94%和25.76%；投向节能环保产业和生态环境产业资金占比分别为17.51%和10.01%；支持清洁生产产业和绿色服务产业资金占比分别为3.56%和3%；6.36%的绿色信托资金支持了多元绿色产业。

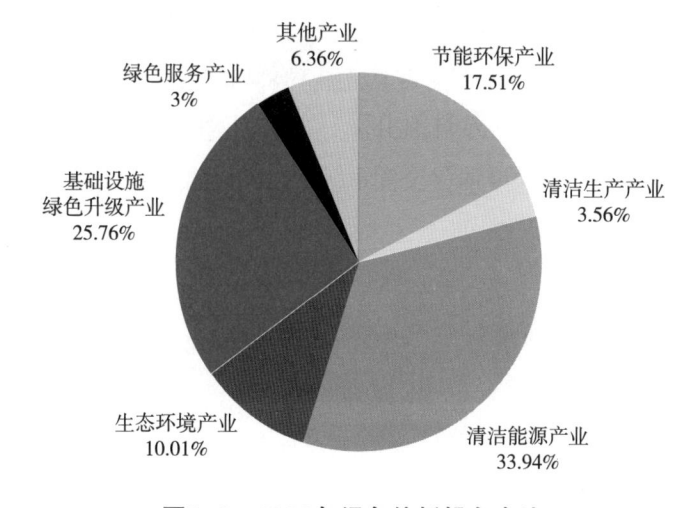

图3-6　2020年绿色信托投向占比

专栏3-8

绿色信托创新案例

粤财信托"绿金1号第一期财产权信托计划",以委托人广东绿金融资租赁有限公司持有的融资租赁应收账款为底层资产,在北金所发行国内首单租赁类绿色债权计划,也是粤港澳大湾区首单绿色债权融资计划。底层资产涉及民生工程的市政污水污泥、垃圾发电、垃圾填埋场、沼气发电等环保项目。据测算,其中"污水处理类项目"每年可减排生化需氧量约438吨、化学需氧量约2 321.40吨、悬浮物约620.50吨、氨氮约397.12吨、总氮约638.75吨、总磷约46.94吨;2020年,"垃圾发电类项目"实现替代化石能源量约1.32万吨,协同二氧化碳减排量约3.53万吨、协同二氧化硫减排量约346.90吨、协同氮氧化物减排量约298.08吨、协同粉尘减排量约144.72吨,环保效益显著。

"兴业信托·绿金优选集合资金信托计划",为业内首单开放净值型标准化绿色资产投资信托,由兴业信托主动管理,优选标准化绿色金融资产进行配置,并依据各因素的动态变化进行及时调整。该信托计划为固定收益型产品,信托规模100亿元,首期成立2 100万元,期限5年,每月开放。

中航信托创新"股权+债权"投贷联动金融方案,为废弃物处理企业诺客环境提供中、短期必要资金,以专业化视角帮助其加快形成核心资产,提升其在细分行业的核心竞争能力。合作关系建立以来,诺客环境共收集各类危废约10.68万吨,处置约8.92万吨,其中2020年全年共收集各类危废约8.48万吨,处置约6.77万吨,取得了良好成效及广泛的社会效益。

第四章　绿色金融基层实践成效显著

中国绿色金融发展和改革创新实践，需要激发地方创新的积极性和创造性，用基层实践来检验并不断丰富和完善改革政策。2020年，绿色金融改革创新试验区建设在不断总结和改革创新中取得新成效。

一方面，绿色金融改革创新试验区建设深入推进。六省（区）九地试验区立足生态环境资源禀赋，探索形成各具特色的绿色金融改革创新之路，形成一系列可复制、可推广的有益经验，有力支持绿色产业发展和经济低碳转型。其中，作为习近平总书记提出的"绿水青山就是金山银山"理念的诞生地，浙江湖州通过绿色金融规范发展、生态环境资源有效转化、科技赋能有力支撑、央地政策协同发力，初步形成绿色金融改革"湖州经验"。

另一方面，其他非试验区坚持贯彻绿色发展理念，在吸取试验区经验基础上，积极引导区域绿色金融改革发展进入"快车道"，切实推动经济社会低碳绿色转型。例如，在长江经济带发展、长江三角洲区域一体化发展、粤港澳大湾区建设等国家重大区域发展战略中，大力推动绿色金融改革创新，实现绿色金融发展与区域经济发展有机结合。

此外，为践行"绿水青山就是金山银山"理念，部分地区还开展绿色金融支持清洁供暖、畜禽养殖废弃物处置和资源化利用、绿色建筑等重点民生工程和污染防治关键领域的相关实践，积极探索符合市场原则的可持续金融支持模式。

第一节　绿色金融改革创新试验区建设深入推进

2020年是"十三五"收官之年，也是绿色金融改革创新试验区建设的关键之年。三年多来，浙江湖州和衢州，江西赣江新区，广东广州，贵州贵安新区，新疆昌吉、哈密和克拉玛依，甘肃兰州新区六省（区）九地，充分发挥绿色金融改革创新优势，以金融创新推动经济绿色低碳转型为主线，以建立健全体制机制为动力，着力支持区域经济绿色、高质量发展。

一、绿色金融改革创新机制持续落地

一是建立健全体制机制，持续推动绿色金融标准落地。2020年，各试验区通过加强完善组织协调、优化政策环境、制订发展计划和考核激励机制等举措，大力推动体制机制建设和政策细则落地落实，出台绿色金融相关政策20余项。

表4-1　2020年试验区出台的主要政策制度

地区	政策制度
浙江	《关于金融支持衢州生猪产业绿色高质量发展的指导意见》（衢银发〔2020〕34号）
	《湖州市重大项目专项贷款和财政绿色专项贴息资金实施办法》
	《湖州市国家绿色金融改革创新试验区建设2020年推进计划》（湖政办发明电〔2020〕6号）
江西	《江西省绿色票据认定和管理指引（试行）》
	《关于运用再贴现工具支持绿色票据发展的通知》
	《关于做好2020年江西省绿色项目融资对接工作的通知》
广东	《广州市地方金融监督管理局关于印发推动广州绿色金融改革创新试验区建设2020年工作方案的通知》
	《花都区支持绿色金融创新发展实施细则》（花府办规〔2020〕1号）
	《广州市黄埔区、广州开发区促进绿色金融发展政策措施实施细则》（穗埔府规〔2020〕11号）
	《广州市绿色金融改革创新试验区绿色企业与项目库管理实施细则（试行）的通知》（穗金融规〔2020〕5号）
	《广州市黄埔区广州开发区绿色项目、绿色企业认定管理办法（试行）》（穗开金融规字〔2020〕4号）
	《关于金融支持粤港澳大湾区建设的意见》（银发〔2020〕95号）

续表

地区	政策制度
贵州	《关于同意成立贵阳市贵安新区共建绿色金融改革创新工作领导小组的批复》（筑委办函字〔2020〕34号）
	《关于印发〈金融支持贵安新区高质量发展工作方案〉的通知》（黔金监发〔2020〕11号）
新疆	《绿色金融标准试验工作方案》
	《哈密市绿色金融改革创新试验区绿色金融标准实施方案（试行）》（哈银办〔2020〕11号）
	《克拉玛依绿色金融改革试验区标准实施方案》
	《自治州绿色金融改革创新试验区建设2年半倒计时工作推进方案》
甘肃	《兰州新区建设绿色金融改革创新试验区实施方案》（甘政办发〔2020〕60号）
	《兰州新区绿色金融五年发展规划（2020—2024年）》
	《兰州新区绿色金融发展奖励政策（试行）》

二是加强货币政策支持力度，运用再贷款、再贴现等货币政策工具扩大绿色信贷投放。2020年，湖州开启再贷款"网上贷"模式，创新推出"央行政策支持贷"线上服务，全年累计发放再贷款150.46亿元，加权平均利率4.62%，其中线上融资90笔、1.75亿元；赣江新区获得绿色票据再贴现支持1.31亿元；广州继续划出绿色再贴现专项支持额度，全年支持广州地区金融机构办理绿色票据再贴现业务23亿元，并引导东莞、佛山等地区创新开办绿色票据业务，发放绿色票据再贴现资金超19亿元；昌吉实现辖区绿色再贴现业务零突破，共发放绿色再贴现0.36亿元。此外，各地均将存款类金融机构绿色信贷业绩评价结果纳入央行金融机构评级。

二、绿色金融服务质量稳步提升

（一）绿色金融组织体系健全发展

一是银行业绿色专营机构快速发展，绿色金融服务意识和服务质量不断提高。截至2020年末，湖州共设立16家绿色专营支行、23家绿色金融事业部。衢州建立绿色专营支行和绿色金融事业部共计54家。赣江新区共设立绿色专营支行7家、绿色金融事业部3家。广州成立12家银行业绿色专营机构，包括5家绿色分行、3家绿色支行、1家绿色金融创新中心及3家绿色金融事业部。贵安新区设立15家银行业绿色金融机构，其中，贵州银行宣布采纳赤道原则，成为国内第六家"赤道银行"。哈密、昌吉、克拉玛依三地实现银行业金融机构绿色专营机构全覆盖,共有绿色专营机构59家,其中哈密14家、昌吉25家、克拉玛依20家。兰州新区成立3家绿色支行。

二是非银行业绿色专营机构多层次、多元化发展。截至2020年末,湖州设立绿色保险产品创新实验室2个,其中浙商财产保险设立长三角绿色保险创新实验室。衢州保险机构设立绿色金融事业部10个,其中人保财险衢州分公司成立浙江省首家绿色保险营业部。赣江新区设置绿色保险实验室(事业部)4家。广州设立13家非银行业绿色金融专营机构,包括1家绿色金融事业部、3家绿色金融实验室、3家绿色基金、2家交易场所及4家其他非银行业绿色专营机构。贵安新区设立非银行业绿色金融机构8家,包括3家绿色担保事业部和1家绿色证券事业部。新疆成立6家绿色金融事业部和1家绿色担保事业部;其中,哈密人保财险、申万宏源证券和银河证券分别成立1家绿色金融事业部,克拉玛依设立3家非银行机构绿色金融事业部,分别覆盖保险公司、金控公司和担保公司。

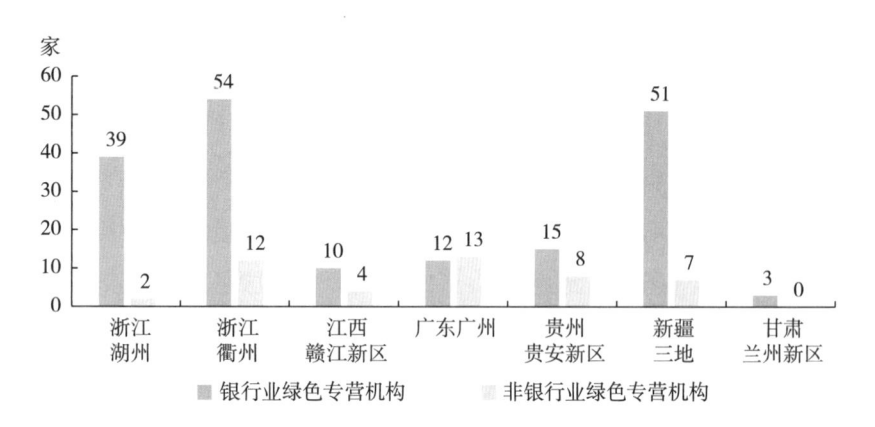

图4-1 2020年末各试验区绿色金融事业部或专营机构数量

(二)绿色金融产品和服务质量不断提高

一是绿色信贷供给能力显著提升,资产质量保持较好水平,产品服务创新持续推进。截至2020年末,试验区绿色贷款余额合计6 066.5亿元,较年初增长36.04%。其中,广州绿色贷款余额最高,达3 820.68亿元;赣江新区和兰州新区绿色贷款增长最快,分别较年初增长96.25%、81.64%。试验区绿色贷款余额占其本外币贷款余额比重为8.83%,高于全国平均水平。其中,哈密占比最高,达34.5%;兰州新区、湖州、克拉玛依等6个试验区占比均超10%。试验区绿色信贷资产质量较好且保持稳定,平均不良率仅0.16%,远低于全国贷款不良率平均水平。其中,新疆三地和兰州新区绿色贷款不良率为0。此外，试验区主动对接市场需求，全面提升产品和服务质量。例如，衢州常山农商行结合本地胡柚特色产业创新推出"金柚贷"，截至2020年末，共发放"金柚贷"143笔，金额达2 115万元。广州创新推出全国首个汽车绿色供应链金融服务，满足车企节能环保方面的融资需求。克拉玛依创新"应收账款质押+特种设备""收费权质押+光伏设备"等方式，发放绿色信贷11.2亿元，用于支持天然气净化、光伏发电等项目。

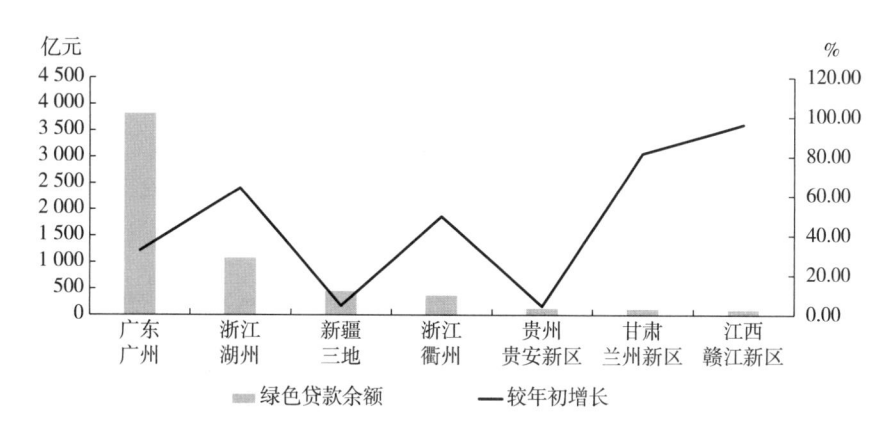

图 4-2 2020年试验区绿色贷款情况

二是大力推动企业和金融机构绿色债券发行，鼓励和支持符合条件的企业上市、挂牌融资，融资渠道多样化建设不断深化。截至2020年末，各试验区发行绿色债券余额887.76亿元，同比增长34.5%。2020年，衢州发行绿色债券5亿元；广州6家企业共发行绿色债券123.5亿元；兰州新区发行绿色债券22.04亿元，主要用于支持雨水调蓄工程等绿色项目。此外，各试验区积极支持主营业务收入主要来自绿色产业和领域的企业上市融资。截至2020年末，各试验区在新三板挂牌的绿色企业共9家，全年合计融资1461.26万元。广东股权交易中心绿色环保板挂牌展示企业233家，注册资本金27.68亿元。2020年，广州侨银环保、洁特生物、小鹏汽车等7家企业分别在中小板、创业板和纽交所上市，募集资金达55亿元，上市企业绿色股权融资额占比为87%。

三是不断壮大绿色基金规模，有效激励更多金融机构和社会资本开展绿色投融资，化解金融创新中的资金瓶颈问题。截至2020年末，湖州共设立绿色产业基金65只、总规模达486.49亿元，资金实际到账120.44亿元，实际使用资金108.13亿元，已投项目为175个。衢州设立各类绿色产业投资基金规模达189.93亿元，资金已到位75.89亿元。2020年，广州设立绿色产业基金6只，管理基金规模共计270余亿元；昌吉设立政府性产业引导绿色产业基金4只，总规模达87.1亿元；哈密成立"哈密市科创产业股权投资基金"，提供3 000万元支持科技型中小企业绿色发展；克拉玛依设立政府性产业引导基金2只，新增募集资金1.7亿元；兰州新区设立绿色金融改革创新试验区发展基金，总规模达30亿元。

四是持续推进环境污染责任险、安全生产责任险、农业保险等绿色保险产品，开展绿色建筑保险等试点。湖州探索绿色建筑工程履约保险、绿色建筑安全生产责任保险，创新推出绿色能效保险、绿色装修工程保险、绿色建设工程质量潜在缺陷保险等产品。截至2020年末，昌吉开展环境污染责任保险业务，更新完善365家高危行业重点企业的目录清单，安全生产责任保险实现100%全覆盖，依托"棉花保险+期货"试点，探索开展绿色农业保险改革创新，保费收入为2.97亿元。哈密各财险公司共承保绿色保险23 864笔，保费收入为1.44亿元，保障金额为147.37亿元。

五是深化个人绿色金融产品发展。湖州依托"智慧支付"系列工程，运用金融科技手段，积极探索面向个人的绿色金融产品。安吉农商行开出全国首张绿色存单，并创新线上"绿意存"产品，吸收的存款专项用于支持县域绿色发展。绿色存款在安吉农商行产生的效益将回馈激励居民开展绿色生活，如奖励居民垃圾分类、低碳出行和绿色支付等。衢州对"个人碳账户"数据进行大数据分析，针对不同主体有限制地开放查询和应用，并鼓励金融机构提供优惠绿色金融服务，促进市民养成绿色支付的习惯。

六是积极支持复工复产。湖州充分利用再贷款支持政策，扩展"绿贷通"平台功能，增设"央行政策支持贷"模块，上线"央行惠农政策支持贷""央行惠小政策支持贷""央行防疫政策支持贷"3款产品。通过对目标客户、利率、条件等要素进行标准化定制、系统化展示，有效提升企业融资可获得性。2020年，克拉玛依安排复工复产专项额度共3亿元，摸排绿色中小微企业办理票据贴现需求，并给予其30个基点的贴现价格优惠。

三、绿色金融基础设施逐渐完善

一是加快推进绿色项目库建设。湖州搭建绿色融资主体认定评价系统（"绿信通"）和ESG评价系统，实现绿色评价智能化、全量化、价值化。截至2020年末，累计认定绿色融资企业763家、绿色融资项目98个。昌吉出台《昌吉州绿色企业认定办法（试行）》和《昌吉州绿色项目认定办法（试行）》，兰州新区制定《兰州新区绿色企业认证和评价办法》《兰州新区绿色项目认证和评价办法》，为科学建设绿色项目库提供了政策依据，打通了绿色金融落地的瓶颈。截至2020年末，各试验区绿色项目库项目总数超2 900个，同比增长近30%，累计投资约1.75万亿元；各试验区共遴选了2 299个项目在北京绿色交易所（原北京环境交易所）挂牌交易，同比增长407.51%。

二是信息披露共享机制持续完善。各试验区政府和金融机构在绿色金融实践和环境信息披露等方面达成共识，环境信息披露质量不断提高。在环境信息披露方面，2020年2月，人民银行组织试验区试用《金融机构环境信息披露指南（试行）》。湖州发布全国首个区域性环境信息披露报告，包含1份环境信息披露区域报告和19家主要银行业金融机构环境信息披露报告，有效发挥绿色金融改革"窗口"展示作用。江西省四家法人城商行开展金融机构环境信息披露工作，成为全国首个法人城商行环境信息披露全覆盖的省份。在环境信息共享方面，昌吉州向金融机构及社会投资主体开放绿色项目库，并在州人民政府网站上公开建设项目公示信息、执行法规条例、行政审批、水环境质量、空气质量等信息。兰州新区将企业环境行政处罚信息纳入征信系统，为金融机构支持绿色产业发展提供信息支撑，2020年末已实现1 487家企业环境行政处罚信息、1 297家企业环保"一考双评"信息的共享。

专栏4-1

湖州发布全国首个区域性环境信息披露报告

2020年，湖州在全国率先落地实施《金融机构环境信息披露指南（试行）》（以下简称《指南》），发布全国首个区域性环境信息披露报告，包括1份环境信息披露区域报告和19家湖州主要银行业金融机构[①]环境信息披露报告。

一、主要做法

一是统一标准，提升信息披露公信力。湖州根据《指南》制定《湖州市银行业金融机构环境信息披露框架（2020版）》，明确规范性引用文件和金融术语及定义，确定总体概况、战略与目标、治理结构等8大项19小项披露内容。

---

① 当年资产规模在100亿元以上的湖州市主要银行业金融机构。

二是注重细节，提升信息披露真实性。第一，明确法人机构在公司治理层面的环境机制设计，要求法人机构董事会要对环境相关风险和机遇进行分析与判断。第二，指导机构强化环境风险、机遇的分析与管理，要求机构提升对环境风险的分析测算能力。第三，强化基础设施建设，要求机构特别是法人机构确保绿色信贷数据的准确性，加强对绿色信贷客户隐私数据的保护。

三是加强指导，强化银行机构责任担当。湖州开设环境信息披露视频课，就银行机构环境信息披露的相关政策、统计方法、监管要求等进行针对性的指导和培训。同时，强调银行机构从总量、人均、多种温室气体排放等角度开展披露。

二、主要成效

截至2019年末，19家主要银行机构绿色信贷余额为549.67亿元[①]，当年投放的绿色贷款形成的二氧化碳减排量为266.52万吨[②]。截至2020年末，湖州已有16家银行建立环境风险管理流程和措施，绿色信贷风险防范机制得到健全完善。

三是金融科技助推绿色可持续发展。截至2020年末，各试验区开发上线绿色金融相关系统或平台17个（见表4-2），在绿色金融系统化、信息化、标准化方面实现新突破。

表4-2　　各试验区运用金融科技开发绿色金融系统（平台）情况

试验区	系统（平台）名称	主要功能	主办方
湖州	绿色金融信息管理系统	集数据实时采集、处理、分析、应用为一体的绿色金融信息监管平台	人民银行研究局、人民银行湖州中支
	绿色金融综合服务平台	绿色融资主体认定（绿信通）、银企对接服务（绿贷通）、项目资本对接（绿融通）	湖州市金融办
	绿色银行监管评级及信息分析综合系统（绿茵系统）	通过信息系统量化银行绿色化程度，为监管政策提供参考依据	银保监会湖州监管分局
	绿色信贷管理系统	绿色信贷识别及环境风险管理	湖州银行

[①] 根据银保监口径统计。
[②] 根据银保监绿色信贷项目节能减排量测算指引计算。

续表

试验区	系统（平台）名称	主要功能	主办方
衢州	绿色贷款专项统计信息管理系统	生成各类绿色信贷统计数据、环境效益计量结果、绿色信贷业绩评价	人民银行衢州中支
	金融服务信用信息平台	政银企交互、绿色企业（项目）识别评价和培育、风险预警监测、信保基金增信融资、可视化统计分析	衢州市政府
赣江新区	小微客户融资服务平台	推动绿色项目与金融机构融资对接	人民银行南昌中支
	绿色企业信息平台	展示绿色企业信息和融资需求	江西联合股权交易中心
广州	广州市绿色金融改革创新试验区融资对接系统（绿穗通）	政策支持、融资对接、项目管理、孵化和培育的综合平台	花都区人民政府、人民银行广州分行
	绿色融资租赁线上平台（绿色银赁通）	融资租赁公司与银行授信叠加，支持绿色产业	九江银行广东自贸试验区南沙支行
	绿色金融体系生态补偿平台（生态补偿平台）	通过金融科技手段实现生态补偿产品及项目的线上交易和对接	广州碳排放权交易中心
	绿色企业供应链融资平台	为新能源汽车办理供应链融资	中国建设银行广州分行、中国工商银行广州分行
贵安新区	贵州省绿色金融综合服务平台	公布绿色金融项目、展示绿色金融机构、发布绿色金融政策与动态	省地方金融监督管理局、贵安新区管委会
新疆	绿色金融服务平台	展示绿色项目信息，与金融机构及社会投资者共享	新疆自治区绿金办
	昌吉绿色小额农户贷款管理系统	追溯绿色信贷资金流向、防范绿色贷款风险	昌吉农村商业银行
	克拉玛依政金企信息共享平台	绿色项目库信息发布	克拉玛依市金融办
兰州新区	兰州新区绿色金融综合服务平台	银企融资对接、绿色专业服务以整合企业部分社会信息数据	兰州新区管委会

四是环境权益交易市场不断壮大。截至2020年末，试验区完成各类环境权益交易超58亿元，同比增长22.61%。初步形成包含碳排放配额交易市场、温室气体自愿减排交易市场、碳普惠市场的多层次碳交易市场体系。广东试点碳市场碳排放配额累计成交量为1.72亿吨，成交金额为35.45亿元，居全国首位，是国内首个配额现货成交额突破30亿元大关的试点碳市场。昌吉和克拉玛依对辖内205家企业核发了排污许可证，对1 809家企业完成排污登记工作。

表4-3　　　　　　　　　　试验区环境权益市场交易金额

地区	交易金额（亿元）
湖州	6.02
衢州	9.49
赣江新区	0
广州	40.02
贵州	1.2
新疆哈密、昌吉、克拉玛依	1.3
兰州新区	0

注：贵州绿色金融改革创新是立足贵安新区、辐射全省，鉴于数据可得性，此表统计的是贵州省。

五是加强绿色金融智库平台建设。各试验区通过设立绿色金融专业委员会、绿色金融学院等方式，加快培育绿色金融专业人才，不断提升绿色金融研究能力。2020年7月，广州绿色金融研究院成立。9月，广东省组织举办广东金融学会绿色金融专业委员会（以下简称广东绿金委）2020年会，调整完善广东绿金委组织架构，组建多个专项工作小组，加强广东绿色金融政产学研联动。12月，湖州市人民政府与中国银行、北京绿色金融与可持续发展研究院签订《关于共同筹建"两山绿色金融学院"框架合作协议》。

四、改革创新工作保障举措水平逐步提高

一是完善绿色金融司法保障和纠纷调解机制。各试验区持续推进法治建设，加强金融司法协作，建立纠纷调解机制，提高法律保障力度。湖州市中级人民法院、湖州市金融办、人民银行湖州市中心支行等4方签署金融司法合作框架协议，湖州市中级人民法院、华东政法大学、人民银行湖州市中心支行等5方签署《绿色金融法治保障与风险治理合作协议》；设立全国首个绿色金融纠纷调解中心，成立以"法润绿金"为品牌的湖州绿色金融纠纷调处法官工作室。截至2020年末，已成功调解银企纠纷案件88件，涉及标的金额1.49亿元。

二是推动财政奖补等激励机制建设。各试验区创新政策引导机制，明确绿色融资风险补偿、担保及绿色保险保费补贴等机制，增强绿色金融改革支撑力，撬动金融资源助力绿色产业发展。2020年，衢州财政部门以30%权重将绿色金融发展绩效纳入财政资金竞争性存放评价指标体系；推动出台绿色企业（项目）专项贴息政策，对深绿、中绿、浅绿企业（项目）分别给予15%、10%、5%的贴息；开展的6次财政资金（合计87.33亿

元）竞争性存放中，绿色金融发展较好的5家银行机构获得51.2%的资金。昌吉出台《昌吉州绿色金融发展专项资金使用管理办法（试行）》，明确财政每年至少安排2 000万元专项资金，用于绿色金融补贴、风险补偿和奖励。克拉玛依重点支持绿色企业复工复产，共为各类绿色企业节省费用3.13亿元，同比增长2.4倍。兰州新区制定出台《兰州新区绿色金融发展奖励政策（试行）》，试点期间安排10亿元财政专项资金，引导金融资源向兰州新区绿色产业、绿色项目集聚。

三是落地绿色贷款担保增信机制。针对绿色项目"融资难""担保难"问题，各试验区创新绿色信用担保产品，根据绿色等级提供差异化担保支持。湖州创新打造"政策性担保定向支持""绿色小额贷款保险""绿色信用保证"三大绿色担保模式，对"深绿""中绿"企业，最高补助75%、50%的担保费用。截至2020年末，湖州累计为153家绿色小微企业提供担保授信2.56亿元，为1 009户提供政策性融资担保14.54亿元。贵阳农商行创新引入"4321"担保方式（本级担保公司承担40%，省财政风险补偿金承担30%，银行或保险机构承担20%，市县担保机构本级财政风险补偿金承担10%），对贵阳清镇市环红枫湖元宝枫种植及加工一体化产业园项目建设提供贷款7.4亿元，预计可带动清镇1 600名建档立卡贫困户脱贫致富。

五、绿色金融国际合作进一步扩展

试验区主动参与国际交流活动，促进绿色金融提质增效。2020年4月，赣江新区九江银行加入联合国环境规划署金融倡议（UNEP FI），是全国首家签署《负责任银行原则（PRB）》的城商行。12月，湖州银行与亚洲开发银行签订合作备忘录，成为境内首家与亚开行签订合作备忘录的银行机构。

第二节 其他地区绿色金融改革创新广泛开展

除六省（区）九地试验区外，长三角（上海市、江苏省和浙江省）、粤港澳大湾区（广东省、香港特别行政区和澳门特别行政区）、成渝地区双城经济圈（重庆市、四川省）等国家重大发展区域及其他部分代表性省（区、市），也大力推动绿色金融改革创新，积极探索绿色金融支持区域发展的新路径，着力实现绿色金融与经济转型发展的有机结合。

一、国家重大区域发展战略大力推动绿色金融发展

（一）绿色金融为粤港澳大湾区发展带来新机遇

2020年9月，深圳绿金委、广东绿金委、香港绿色金融协会、澳门银行工会联合发起设立"粤港澳大湾区绿色金融联盟"，联盟秘书处常设深圳。作为全国首个区域性绿色金融联盟，粤港澳大湾区绿色金融联盟的成立是落实《关于金融支持粤港澳大湾区建设的意见》（银发〔2020〕95号）及粤港澳绿色金融合作的重要举措，将为深化粤港澳金融合作带来新的动力。联盟将在绿色供应链金融（汽车制造业）、固体废弃物处置、绿色建筑项目、区块链光伏项目等领域展开创新探索，并形成粤港澳统一碳市场研究工作组、绿色资产交易研究工作组等5个工作组。

（二）绿色金融服务长三角一体化发展

为贯彻落实党中央、国务院决策部署，经国务院同意，2020年2月14日，人民银行、银保监会、证监会、外汇局、上海市政府联合发布《关于进一步加快推进上海国际金融中心建设和金融支持长三角一体化发展的意见》（银发〔2020〕46号），从积极推进临港新片区金融先行先试、在更高水平加快上海金融业对外开放和金融支持长三角一体化发展等方面提出30条具体措施，进一步加快推进上海国际金融中心建设和长三角一体化发展。

长三角地区积极推进金融先行先试，探索建立符合一体化绿色发展要求的金融体制。2020年4月，浦发银行长三角一体化示范区管理总部在上海成立，重点服务自贸、科创、绿色生态的创新平台，加快发展绿色金融和产品创新，全力支持上海国际金融中心建设。8月，上海农商银行设立长三角金融总部，计划未来3年为长三角地区（不含上海）客户提供授信不少于1 200亿元。截至2020年末，长三角全部银行业存款类金融机构绿色贷款余额为2.79万亿元。

（三）绿色金融支持长江经济带绿色发展

2020年11月，习近平总书记在南京主持召开全面推动长江经济带发展座谈会，提出要使长江经济带成为我国生态优先绿色发展主战场，要求长江经济带要努力建设人与自

然和谐共生的绿色发展示范带,并再次强调要加强生态环境系统保护修复,要把修复长江生态环境摆在压倒性位置。

金融机构积极支持长江经济带11省(市)生态优先、绿色发展,成为推动经济社会发展全面绿色转型的重要力量。2020年12月8日,国家开发银行面向全球投资人发行"长江大保护"专题"债券通"绿色金融债券,发行规模为35亿元。募集资金专项用于长江流域经济带污染防治、资源节约与循环利用及生态保护和适应气候变化等类别的绿色产业项目。

二、其他地区主动开展绿色金融改革创新

(一)北京:以绿色金融改革创新支持首都绿色低碳循环发展

2020年,北京将创建绿色金改试验区工作列入"十四五"规划,统筹全市力量推进试验区申创和各项落地准备工作。一是推动金融精准支持绿色产业高质量发展。绿色技术创新全国领先,相关领域重点实验室达115家、工程技术中心达51家。绿色建筑实现规模化发展,全市累计通过绿色建筑标识项目共531项,二星级及以上建筑面积占比达93.9%。绿色债券发行规模居全国首位,支持多家绿色企业上市融资,配合国家碳达峰、碳中和目标战略实施,率先发行碳中和债。节能环保、清洁能源、绿色建筑、绿色交通类贷款占全部绿色贷款比重近90%。二是高起点推动城市副中心加大绿色金融资源聚集力度。围绕绿色金融先导承载地建设,引导各类绿色低碳基金、ESG理念投资机构、绿色金融智库相继落地。三是高标准开展绿色金融国际交流合作。举办《"一带一路"绿色投资原则》(GIP)第二次全体会议、中欧绿色金融论坛、第二届中国资管行业ESG投资高峰论坛等大型活动。四是高水平深化碳排放权交易市场建设。2020年碳配额成交价格为全国平均成交价格的4倍,北京环境交易所更名为北京绿色交易所,绿色金融基础设施建设工作持续加快。

(二)重庆:加速推进绿色金融改革创新试验区申建

2020年,重庆按照碳达峰、碳中和战略部署,加速推进创建绿色金融改革创新试验区。一是做好顶层设计。明确建设试验区的碳减排目标,初步建立"1+N"绿色金融与绿色制造、绿色建筑、绿色交通、绿色农林等绿色产业融合发展机制。二是对接高标

准。按全国统一绿色金融标准，制定以碳排放效益为核心指标的绿色项目（企业）评价规范，搭建全国首个碳减排项目库。三是完善基础设施。上线"长江绿融通"系统，实现统计监测、绿色项目智能识别、电子政务等功能。四是健全激励约束。推动部分区县出台绿色金融奖补细则，实现全市绿色信贷业绩评价智能化一键生成。五是强化创新。全辖金融机构推出140款绿色金融产品，绿色贷款、绿色债券余额合计超3 000亿元，较年初增长超30%，重庆农村商业银行成为中西部首家"赤道银行"和参加"中英金融机构气候与环境信息披露试点"的银行机构。

（三）深圳：绿色金融支持粤港澳大湾区开放创新

为贯彻落实中共中央、国务院印发的《粤港澳大湾区发展规划纲要》，深圳以绿色发展为契机，积极开展绿色金融改革实践探索，深入推进绿色金融体系建设。2020年，深圳出台全国首部绿色金融法规《深圳经济特区绿色金融条例》，并荣获国际金融论坛（IFF）"全球绿色金融创新奖"；积极开展垮区域合作交流，深圳绿金委联合广东绿金委、香港绿色金融协会、澳门银行工会联合发起设立"粤港澳大湾区绿色金融联盟"，联盟秘书处常设深圳。同时，深圳绿金委与联合国环境规划署全球金融中心城市绿色金融联盟（简称C4S）共同推动设立的"绿色金融服务实体经济实验室"正式启动，开展大湾区"固体废物处置研究与实践探索"项目研究，发挥绿色金融对"无废城市"建设的支撑作用。

第三节 绿色金融支持污染防治和民生重点领域

2020年，绿色金融继续加大对生态价值补偿、"无废城市"、绿色建筑、垃圾分类、清洁供暖、畜禽养殖废弃物处置和资源化利用、黑臭水体治理等污染防治重点项目和重点民生领域的支持力度，继续探索可持续的金融支持路径，不断满足低碳循环发展和人民群众日益增长的对优美生态环境的需要。

一、绿色金融推动实现生态价值补偿取得成效

建立生态产品价值实现机制，是落实党中央、国务院绿色发展要求的重要战略抓

手。国家层面的生态产品价值实现以财政转移支付为主，包括纵向生态保护补偿和横向生态保护补偿。例如，天然林保护和退耕还林工程中，国家级公益林平均补偿标准为每亩每年5元，集体和个人所有的国家级公益林补偿标准为每亩每年15元；中央财政每年从水污染防治资金中安排一部分资金作为引导和奖励资金，支持长江流域19个省（区、市）健全完善流域横向生态保护补偿机制。此外，我国开展碳排放权交易试点已有10余年，进一步丰富了生态产品价值实现渠道。

地方层面的生态产品价值实现，既有政府主导型的生态保护补偿，也有市场主导型的产业化经营。其中，2019年以来，推动长江经济带发展领导小组办公室先后批复浙江丽水和江西抚州开展生态产品价值实现机制试点，两地探索形成生态产品变生态资本的"生态贷"模式。浙江安吉探索形成生态产品产业化经营的"两山银行"模式。丽水建立生态行为与金融信贷挂钩的联动激励机制，创新推出"两山信用贷"和"生态主题卡"。广州建立了碳市场和碳普惠相结合的市场化生态补偿机制。重庆结合脱贫攻坚战工作部署，从碳履约、碳中和和碳普惠3条路径开展"碳汇+"生态产品价值实现试点，万州、酉阳、忠县林业碳汇项目产生碳汇量约190万吨。

二、绿色金融支持"无废城市"建设持续推进

2020年，"11+5"个试点城市和地区[①]发挥绿色金融支撑作用，持续推进"无废城市"建设，并取得积极成效。其中，深圳排放权交易所依托"绿色金融服务实体经济实验室"平台，发挥绿色金融对"无废城市"建设支撑作用，开展大湾区"固体废物处置研究与实践探索"项目研究，构建大湾区固废处置政府间沟通协调机制、固废处置设施布局及监管协调机制、固废处理技术协同网络和广东省（深圳）固废交易平台四大固体废物处理协同网络。截至2020年末，"深圳危险废物交易平台"系统设计和功能开发已完成。该平台将覆盖深圳1万余家危险废物相关企业，可为企业提供签约、检测、支付"一站式"线上服务。浙江绍兴通过保险机构、环境监管部门和企业联动试点打造"保险保障+信用评价+平台监管"的业务模式，形成涉废企业一体化绿色金融环境风险防

---

① 广东省深圳市、内蒙古自治区包头市、安徽省铜陵市、山东省威海市、重庆市（主城区）、浙江省绍兴市、海南省三亚市、河南省许昌市、江苏省徐州市、辽宁省盘锦市、青海省西宁市11个城市作为"无废城市"建设试点。同时，将河北雄安新区、北京经济技术开发区、中新天津生态城、福建省光泽县、江西省瑞金市作为特例，参照"无废城市"建设试点一并推动。

控体系，将固体废物特别是危险废物环境风险降至最低。截至2020年末，绍兴已为参保的20家企业共排查环境风险隐患点150余个，缴纳保费92.96万元，保险金额达到1.35亿元。

三、绿色金融与绿色建筑协同发展

2020年7月，住房和城乡建设部、发展改革委、教育部、工业和信息化部、人民银行、国管局、银保监会七部委联合印发《绿色建筑创建行动方案》（建标〔2020〕65号），明确到2022年，当年城镇新建建筑中，绿色建筑面积占比达70%，并提出要加强财政金融支持，积极完善绿色金融支持绿色建筑的政策环境。8月，住房和城乡建设部、教育部、科学技术部、工业和信息化部、自然资源部、生态环境部、人民银行、市场监督管理总局、银保监会九部委联合印发《住房和城乡建设部等部门关于加快新型建筑工业化发展的若干意见》（建标规〔2020〕8号），提出要加大金融扶持，支持新型建筑工业化企业通过发行企业债券、公司债券等方式开展融资，对达到绿色建筑星级标准的新型建筑工业化项目给予绿色金融支持，并提出在不新增隐性债务的前提下鼓励各地设立专项基金支持建筑工业化发展。

在信贷领域，建筑节能与绿色建筑有关内容纳入人民银行绿色贷款专项统计制度、银保监会绿色信贷统计制度。在保险领域，积极推动开展绿色建筑性能保险、超低能耗建筑性能保险等绿色保险应用试点，打造"保险+服务+科技+信贷"，为绿色建筑项目提供事前信用增进、事中风控服务、事后损失补偿。2020年8月，人保财险绿色建筑性能保险"保险+服务+科技+信贷"新模式签订首单协议。在债券领域，地产及城投公司通过发行企业债、公募公司债、私募债、中期票据等方式支持绿色建筑开放建设。

专栏4-2

绿色金融与绿色建筑协同发展案例

一、湖州经验

2020年3月，住房和城乡建设部、人民银行、银保监会联合批复湖州在绿色金融改革创新试验区框架下开展绿色建筑和绿色金融协同发展实践，并围绕绿色建筑标准实施体系建设、绿色金融支持方式创新及配套支持政策制定三个维度开展工作。湖州成为全国首个绿色建筑和绿色金融协同发展试点城市，一年来成效显著。

一是试点政策加快落地。制定《湖州市建设绿色建筑和绿色金融协调发展城市推进计划》，明确至2021年，全市城镇绿色建筑占新建建筑比例达到99%以上；制定《关于加快绿色建筑提质发展若干意见》，出台产业、财政、金融、政府投资管理等16项支持措施；允许绿色装配式建筑的容积率由4%提高到7%；绿色建筑公积金贷款额度提高10%。

二是标准体系先行先试。完善绿色建筑评价地方标准，编制全国首个绿色建筑贷款认定规则，明确绿色建筑项目在符合5个条件下（取得绿色建筑预认证、土地出让合同或项目备案为绿色建筑、承保绿色建筑性能保险、相关主体有良好信用记录、接入信息披露自律机制），金融机构对其发放的贷款可统计为绿色信贷，有效解决绿色金融支持绿色建筑期限错配、信息不对称等障碍。此外，市住建局与市金融办共同组织制定绿色建筑项目认定标准及绿色建筑开发贷款、消费贷款等系列贷款标准。

三是金融产品多点开花。湖州36家银行机构先后开发了"绿地贷""绿色购建贷""绿色建筑企业按揭贷"等创新产品114个，建立15亿元绿色投资联动专项资金，设立总规模达304亿元的绿色产业基金。安吉县创新设立全国首个"农房绿色建筑贷"。全国首单"保险+服务+信贷"绿色建筑性能保险落地湖州。

截至2020年末，湖州绿色建筑贷款余额75.44亿元，较年初增长129.86%，支持建筑领域的绿色贷款余额占全部绿色贷款的比重提高到7.25%。

二、青岛经验

2020年12月，住房和城乡建设部、人民银行及银保监会共同批复青岛市开展绿色城市建设发展试点工作。在试点起步阶段，青岛市从政策实施、产品创新应用等方面推动绿色金融支持城市绿色发展建设。

一是青岛市人民政府印发《关于加快推进绿色城市建设发展试点的实施意见》，将试点工作细化为4大类27项具体任务。该实施意见明确以探索推广市场应用模式、搭建电子化常态化金企对接平台、设立绿色发展基金、推进绿色债券发展等为主要内容的绿色金融体系构建任务，建立以绿色融资为特色的城乡建设市场化资源配置结构，完善绿色城市与绿色金融联动发展机制。

二是探索绿色金融支撑机制。重点加强与金融机构、企业主体合作，引导银行机构积极对接绿色城市领域融资需求，先后与中国建设银行等6家金融企业（机构）达成战略合作意向，获得意向性绿色城市金融支持资金达3 500亿元。同时加大绿色信贷规模和产品创新力度，开出全国首张超低能耗建筑性能保单、"减碳保"建筑节能保险保单，发放全省首笔1 000万元"碳中和"贷款和首笔5亿元"碳中和"债券，努力趟出资本力量助推绿色城市建设发展新路径。

三是开展绿色保险试点。中德生态园被动房住宅推广示范小区项目（二期）业主单位，就超低能耗建筑投保。参保后，保险公司组织第三方风控服务机构，全过程监督超低能耗建筑的建造过程。若投保项目的供暖年耗热量、供冷年耗冷量、气密性三项指标未达到超低能耗建筑的性能要求，保险公司将根据保险合同约定，赔偿项目节能整改费用，或对能耗超标进行经济补偿，并承担相应的鉴定费用和法律费用。

四、绿色金融助力垃圾分类工作有序开展

各地运用绿色金融工具，助力控制垃圾增长速度，提高垃圾处理效率。湖州创新推出"园区贷"、银行卡加载积分、绿色信用贷等产品，一方面推动"低小散"企业集中进入产业园区、统一进行污染处理，另一方面培养居民垃圾分类意识，形成绿色生活方式。广州创新药品置换保险，发挥政府、药企、保险公司合力，为居民提供免费的过期药品置换服务，减少过期药品对空气、土壤和水源环境的污染。

五、绿色金融支持清洁供暖工作持续推进

金融支持清洁供暖，是助力打好污染防治攻坚战、打赢蓝天保卫战的重要路径。综合来看，跨部门协作、信息共享机制建设、金融产品与服务创新等是推动金融支持清洁供暖的重要抓手，特别是相关信贷标准的完善，进一步提高了金融支持清洁供暖的效率和精准性。

（一）山西长治多措并举

作为京津冀大气污染传输通道"2+26"重点城市之一，山西长治从"凝聚合力、

编制标准、优化服务、数据平台"四方面着力，稳步推进绿色金融支持清洁供暖工作。2017—2020年，长治各金融机构累计向清洁供暖企业发放贷款共7.98亿元，截至2020年末，贷款余额为3.73亿元，同比增长69.17%，信贷满足率为85.7%。长治完成清洁供暖改造29.8万户，同比增长16.41%。长治主城区及县城建成区清洁供暖覆盖率达100%，农村清洁供暖覆盖率达88%。

长治的主要做法有：一是制定《清洁供暖贷款规范标准》，明确贷款主体条件、贷款申请、发放流程、贷后管理及相关罚则等内容，为银行和企业提供清洁供暖信贷产品统一标准。二是通过支小再贷款、货币政策直达工具、产品创新等举措，不断优化金融服务。以长子农商行为例，截至2020年末，使用支小再贷款专用额度向清洁供暖企业放贷930万元，年利率4.35%；运用直达工具为清洁供暖企业办理无还本续贷1 440万元，返还利息66.9万元；推出"燃电贷""沼气贷"产品，带动450余户农户实现清洁取暖。三是加强清洁供暖监测平台和信息平台建设。截至2020年末，监测平台共录入56.6万户清洁取暖农户基础资料，同比增长18.7%，为金融机构对清洁供暖企业的信贷服务及风险防控提供了数据支撑。截至2020年末，长子县辖区内8家金融机构、8家清洁供暖企业全部接入信息平台，促进了政、银、企信息交流和资金对接。

（二）新疆创新信贷模式

截至2020年末，新疆城镇集中供热系统清洁化建设运营和改造绿色贷款余额38.92亿元，占基础设施绿色升级绿色贷款余额的6.18%。新疆各金融机构加强信贷模式创新，有效解决了企业难题。中国建设银行昌吉分行以"PPP+特许经营权"模式向5家渠首热鸿达热力有限公司提供项目建设缺口部分基本建设贷款5.8亿元，助力企业实现电厂余热综合利用供热。昆仑银行研发"蓝天贷"产品，在客户准入和利率方面无差别对待国有企业和民营企业，有效解决了民营企业融资难、融资贵问题。截至2020年末，金融机构已为20家发电和供热企业累计授信41.69亿元，累计投放金额23.24亿元。

六、绿色金融支持畜禽养殖废弃物处置和资源化利用取得新经验

2020年，江西共青城、浙江衢州龙游县继续先行先试，探索金融支持畜禽养殖废弃物处置和资源化利用有效途径。江西抚州、重庆荣昌等紧密结合地方实际需求，加大金融支持畜禽粪污资源化利用工作力度。

（一）江西"共青模式"在省内多地推广

江西赣江新区共青组团继续推广"洁养贷"。共青城2家畜禽养殖企业获得"洁养贷"980万元，助力粪污年处置量达到7 855吨，生产的干粪及沼气用于本企业4 000亩农田种植及生活发电等，年节省生产成本84万元。

"共青模式"已在江西省内多地推广。2020年，人民银行九江市中心支行推动修水县制定《修水县畜禽养殖及粪污资源化利用试点方案》，并设立500万元的风险补偿基金；组织九江银行、江州农村商业银行探索创新第三方收益权质押模式，为企业发放环保设施改造项目贷款。抚州东乡区畜牧局、生猪协会等部门合作推出集《发展改革委立项备案书》《环评合格报告》《动物防疫条件合格证》三证合一的"养殖经营权"抵押贷款模式。截至2020年末，东乡农村商业银行向16家生猪养殖企业发放"畜禽智能洁养贷"4 930万元。

（二）重庆荣昌"财金联动"

重庆荣昌区畜禽产业发达，"荣昌猪"为世界八大、中国三大优良地方猪种之一，品牌价值居全国地方猪品牌价值榜首。随着近年来畜禽养殖组织化规模化推进，全区畜禽养殖污染负荷与土地消纳存在较大压力，部分镇街土地承载能力和环境承载能力趋于饱和，资源环境约束进一步趋紧。荣昌区创新"财金联动"模式，整体推进全区畜禽养殖废弃物处置和资源化利用工作。2020年，金融支持畜禽粪污贷款余额1.14亿元，同比增长89.19%。全区20个镇街、290个规模化养殖场和具备条件的中小型养殖场实现设施升级改造，项目总投资9 103.3万元。畜禽粪污综合利用率达到93.23%，规模养殖场粪污处理设施装备配套率达到100%，全区粪污产生量87.2万吨，养殖粪污资源化利用种植面积11.8万亩，替代化肥1.4万吨，产生经济效益2 800万元。

荣昌区主要做法有：一是完善机制和政策体系。人民银行永川市中心支行会同荣昌区财政局、区畜牧局等部门联合出台《金融支持荣昌区畜禽粪污资源化利用绿色发展实施方案》，推动荣昌区政府出台《荣昌区促进生猪产业贷款的指导意见》，引导金融机构支持生猪产业。二是财金联动扶持。加大财政直接补助，2020年财政补助资金4 900万元；加大财政间接支持，设立"助农贷"风险补偿基金1 000万元，1∶10放大，发挥杠杆撬动作用；运用再贷款资金支持畜禽养殖企业，降低企业融资成本。三是创新金融产品和服务。金融机构深入畜禽养殖企业走访，"一企一策"解决养殖企业融资困难。

中国农业银行荣昌支行围绕国家级重庆（荣昌）生猪交易市场"猪交所"平台，开发上线"农业银行资金双向保付系统"，日均交易额1 500万~4 000万元；结合"猪交所"平台推出"生猪电商e贷"，2020年发放贷款共82笔，金额达2 051万元。

七、绿色金融支持黑臭水体治理等污染防治重点领域

住房和城乡建设部、生态环境部、人民银行等部门积极支持金融机构借助市场机制加大对黑臭水体的治理力度，直辖市、省会城市、计划单列市建成区黑臭水体消除比例显著提高。截至2020年末，全国地级及以上城市2 914个黑臭水体消除比例达到98.2%，并力争在"十四五"时期基本消除县级城市建成区的黑臭水体。

专栏4-3

绿色金融支持黑臭水体整治的广东实践

广东通过完善政策框架，加强政银联动合作，强化绿色金融产品和服务创新，探索多元化融资模式等措施不断加大金融对黑臭水体治理的支持力度。截至2020年末，广东城市黑臭水体整治绿色信贷余额151.04亿元，同比增长31.23%。广东大部分城市黑臭水体基本消除。

一是引导政策性银行运用抵押补充贷款（PSL）资金，支持黑臭水体项目开展。农发行云浮分行使用PSL资金向郁南县"整县生活污水处理捆绑"PPP项目授信3亿元，发放贷款2.29亿元，贷款利率4.45%，比该行自有资金贷款利率低0.46个百分点。

二是加强政银、政银企合作。平安银行广州分行与广东粤科集团、广东建工集团签订广东环保基金《合作备忘录》。三方共同发起总规模为63亿元的广东环保基金母基金，撬动社会资本投向粤东西北等地区生活垃圾和污水治理领域。

三是探索多元融资模式。广东省人民政府发行全省首只、全国水资源领域首只绿色地方政府专项债券，发行总额27亿元，用于珠江三角洲水资源配置工程项目建设。国家开发银行广东省分行利用PPP模式加大对水环境整治、污水处理等基础设施

建设项目投入，重点支持广州水生态项目、东莞水生态项目、遂溪县镇村生活污水处理及配套管网工程PPP项目等项目建设。广东南海农村商业银行通过发行绿色金融债券筹集资金，累计向绿色产业和项目投放27.97亿元，支持南海区里水镇河涌水环境治理项目等环境基础设施项目建设。

第五章　绿色金融国际合作深入开展

绿色金融是我国参与全球经济金融治理的重要领域。2020年，中国积极推动绿色金融服务人类命运共同体，在全球范围内广泛开展合作，与多个国家和国际组织达成多项绿色发展共识，在落实《"一带一路"绿色投资原则》、环境信息披露、气候与环境风险评估等方面取得重大成果。2020年9月，在第75届联合国大会一般性辩论上，国家主席习近平向全世界郑重宣布，中国二氧化碳排放力争于2030年前达到峰值，努力争取2060年前实现碳中和。这是中国第一次在全球正式场合提出碳中和计划时间表，彰显大国担当，得到国际社会普遍认可。随后，在联合国生物多样性峰会和气候雄心峰会上，国家主席习近平多次表明中国参与全球环境治理的决心，并明确了2030年减少碳排放的系列举措。到2030年，中国单位国内生产总值二氧化碳排放将比2005年下降65%以上，非化石能源占一次能源消费比重将达到25%左右，森林蓄积量将比2005年增加60亿立方米，风电、太阳能发电总装机容量将达到12亿千瓦以上。国际社会普遍认为，中国的倡议与举措发挥了表率作用，是推动构建人类命运共同体的一项重要行动。

第一节　"一带一路"绿色金融合作取得积极进展

《"一带一路"绿色投资原则》（GIP）作为一套自愿性准则，获得相关投融资方更加普遍的认可。截至2020年末，来自14个国家和地区的38家国际大型金融机构和企业签署了GIP，其资产总规模超过41万亿美元；支持机构数量扩大至12家，包括四大会计师事务所等全球和区域性金融服务提供商。

一、积极落实《"一带一路"绿色投资原则》

（一）召开GIP首次指导委员会会议

2020年4月6日，GIP指导委员会召开首次会议。会议讨论了GIP中长期规划，研究了完善GIP治理结构和构建专业化秘书处等问题，并就进一步推动落实GIP提出了建议，包括强化GIP签署机构的环境信息披露、追踪流入共建"一带一路"国家的绿色投资、与其他国际性倡议和共建"一带一路"国家的政府部门开展合作等。

（二）召开GIP第二次全体会议

9月24日，GIP第二次全体会议在北京召开。来自全球四十多个金融机构和国际组织的近140名代表参会。会议发布了《"一带一路"绿色投资原则2020年度报告》。一是评估了GIP落实情况。大部分GIP成员机构公布了可持续发展战略和绿色转型目标，按照国际标准建章立制工作取得积极进展。但从最佳实践要求看，各成员机构仍有较大进步空间。二是明确了GIP未来的重点工作，包括指导成员机构进一步将绿色发展目标整合入公司业务与治理结构，提升成员机构的可持续性评估、风险评估和管理等能力，组织撰写绿色投资最佳实践和环境信息披露的手册，鼓励成员机构创新更多绿色金融产品，支持绿色"一带一路"建设，并按照气候相关财务信息披露工作组（TCFD）要求为成员设立信息披露改进目标等。三是提出了GIP中长期规划。GIP"2023愿景"包括自我评估、信息披露、绿色承诺、加大投资和成员机构发展五个关键支柱。

二、深化"一带一路"绿色金融能力建设

（一）开发GIP气候与环境风险评估工具

2019年末，GIP第一工作组启动了研制"一带一路"项目环境与气候风险测算工具的工作。2020年，中国工商银行与秘书单位普华永道及GIP秘书处牵头15家成员机构，共同推动环境风险分析，开发了GIP气候与环境风险评估工具CERAT，并进入内部测试研究阶段，用于测算能源、交通、电力等行业项目的碳排放。目前，CERAT对GIP会员单位开放测算功能，并支持游客浏览。

专栏5-1

气候和环境风险评估工具箱简介

中国工商银行、普华永道及GIP秘书处牵头15家成员机构，完成了气候和环境风险评估工具箱（The Climate & Environmental Risk Assessment Toolbox，CERAT）第一阶段开发，并在GIP成员机构范围内进行了内部测试。

CERAT是针对项目的综合性碳减排核算工具，内嵌了不同项目类型、项目技术等指标，实现不同绿色项目、棕色项目的碳排放核算。CERAT提供中英双语版本和相应语言的软件界面，在界面中还提供用户操作指南、碳排放计算逻辑说明、不同地区（如欧盟、中国等）碳排放标准等参考信息，便于使用者根据实际项目填报与测算。使用者能够直接下载项目碳排放情况报告。

下一步，GIP第一工作组拟持续优化CERAT，适时增加污染物排放、水风险、生物多样性等测算模块。

（二）制定"一带一路"环境和气候信息披露框架

2020年，兴业银行和东方汇理银行共同牵头GIP环境和气候信息披露工作组，在总结市场优秀实践的基础上，结合气候相关财务信息披露工作组（TCFD）的建议和GIP成员机构的实际情况，形成了成员机构落实GIP原则和开展环境信息披露的报告框架。GIP秘书处以此为基础，对成员机构落实GIP和开展信息披露有关情况进行评估，并对表现优秀的成员机构颁发"GIP最佳实践奖"，以鼓励落实绿色投资原则并提升信息披露的广度和深度。

（三）积极开展"一带一路"绿色金融能力建设合作

GIP举办五场线上研讨会，议题涵盖碳排放计算工具，环境、社会和治理（ESG）信息披露、绿色金融产品创新等，推动共建"一带一路"国家金融机构加强知识共享和经验交流。中国工商银行牵头发起的"一带一路"银行家圆桌会已成为沿线国家商业金融机构间互助合作和能力建设的重要平台；国家开发银行、中国进出口银行、中国农业银行、中国银行等机构也结合市场需求与自身优势,提供了与"一带一路"建设可持续发展相关的培训。

清华大学绿色金融发展研究中心支持蒙古、哈萨克斯坦、巴基斯坦等沿线国家制定绿色金融界定标准、开发绿色项目环境效益评估工具,并与国际金融公司等共同发起绿色金融能力建设项目(GFLP)。2020年,GFLP集中举办两次大型能力建设活动,主题分别为"金融机构和绿色债券发行人的环境信息披露"和"后疫情时代的绿色复苏和绿色金融促进保护生物多样性"。来自60多个国家和地区的3 000位金融行业政策制定者、企业高管、专业服务机构专家和各界人士参加了活动。

(四)发布"一带一路"海外项目分级分类体系

2019年,生态环境部与中外合作伙伴共同发起成立"一带一路"绿色发展国际联盟。2020年12月,该联盟发布"一带一路"海外项目分级分类体系,为利益相关方识别和应对海外投资的生态环境风险、筛选重点项目提供指引。该体系建议依据投资项目在环境污染防治、气候变化减缓和生物多样性保护三个维度上的影响,将项目划分为鼓励合作类(绿色)、一般影响类(黄色)和重点监管类(红色)三种类型。

三、金融机构积极支持"一带一路"建设

(一)中国进出口银行"一带一路"绿色投资实践

一是将可再生能源项目作为2020年境外投资重点,为巴基斯坦苏基—克纳里水电站项目、乌兰巴托污水处理厂项目、迪拜哈斯彦2 400兆瓦清洁燃煤电站项目等多个"一带一路"绿色项目提供了信贷支持。二是在参控股的股权投资业务中,定向支持绿色经济领域的出资金额共计3 700万美元及3.3亿元人民币,包括东盟基金投资绿色经济领域项目1个,出资1 950万美元;中日节能环保基金累计投资项目13个,总投资金额3.3亿元人民币,推动2个项目实现上市;中国—中东欧投资合作基金二期投资波兰250兆瓦光伏发电站,出资1 750万美元。三是区域信用担保与投资基金(CGIF基金)以增信担保方式支持绿色经济发展,累计为3个境外绿色债券提供担保,担保责任余额约3.53亿美元。

(二)丝路基金"一带一路"绿色投资实践

丝路基金积极贯彻新发展理念,将可持续投资原则融入公司投资决策和管理,扎

实推进高质量共建"一带一路"。2020年8月，在签署《区域全面经济伙伴关系协定》（RCEP）的背景下，丝路基金与美国KKR集团（Kohlberg Kravis Roberts & Co.）共同投资韩国废弃物处置项目，学习和探讨引入韩国医疗固废处理领域领先的技术标准和管理经验，助力我国固废产业优化升级。9月，丝路基金投资的迪拜光热和新能源平台项目荣获GIP年度"最佳绿色融资项目"奖项。

丝路基金积极推进已投项目公司的绿色治理。其中，俄罗斯西布尔公司在节能减排方面持续努力，其2020年考核排名已超过欧洲公司和世界石化企业的平均排名。凭借在节约燃料和提升效率方面的出色成就，东方海外公司获得2020年香港环境卓越大奖和Seatrade Maritime亚洲海事大奖的"燃油效益大奖"。

第二节　参与和引领绿色金融多边国际合作

一、在央行与监管机构绿色金融网络（NGFS）治理和研究中发挥重要作用

央行与监管机构绿色金融网络（NGFS）是中国参与国际绿色金融合作的重要平台。人民银行是NGFS指导委员会成员之一，参与决策NGFS发展的重要事项。截至2020年末，NGFS的正式成员增至84家央行和金融机构，同时有13个观察员。其中，12月15日，美联储宣布加入NGFS，是第84个成员。

人民银行自2018年起担任微观审慎工作组主席，重点关注如何将环境气候风险纳入审慎监管框架、金融机构披露环境气候风险的实践等议题。2020年9月，微观审慎工作组完成了《金融机构环境风险分析综述》（Overview of Environmental Risk Analysis by Financial Institutions）和《环境风险分析方法案例集》（Case Studies of Environmental Risk Analysis Methodologies），总结了环境风险分析的关键步骤，为银行、资管和保险公司开展环境风险分析提供了方法、工具和应用案例，为金融行业提高环境风险评估和管理水平提供了重要的公共产品。

同时，为满足NGFS对气候相关宏观研究的需求，2020年9月，NGFS正式设立研究工作组，由人民银行担任主席。研究工作组计划2021年重点关注生物多样性损失对金融

系统的影响，以及如何动员更多资金保护生物多样性。

> 专栏5-2
>
> ## 《金融机构环境风险分析综述》简介
>
> 《金融机构环境风险分析综述》（以下简称《综述》）介绍了环境风险传导演化成金融风险的典型案例，用较为通俗的语言介绍了银行、资管和保险公司常用的环境风险分析工具和方法。
>
> 《综述》指出，环境风险分析在金融业的推广应用仍面临较多挑战。例如，金融业尚未充分了解环境风险和意识到其与金融风险的相关性；可用于评估环境风险的公开数据和方法普遍缺失；金融机构对环境风险分析的投入和能力不足；与污染相关的风险分析和新兴经济体环境风险分析不足；已有的环境风险分析方法仍不完善，数据质量也存在问题。
>
> 为推动金融机构开展环境风险分析，《综述》提出以下六项建议：一是央行和其他金融监管机构应带头开展宏观层面的环境风险分析，向金融机构释放清晰的政策信号，明确推广环境风险分析的决心，制定相关的标准，推动金融机构开展环境风险分析。二是将环境风险分析方法作为公共产品，向金融业推广。三是扶持重点行业或重点地区的示范研究项目。四是建立国际通用的、健全的环境披露框架，鼓励金融机构根据TCFD建议披露其对环境和气候因素的风险敞口及环境风险分析结果。五是建立关键风险指标（Key Risk Indicators, KRI）和相关统计数据库，帮助金融机构和监管部门识别、评估与管理环境和气候相关风险，并提升数据的可比性。六是建立绿色和棕色经济活动分类体系。

二、延续二十国集团（G20）绿色发展共识

2020年，在人民银行等多方推动下，G20延续了对可持续金融议题的关注，重点讨论如何支持疫情后经济实现低碳绿色复苏，在2020年10月G20财长和央行行长视频会议上，各方普遍认为应抓住疫后复苏这一窗口期推动经济低碳转型，绿色金融是撬动私人

部门资金的重要抓手，可弥补应对气候变化存在的资金缺口，各方呼吁金融机构和企业将可持续因素纳入投资决策和经营活动，加速和放大政府低碳政策的效果。

2020年11月，G20举行领导人利雅得峰会，核准通过了《G20领导人利雅得峰会宣言》，该宣言肯定了可持续金融对全球经济增长和稳定的重要作用，明确表示"发展可持续金融和普惠金融对全球经济增长和稳定至关重要"。

在人民银行和欧洲等多方支持下，意大利作为2021年G20轮值主席国，考虑将可持续金融作为2021年G20重点工作，计划重启2016年由人民银行牵头成立的可持续金融研究小组。

三、参与可持续金融国际平台（IPSF）合作

IPSF由欧盟委员会、人民银行等8家成员于2019年10月正式发起，旨在深化绿色和可持续金融领域的国际协调合作，动员私人部门资金开展环境可持续投资。截至2020年末，IPSF成员数发展至14家，成员所在国占全国经济体量、人口总量和碳排放量的50%。

2020年10月，IPSF举行一周年线上视频活动，发布首份进展报告。报告指出，新冠肺炎疫情凸显了各方采取协调行动、为全球经济可持续发展提供融资支持的迫切需求。近年来，可持续金融市场在规模和多元化方面发展较快，但还不足以实现《巴黎协定》目标。IPSF初步梳理了成员所在国在绿色金融相关领域的进展情况，认为在绿色分类标准方面，IPSF成员处于初期阶段，许多IPSF成员所在国都在考虑开发各自的绿色分类标准。为此，欧委会方面与人民银行牵头在IPSF下成立了绿色分类标准工作组，重点对比中欧绿色金融分类标准的异同，在此基础上提出共同分类方案，以推动国际绿色金融市场协调发展，降低绿色跨境投资成本。在可持续信息披露方面，多数IPSF成员出台了可持续信息披露监管要求，并考虑向强制性监管方向过渡。在绿色标签标准方面，越来越多IPSF成员正在开发制定可持续金融产品的标准或标签，并配套监管标准或指引文件，以提高透明度和准确性，解决洗绿风险。

> 专栏5-3

绿色金融标准中外一致性研究取得积极进展

随着主要经济体绿色金融/可持续金融标准的建立，在全球范围内跨境绿色资本流动趋势愈发明显的趋势下，促进不同绿色金融标准的兼容发展显得日益迫切。2019年10月，人民银行代表中国加入可持续金融国际平台（IPSF），与欧洲多国和阿根廷、加拿大、摩洛哥等成员共同推动绿色与可持续金融领域的国际合作。2020年7月，中欧牵头成立工作组，开展中欧绿色金融/可持续金融分类标准的对比研究，通过梳理双方标准在分类框架、支持范围和技术标准等方面的异同，旨在提出中欧共同标准方案的建议。技术工作组秉持开放性态度，过程中也积极吸收其他国家成员参与并汲取建议。目前，加拿大、日本、新加坡等国家技术专家陆续加入技术工作组，技术工作组代表性和影响力日益增加。

目前，技术工作组对中欧绿色金融标准的比较分析已取得初步共识性成果，为下一步建立共同认可的一致性标准奠定了基础。

一、中欧绿色金融/可持续金融标准在环境目标维度高度一致

欧盟《可持续金融分类方案》旨在为政策制定者、业界和投资者提供实用性工具，识别具有环境可持续性的经济活动和投资机会。《可持续金融分类方案》明确了六大环境目标，至少对六大环境目标之一有显著贡献且对其他环境目标无重大损害的经济活动，被纳入绿色经济活动。六大环境目标包括：气候变化减缓，气候变化适应，海洋与水资源可持续利用和保护，循环经济、废弃物防治和回收，污染防控，保护健康的生态系统。与此相对，中国代表性的绿色金融标准《绿色债券支持项目目录（2020年版）》（征求意见稿）展现了三个维度的环境目标，分别为：环境改善、应对气候变化和资源节约高效利用。虽然分类维度和定义表述有所不同，但双方环境目标的实质覆盖范围基本重合，高度一致。

表5-1 中欧主要绿色金融标准的目标对比

欧盟目标	中国目标
气候变化减缓	应对气候变化
气候变化适应	
海洋与水资源可持续利用和保护	环境改善
循环经济、废弃物防治和回收	
污染防控	
保护健康的生态系统	资源高效利用：循环经济、废物回收利用和污染防控

二、中欧绿色金融标准绿色经济活动覆盖范围重合度较高且具有互补性

虽然双方绿色金融标准分类框架、分类方法不同，但支持的具体绿色经济活动对象具有较高重合度。目前，欧盟《可持续金融分类方案》已经完成气候变化减缓、气候适应环境目标维度的绿色经济活动识别，其他环境目标维度绿色经济活动识别将在后续年度陆续完成。中国《绿色债券支持项目目录（2020年版）》（征求意见稿）则完成了全部环境目标维度的绿色经济活动界定。因此，欧盟《可持续金融分类方案》暂未列示生态保护、污染防控等环境目标绿色经济活动，并不意味着反对和排斥为上述环境目标作出显著贡献的经济活动，不代表在上述领域双方绿色金融标准存在重大差异。在双方都已完成的气候变化减缓环境目标维度绿色经济活动界定中，具体绿色经济活动的覆盖范围重合度较高，特别是在可再生能源领域，双方共识性的支持对象基本一致。在工业能效领域，双方对于绿色经济活动涉及的具体类型则存在相对较大的差异，上述现象体现了双方产业结构的差异，以及产业低碳转型技术路径等方面的多样性。上述现象也提示，提升绿色金融标准的兼容性，需考虑不同国家、不同经济体产业结构、产业发展阶段特点，在坚持共识性环境目标的前提下，将所在国家或经济体对特定环境目标具有重大影响的行业纳入评估范围，从中识别具有显著环境目标贡献的经济活动，将提升绿色金融标准的代表性和广泛接纳度。

三、中欧绿色金融标准存在相互借鉴的空间

目前，除绿色金融标准一致性研究的发起者和牵头者中欧双方之外，越来越多的国家、国际组织加入绿色金融标准一致性研究合作，这对建立具有国际共识性的

绿色金融标准奠定了良好的基础。作为绿色金融标准研究的领先者，中欧双方绿色金融标准具有各自独特的优点，也存在相互借鉴、完善的空间。例如，欧盟《可持续金融分类方案》在技术标准基准方面的相对明确清晰，中国《绿色债券支持项目目录》在绿色经济活动领域、范围方面的广泛代表性。中国在推进国际共识性绿色金融标准建立的过程中，需要积极汲取包括欧盟《可持续金融分类方案》在内的其他绿色金融标准良好经验，同时反映自身和其他处于同类发展阶段的国家和经济体实际，积极发挥中国绿色金融标准的影响力和话语权。

四、加入可持续金融专项工作组（STF）

2020年2月，国际证监会组织（IOSCO）成立了理事会层面的可持续金融专项工作组（STF），重点研究发行人可持续相关信息披露、投资者保护等监管问题。中国证监会加入STF并积极参与了发行人可持续信息披露等具体工作，通过填报问卷、提交行业座谈报告等方式分享了中国的监管动态和业务实践。

五、证券交易所积极参与绿色金融国际合作

2020年7月，深圳证券交易所加入联合国可持续证券交易所倡议（UNSSE）气候信息披露专题顾问工作组。该工作组由伦敦证券交易所和约翰内斯堡交易所联合牵头，旨在推动全球交易所披露气候相关信息，为发行人提供符合TCFD框架规范的工作流程指南和相关综合信息披露指导。8月，上海证券交易所在获得中国证监会同意后，加入UNSSE气候信息披露咨询顾问组。2021年6月29日，UNSSE正式发布《气候信息披露指南》及《推动市场积极应对气候变化的行动计划》，上海证券交易所反馈的相关意见均获得采纳，5个上交所绿色金融案例入选该行动计划。9月，上海证券交易所获选世界交易所联合会（WFE）可持续发展工作组副主席，持续深入参与国际组织绿色金融工作。一是参与ESG数据库建设项目，反馈绿色债券、绿色ETF及指数等指标信息。二是参与全球交易所可持续发展调研，分享践行可持续发展倡议的有力举措，及践行联合国可持续发展目标（SDGs）具体落实工作。三是参与全球ESG相关标准的制定，11月，针对国际财务报告准则（IFRS）发布的《关于可持续发展报告咨询意见》，上海证券交易所作

为WFE可持续工作组副主席，组织了多次会议听取会计审计机构和国际资产管理公司等市场机构意见，与工作组主席一起召集成员交易所讨论，最后形成了WFE关于IFRS制定一套全球统一的可持续发展报告标准的支持意见。

六、部分金融机构积极加入绿色金融国际平台

《可持续蓝色经济金融原则》（Sustainable Blue Economy Finance Principles）由联合国环境规划署管理，旨在利用蓝色金融力量重建海洋繁荣，恢复海洋健康和生物多样性，是世界上第一个为银行、保险公司和投资者提供可持续蓝色经济融资的全球性指导框架。截至2020年末，兴业银行、青岛银行自愿签署了《可持续蓝色经济金融原则》。

专栏5-4

可持续蓝色经济金融原则

2018年，欧盟委员会、世界自然基金会、威尔士亲王国际可持续发展部和欧洲投资银行（EIB）共同制定了《可持续蓝色经济金融原则》。

1. 保护原则

我们将支持那些采取一切可能措施来恢复、保护或维持海洋生态系统的多样性、生产力、复原力、核心功能、价值和整体健康，以及依赖海洋生态系统的生计和社区的投资、活动和项目。

2. 合规原则

我们将支持那些符合可持续发展和海洋健康相关的国际、区域、国家法律和其他相关框架的投资、活动和项目。

3. 风险意识原则

我们将努力以对经济、社会和环境价值、量化风险和系统影响的整体和长期评估为基础，作出投资决策；并将根据对与业务活动相关的潜在风险、累积影响和机遇的新认知调整我们的决策流程和活动。

4. 系统性原则

我们将努力识别我们的投资、活动和项目在整个价值链上的系统性影响和累积

影响。

5. 包容原则

我们将支持那些包含、支持和提高当地生计的投资、活动和项目，并与利益相关方进行有效沟通，来识别、回应和减缓受影响方相关问题。

6. 合作原则

我们将与其他金融机构和相关利益方合作，共同推动和实施这些原则，分享有关海洋的知识、可持续蓝色经济最佳实践、经验教训及观点和想法。

7. 透明原则

在不涉密的情况下，我们将披露投资及其对社会、环境和经济的（正面和负面）影响。我们将努力报告这些原则的落实进展情况。

8. 目的性原则

我们将努力引导资金投向直接有助于实现可持续发展目标（SDG）14（"保护和可持续利用海洋和海洋资源以促进可持续发展"）和其他可持续发展目标的项目和活动，尤其是有助于海洋治理的。

9. 影响力原则

我们将支持那些不仅要避免损害，更要为当代和后代提供海洋所带来的社会、环境和经济效益的投资、项目和活动。

10. 预防原则

我们将支持那些已根据可靠科学证据评估环境社会风险及影响的海洋相关投资、活动和项目。坚持预防原则优先，特别是在缺乏科学数据的情况下。

11. 多元化原则

中小企业在蓝色经济中发挥着重要作用，我们将努力开发多元化的投资工具，以覆盖更广泛的可持续发展项目，例如传统的和非传统的海洋行业、小型的和大型的项目。

12. 解决方案导向原则

我们将努力引导资金投向解决海洋问题（包括陆上和海上）的创新商业方案，为海洋生态系统和依赖海洋的生计带来积极影响。我们将努力识别和培育此类项目的商业案例，并鼓励推广由此形成的最佳实践。

13. 伙伴原则

我们将与公共、私营和非政府部门机构合作，加快实现可持续蓝色经济，包括编制和落实沿海及海洋空间规划实施方案。

14. 科学引领原则

我们将积极学习和蓝色经济投资相关的潜在风险和影响、开发相关数据，并鼓励蓝色经济中的可持续投资机会。更广泛地说，我们将努力分享海洋环境相关的科学信息与数据。

此外，2020年，重庆农村商业银行、绵阳市商业银行、贵州银行正式采纳《赤道原则》，成为继兴业银行（2008年）、江苏银行（2017年）、湖州银行（2019年）后中国又一批赤道银行。九江银行加入负责任银行原则（PRB），成为继中国工商银行、兴业银行、华夏银行之后第四家加入的中资银行。

第三节 绿色金融双边合作取得新进展

一、中英环境信息披露试点不断深化

2020年，中英金融机构环境信息披露试点工作持续推进。

一是试点机构覆盖所有类型金融机构。继2019年增加平安集团、中航信托、人保财险三家机构后，2020年，海通证券、重庆农商行及湖州市绿色金融改革创新试验区领导小组加入试点，中国银行、江西银行、九江银行成为观察员。中方试点机构由最初的6家（中国工商银行、兴业银行、江苏银行、湖州银行、华夏基金、易方达基金）扩展到15家（含观察员），覆盖银行、资管、保险、证券等多个行业，参与机构管理的资产总额达90多万亿元人民币。

二是试点机构环境信息披露水平提升。中英共同发布第二份《中英金融机构气候与环境披露试点进展报告》。分机构看，中国工商银行连续两年发布专题报告，并以附录的形式将报告与TCFD框架的内容进行了对标和索引。平安银行根据TCFD框架发布了年度《气候变化报告》。湖州银行发布了专题报告，部分保险和信托机构在社会责任报告或年度报告中开辟专栏进行了环境信息披露。

三是试点经验加快复制推广。12月21日，金融机构环境信息披露研讨会暨中英金融机构环境信息披露试点工作组第八次会议在北京召开。在会上，中方工作组发布了《中英金融机构环境信息披露框架（中方）》。在此基础上，中国工商银行牵头研制了《金融机构环境信息披露指南》，并在绿色金融改革创新试验区先行试用，指导浙江湖州实现辖内金融机构环境信息全披露。此外，江西银行、兴业银行、江苏银行、海通国际四家试点机构分别发布了环境信息披露最新成果和报告，其中兴业银行和江苏银行披露了绿色建筑和医药化工行业的压力测试成果，海通国际分享了到2025年实现集团碳中和目标及实现路径。

二、加强中欧绿色金融合作，构建绿色发展伙伴

6月22日，国家主席习近平在北京以视频方式会见欧洲理事会主席米歇尔和欧盟委员会主席冯德莱恩，在绿色低碳、数字经济等广泛领域达成共识。

7月28日，国务院副总理刘鹤与欧盟委员会执行副主席东布罗夫斯基斯以视频会议形式共同主持了第八次中欧经贸高层对话。双方围绕"开启后疫情时代中欧合作新局面，引领全球经济稳健复苏增长"主题，进行了深入、坦诚、务实、高效的讨论，将绿色金融相关内容纳入对话第14项成果。未来将在数字货币领域、可持续金融、金融科技等领域加强信息共享和交流合作，探讨推动中欧绿色金融标准趋同。

三、第七次中法高级别经济财金对话强化绿色金融合作

7月21日，国务院副总理胡春华与法国经济和财政部长布鲁诺·勒梅尔共同主持了第七次中法高级别经济财金对话，双方就中法抗疫合作和国际宏观经济政策协调、中法双边重点领域和大项目合作等内容进行深入探讨，将绿色金融相关内容纳入对话第21项成果。双方同意继续促进两国金融监管机构之间的合作，包括可持续金融。中方欢迎符合条件的法国机构投资者积极投资中国债券市场，愿与法国就银行间债券市场投资、发债有关问题保持沟通，并提供必要的支持与便利。中方欢迎法国银行和金融市场基础设施申请接入人民币跨境支付系统（CIPSX），中法两国共同发起并致力于推动央行和监

管机构绿色金融网络（NGFS）的有关工作。双方将继续加强在绿色金融市场领域的合作，包括ESG信息披露，绿色资产风险权重，以及绿色金融支持生物多样性等议题，共同推动可持续金融发展。

四、第二次中意财长对话强化双边绿色金融合作

11月11日，财政部长刘昆与意大利经济和财政部部长瓜尔蒂耶里共同主持了第二次中意财长对话，为进一步深化中意经济财金合作，双方就抗击疫情、宏观经济政策协调、全球经济治理合作、财金合作等领域进行了深入探讨，达成了多项共识，并将绿色金融相关内容纳入对话第14项成果。双方将继续加强绿色金融领域的合作，包括在NGFS框架下开展合作。双方将鼓励两国金融机构签署《"一带一路"绿色投资原则》。

第四节　市场机构的国际合作实践更加丰富

一、不断扩大国际合作支持的绿色领域

2020年，中国金融部门与国际金融组织合作支持的绿色产业范围扩大至水泥余热发电、新能源汽车、河流综合治理、大气污染防治等节能环保产业，医疗固废处理等清洁生产产业，水力发电、光伏发电、煤炭清洁利用、可再生能源等清洁能源产业，绿色智慧公交等基础设施绿色升级及绿色金融研究等领域。其中，在证监会支持下，中证金融研究院申报并获批亚洲开发银行知识服务技术援助项目《可持续绿色投融资发展与企业环境信息披露指标体系建设研究》，积极助力绿色金融市场生态的不断优化。

专栏5-5

积极发挥转贷优势，推动国际可持续发展

中国继续与新开发银行、欧洲投资银行、德国复兴信贷银行等国际金融机构开

展转贷合作，推动节能减排可持续发展。

2020年，中国进出口银行争取新开发银行专项贷款10亿美元，用于节能环保、新能源和可再生能源、公共卫生建设等受疫情影响严重、急需复工复产的重点行业和领域。获得中奥财政合作5亿欧元贷款独家转贷行资格，由奥地利监管银行（OeKB）作为上游贷款人，款项专用于支持环保型基础设施建设、气候和环境保护、环境友好型交通建设等领域。利用转贷款支持黄孝河机场河水环境综合治理二期项目39亿元人民币，该项目是集水质净化、排涝提升、湿地景观等多功能于一体的重大工程，也是落实"长江大保护"总体目标而大力推进的四水共治项目之一。利用转贷款支持唐钢佳华焦炉环保升级搬迁项目，该项目可实现煤炭资源高效转化利用，所采用工艺除尘率达99.9%，具有明显经济和节能减排效益。

华夏银行向安徽海螺新能源有限公司发放转贷款1 063万欧元，贷款期限11年，用于淮安海螺新能源有限公司12兆瓦时储能电站项目、张家港海螺新能源有限公司32兆瓦时储能电站项目建设。两个储能项目采用削峰填谷的方式运作，电能全部按照公允价格出售给淮安海螺水泥、张家港海螺水泥两个企业使用。目前，两个储能电站均稳定运行，其成功模式有望在其他水泥厂区复制推广。

二、分享中国经验，强化国际绿色投资教育

（一）积极宣传中国绿色和ESG投资实践

一是生动展示中国上市公司ESG等非财务信息披露进展。在国际证监会组织（IOSCO）的"世界投资者周"活动中，在中国证监会投资者保护局的指导下，上海证券交易所开设主题为"科创板上市公司　社会责任知多少"的特别节目，发布《大数据视角下的沪市A股公司投资者关系全景报告》，介绍中国绿色金融投资者教育的有益实践。近90个国家和地区的证券监管机构、证券交易所及8个全球性或地区性组织、投资者协会参与了"世界投资者周"活动。深圳证券交易所出席美银美林ESG专项路演、联合国负责任投资原则论坛等活动，围绕ESG等境外投资者关心话题，介绍深圳上市公司相关情况。

二是加强国际投资者对中国特色ESG信息披露的理解。10月27—29日，上海证券交易所举办2020年国际投资者大会，专设ESG讨论环节，邀请中国人民银行、联合国贸促会（UNCTAD）、世界证券交易所联合会（WFE）和卢森堡交易所等机构参与"推动疫情后世界经济绿色复苏"等讨论，提升绿色发展意识。在"推动高质量发展——中国公司ESG实践"圆桌讨论环节，境内外大型机构投资者、沪市上市公司和境内外指数公司等从不同角度探讨ESG投资机遇与挑战。

三是将绿色金融国际推介与上市公司ESG能力建设有机结合，推动上市公司从战略发展角度加大对ESG的重视。9月25日，上海证券交易所举办"对话国际投资者：ESG如何赋能上市公司"线上培训，从公司质量和投资价值的角度向上市公司阐释了ESG信息披露的重要性，并积极向国际投资者宣传上市公司ESG优秀实践，近120家国际投资者及上市公司代表踊跃参加。

（二）分享中国推动疫后可持续复苏经验

2020年，新冠肺炎疫情肆虐全球，上海证券交易所积极向WFE及WFE会员交易所提供防控举措和业务连续性计划等材料，以实际行动履行上海证券交易所在抗疫国际合作中的社会责任。上海证券交易所还联合卢森堡交易所，以两所名义向卢森堡当地医院捐赠医疗物资，联合中国金融期货交易所向巴基斯坦证券交易所捐赠防疫物资，同全球同业携手抗疫，共克时艰。WFE官方杂志《聚焦》五月刊上，还特别刊登了上海证券交易所疫情期间IPO不停、支持疫情一线地区为主题的英文文章。

2020年6月，中国工商银行出席全球可持续发展投资者（GISD）联盟"新冠疫情应对与复苏"CEO特别视频会议，宣介中方防控疫情、重启经济的主要经验，以及推动世界经济复苏、加快落实《2030年可持续发展议程》的建设性意见。会议发布GISD联盟行动声明，呼吁全球企业界将可持续发展目标（SDGs）融入自身核心业务模式并引导投资行为，推动后疫情时代世界经济可持续、有韧性的复苏。

第六章 绿色金融任重道远

在过去的几年里,全球关于气候变化的讨论发生了根本性变化。各国已就气候变化是否正在发生形成广泛共识,开始集中就如何应对气候变化进行更具建设性的讨论与实践。截至2020年末,已有126个国家和地区正式宣布或正在考虑提出净零排放目标,其温室气体排放量占全球总排放量的比重达51%[①]。净零排放和碳中和目标将深刻改变全球经济、产业和投资结构,现有金融体系也需顺应历史潮流,为适应和减缓气候变化作出相应调整。绿色金融任重道远、发展空间巨大。

从国内看,做好金融支持绿色低碳高质量发展工作,是党中央、国务院赋予金融体系的光荣使命和重要任务。金融部门要聚焦碳达峰碳中和目标,做好绿色金融顶层设计和规划,充分发挥金融支持绿色发展的三大功能。一是通过货币政策、信贷政策、监管政策、强制披露、绿色评级、行业自律、产品创新等,引导和撬动金融资源向低碳项目、绿色转型项目、碳捕捉与封存等绿色创新项目倾斜。二是通过气候风险分析压力测试、环境和气候风险分析等工具,增强金融体系管理气候变化相关风险的能力。三是推动建设全国碳排放权市场,稳妥有序发展碳金融,为实现碳达峰、碳中和目标积极贡献力量。

为实现上述三个功能,持续提升金融体系支持经济复苏、绿色转型和降碳减排的能力,2021年和今后一段时期,我们应准确理解国家碳减排和经济绿色低碳转型的政策内涵,把握好金融支持碳达峰碳中和的节奏和力度,围绕完善绿色金融五大支柱,重点做

---

① 数据来源:联合国环境规划署,《2020年排放差距报告》。如果美国按照拜登—哈里斯(Biden-Harris)气候计划,到2050年实现温室气体净零排放,这一比例将增加至63%。

好以下几项工作。

第一，构建长效机制，完善金融支持绿色低碳转型的顶层设计，降低经济发展对高碳产业的路径依赖，实现经济可持续发展。研究出台金融支持碳达峰、碳中和目标的一揽子政策措施，在"十四五"金融规划等顶层制度设计中就金融支持绿色低碳发展和应对气候变化作出系统性安排。完善激励约束机制，研究气候和环境因素对货币政策和金融稳定的影响。充分发挥金融市场配置资源的基础性作用，有效抑制不顾资源环境承载能力盲目追求增长的短期行为，加快推动高碳行业转型或有序退出，重点培育绿色建筑、清洁交通、可再生能源等绿色产业板块。支持绿色技术研发与推广，推进清洁生产，发展绿色环保产业，加速工业部门绿色和数字化转型。逐步将绿色消费纳入绿色金融支持范围，推动形成绿色生活方式。

第二，完善政策标准，推动绿色金融自身高质量可持续发展。一是进一步丰富绿色金融政策工具箱。研究出台绿色金融条例等规范性文件。推动建立强制性、市场化、法治化的金融机构气候与环境信息披露制度，不断完善信息披露模板，由易到难、由少到多，逐步实现金融机构计算和披露其资产的碳排放量信息。及时调整和完善绿色金融评价机制，不断扩展绿色金融评价结果应用场景，形成对绿色金融业务的有效激励约束。创设碳减排支持工具，利用优惠再贷款鼓励金融机构增加与碳减排相关的优惠贷款投放。开展气候和环境风险分析及压力测试，及时防范化解经济和产业结构调整可能引发的区域性或行业性金融风险。二是以碳中和为约束条件，进一步完善绿色金融标准体系。尽快出台统一的新版《绿色债券支持项目目录》。根据"需求导向，急用先行"原则，制定新一批绿色金融标准清单。推动成熟标准在试验区先行先试。深度参与ISO/TC 322的可持续金融标准研究工作，持续推进中欧绿色金融标准趋同。

第三，创新产品服务，丰富直达实体的多层次绿色金融市场体系。创新发展绿色资产证券化、绿色资产支持票据等产品。研究推动绿色金融资产跨境交易，提高国内绿色金融产品流动性。创新发展数字绿色金融，加强数字技术和金融科技在环境信息披露和共享等方面的应用，降低金融机构与绿色主体之间的信息不对称。发展碳基金、碳债券等碳金融产品工具，推动期货交易所积极研发碳期货品种，有序拓展碳市场交易的参与主体范围。鼓励社会资本出资设立低碳转型基金。丰富绿色保险产品，鼓励保险资金投资绿色领域。引导金融机构充分考虑我国经济社会发展实际和各行业发展的阶段性和转型难度等因素，紧密跟随有关部门制定的碳减排政策，在确保自身业务可持续性的前提下，积极支持相关企业绿色低碳转型，稳妥有序调整自身资产结构，避免对传统高碳行业简单采取踩踏式、冒进式抽贷。

第四，推进地方试点，加快绿色金融改革创新试验区有益经验的复制推广。鼓励试验区政府多方筹措资金、创新支持方式，探索碳达峰、碳中和新要求下，不断充实和丰富绿色金融改革创新试验区改革创新任务。利用试验区联席会议机制，总结推广试验取得的有益经验，切实发挥好试验区先行先试示范作用。支持试验效果突出的试验区升级为绿色金融示范区，选择一批能承担重大改革创新任务、支持国家重大战略的地区，继续开展绿色金融改革创新试点。

第五，深化国际合作，以绿色金融参与和引领全球金融治理。坚持"互利共赢、共同发展"原则，发挥好中国在绿色金融市场规模巨大、政策体系成熟等方面的先行优势，继续通过G20、金融稳定理事会（FSB）、NGFS、IPSF、国际清算银行（BIS）、巴塞尔银行监管委员会（BCBS）、可持续银行网络（SBN）等多边及双边平台，积极宣传推广中国绿色金融政策、标准和最佳实践，讲好中国故事，贡献中国智慧，将中国的成功经验和优势资源落实到"南南合作"和"一带一路"倡议中，彰显中国负责任大国形象。

控碳减排功在当代、利在千秋。以国家主席习近平2020年9月在联合国大会上的郑重承诺为标志，中国生态文明建设进入到以碳达峰、碳中和为重点战略方向的新阶段，历史赋予了我们新的使命和艰巨任务。支持绿色低碳转型和高质量发展，助力培育具有国际竞争力的绿色产业，是今后一段时期我国金融工作的核心任务和重点内容。金融业应继续以"绿水青山就是金山银山"理念为引领，以更宽广的胸襟砥砺前行，再接再厉，向党、向国家、向全世界人民交出中华民族的答卷。

附录一　2020年绿色金融大事记

1月11日，北京环境交易所举办"2020北京绿色金融研讨会暨绿色项目库启动会"，绿色项目库正式上线，启动全国范围的绿色项目入库工作。

1月15—16日，人民银行研究局在广州市花都区召开绿色金融改革创新试验区第二次联席会议，会议审议了《2019年绿色金融改革创新试验区评估报告》和《2019年绿色金融改革创新经验和复制推广方案》。

2月14日，人民银行、银保监会、证监会、外汇局、上海市政府发布《关于进一步加快推进上海国际金融中心建设和金融支持长三角一体化发展的意见》（银发〔2020〕46号）。

2月22日，中共中央办公厅、国务院办公厅印发。

2月27日，重庆农村商业银行正式宣布采纳赤道原则，成为中国境内第四家赤道银行。

2月，证监会加入国际证监会组织（IOSCO）成立的理事会层面的可持续金融专项工作组（STF），参与发行人可持续信息披露等具体工作。

3月10日，住房和城乡建设部、人民银行、银保监会三部委联合下发《关于支持浙江省湖州市推动绿色建筑和绿色金融协同发展的批复》，浙江省湖州市成为全国首个绿色建筑和绿色金融协同发展试点城市。

4月6日，"一带一路"绿色投资原则（GIP）指导委员会召开2020年首次会议。

5月15日，九江银行正式成为第四家加入《负责任银行原则》的中资银行。

5月27日，深圳证券交易所参加美林美银证券ESG论坛，与中国香港交易所、日本交易所、印度国家证券交易所一同就ESG发展进行探讨，并就深圳市场ESG发展向境外投资者做介绍。

6月15日，深圳证券交易所受联合国负责任投资原则（PRI）邀请作为主旨演讲嘉宾，在PRI论坛中介绍深交所ESG产品。

6月22日，国家主席习近平在北京以视频方式会见欧洲理事会主席米歇尔和欧盟委员会主席冯德莱恩，在绿色低碳、数字经济等广泛领域达成共识。

7月14日，经国务院批准，财政部会同生态环境部、上海市人民政府共同发起设立了国家绿色发展基金，注册资本885亿元人民币。

7月20日，绵阳市商业银行正式宣布采纳赤道原则，成为中国境内第五家赤道银行。

7月21日，中法举行第七次高级别经济财金对话，将绿色金融相关内容纳入对话第21项成果。

7月28日，中欧举行第八次经贸高层对话，将绿色金融相关内容纳入对话第14项成果。

7月，深圳证券交易所加入由伦敦证券交易所牵头的联合国可持续证券交易所倡议（UNSSE）组织的气候信息披露专题顾问工作组。

8月20—21日，人民银行在贵安新区召开全国绿色金融改革创新试验区第三次联席会议，会议审议了《绿色金融改革创新试验区自评价报告》和《绿色金融改革创新经验和复制推广方案》。

8月，上海证券交易所加入UNSSE组织的气候信息披露咨询顾问组，参与首轮咨询小组电话会。

9月4日，在中国金融学会绿金委指导下，深圳绿金委与广东绿金委、香港绿色金融协会和澳门银行公会联合发起成立"粤港澳大湾区绿色金融联盟"，深圳绿金委正式成为联盟秘书处。

9月10日，央行与监管机构绿色金融网络NGFS发布《金融机构环境风险分析综述》和《环境风险分析方法案例集》。

9月19日，绿色金融专业委员会年会暨中国绿色金融论坛在北京召开。

9月24日，《"一带一路"绿色投资原则》（GIP）第二次全体会议在北京召开。

9月25日，上海证券交易所面向沪市上市公司及全球投资者举办了"对话国际投资者：ESG如何赋能上市公司"线上培训。

9月，上海证券交易所当选世界交易所联合会（WFE）可持续发展工作组副主席。

10月，明晟指数（MSCI）就境内外ESG投资发展趋势与深圳证券交易所开展主题交流活动。

10月16日，人民银行行长易纲应邀出席可持续金融国际平台（IPSF）一周年线上活动，与欧盟委员会执行副主席东布罗夫斯基斯共同宣布，成立由中欧联合牵头的IPSF绿色分类标准工作组。

10月26日，生态环境部、发展改革委、人民银行、银保监会、证监会五部门联合印发《关于促进应对气候变化投融资的指导意见》。

10月27—29日，上海证券交易所举办2020年国际投资者大会，会议专设ESG环节，推动国际组织、国内外机构投资者等参与"推动疫情后世界经济绿色复苏""推动高质量发展——中国公司ESG实践"等讨论。

11月11日，中意举行第二次财长对话，将绿色金融相关内容纳入对话第14项成果。

11月13日，兴业银行正式成为联合国《可持续蓝色经济金融倡议》的全球第27家签署机构和第49家会员单位，也是首家中资签署机构和会员单位。

11月15日，国际金融论坛（IFF）正式公布"2020全球绿色金融创新奖"的获奖名单，深圳排放权交易所凭借"助力深圳特区构建绿色金融体系并实现绿色金融立法"项目荣膺奖项。

11月16日，青岛银行获得联合国环境规划署（UNEP）批准，正式成为全球第50家《可持续蓝色经济金融倡议》会员单位。

11月28日，中国金融学会学术年会在京举行。本次年会的主题是"金融支持双循环新发展格局"。与会专家围绕"绿色金融与30·60目标"等开展专题讨论。

11月30日，贵州银行正式宣布采纳赤道原则，成为中国境内第六家"赤道银行"。

12月10日，"绿水青山就是金山银山理念引领下的中国绿色金融改革创新研讨会"在湖州召开。

12月12日，国家主席习近平在气候雄心峰会上通过视频发表题为《继往开来，开启全球应对气候变化新征程》的重要讲话，宣布中国国家自主贡献一系列新举措。

12月16—18日，中央经济工作会议在北京举行。会议将做好碳达峰、碳中和工作列为2021年八大重点任务之一，要求抓紧制定2030年前碳排放达峰行动方案，支持有条件的地方率先达峰，加快建设全国碳排放权交易市场等。

12月，"2020中欧绿色金融论坛——ESG专场"在北京成功召开。

12月21日，金融机构环境信息披露研讨会暨中英金融机构环境信息披露试点工作组第八次会议在京举办。

附录二 2020年绿色金融主要政策文件

《关于在绿色金融改革创新试验区试行部分绿色金融标准的通知》（银办发〔2020〕15号），2020年2月。

《关于进一步加快推进上海国际金融中心建设和金融支持长三角一体化发展的意见》（银发〔2020〕46号），2020年2月。

《关于发布〈深圳证券交易所上市公司规范运作指引（2020年修订）〉的通知》（深证上〔2020〕125号），2020年2月。

《关于构建现代环境治理体系的指导意见》，2020年2月。

《上市公司创业投资基金股东减持股份的特别规定》（中国证券监督管理委员会公告〔2020〕17号），2020年3月。

《关于发布〈上海证券交易所公司债券发行上市审核规则适用指引第2号——特定品种公司债券〉的通知》（上证发〔2020〕87号），2020年3月。

《关于发布〈上海证券交易所科创板企业发行上市申报及推荐暂行规定（2021年4月修订）〉的通知》（上证发〔2021〕238号），2020年4月。

《关于印发〈绿色债券支持项目目录（2020年版）〉的通知（征求意见稿）》，2020年7月。

《关于金融支持粤港澳大湾区建设的意见》（银发〔2020〕95号），2020年5月。

《关于营造更好发展环境 支持民营节能环保企业健康发展的实施意见》（发改环资〔2020〕790号），2020年5月。

《关于绿色融资统计制度有关工作的通知》（银保监办便函〔2020〕739号），2020年6月。

《关于发布〈深圳证券交易所创业板上市公司规范运作指引（2020年修订）〉及有关事项的通知》（深证上〔2020〕499号），2020年6月。

《关于发布〈上海证券交易所科创板上市公司自律监管规则适用指引第2号——自愿信息披露〉的通知》（上证发〔2020〕70号），2020年9月。

《关于促进应对气候变化的投融资的指导意见》（环气候〔2020〕57号），2020年10月。

《关于发布〈深圳证券交易所公司债券创新品种业务指引〉第1-5号的通知》（深证上〔2020〕1173号），2020年11月。

《碳排放权交易管理办法（试行）》（生态环境部令第19号），2020年12月。

《关于印发〈2019—2020年全国碳排放权交易配额总量设定与分配实施方案（发电行业）〉〈纳入2019—2020年全国碳排放权交易配额管理的重点排放单位名单〉并做好发电行业配额预分配工作的通知》（国环规气候〔2020〕3号），2020年12月。

《环境信息依法披露制度改革方案》，2020年12月。

附录三 2020年绿色金融标准体系建设成果一览

序号	政策文件名称	发文单位	发文时间
1	《中国银保监会办公厅关于绿色融资统计制度有关工作的通知》	银保监办发〔2020〕739号	2020年6月
2	《关于发布〈上海证券交易所公司债券发行上市审核规则适用指引第2号——特定品种公司债券〉的通知》	上证发〔2020〕87号	2020年11月
3	《深圳证券交易所公司债券创新品种业务指引第1号——绿色公司债券》	深证上〔2020〕1173号	2020年11月

China Green Finance Progress Report
(2020)

Research Bureau of the People's Bank of China

CHINA FINANCIAL PUBLISHING HOUSE

Compilation Group

Chief Editor:	Wang Xin			
Associate Editor:	Lei Yao			
Edited by:	Yang Ping	Wang Yan	Han Xintao	
Compiled by:	Li Yanni	Yang Hongsen	Guo Lixuan	Yu Jianke
	Guan Xiaoming	Zhang Weiwei	Xu Meng	He Kun
	Xing Bingkun	Ge Zhisu	Cheng Yanfen	Cai Chunchun
	Che Shiyi	Zhang Yantao	Mao Qizheng	Xu Huan
	Qu Weimin	Wang Paihan	Teng Rui	Qi Yalin
	Gao Ming	Liu Weite	Ai Pan	Yang Xin
	Guo Yuan	Cheng Cuiyun	Lin Lanlan	Liu Ninglin
	Yin Shuai	Shi Jiale	Wang Xuan	Ni Gaiqin
	Xu Zheping	Han Ning	Li Qiuju	Dong Yanmeng
	Zhang Xuanchuan	Cai Hengpei	Du Jian	Xiao Kan
	Liu Jialong	Cheng Lin	Yuan Ping	Wen Yaheng
	Wu Yufeng	Liu Hong	Li Haiping	Zhu Zhui
	Liu Lihong	Xu Zhenxin	Yao Min	Xu Shilong
	Xun Zhijian	Chen Simeng	Liu Chuanwei	Yang Bowen
	Chu Wen	Li Rongli	Gao Zhengjiang	Tang Yuqi
	Xu Shaohua	Lan Wangsheng	Shi Yi	Shang Jin
	Cui Yanmei	Gao Wei	Yuan Fang	Li Wei'e
	Chen Wei	Yin Hong	Zhang Jingwen	Shen Zhongquan
	Sun Wei	Ren Qiuxiao	Duan Lian	Li Wenbo
	Peng Chenchen	Chen Yaqin	Chen Quan	Peng Ling
	Long Huan	Dong Shanning	Zhang Pan	Zhou Jianliang
	Hua Nan	Yang Jiehan	Zhou Ran	Tian Bo
	Li Lan	Xiang Fei	Zong Tianhua	Qi Jiuhong
	Jin Zisheng	Lin Yin	Chen Ni	Shen Shuangbo
	Li Yue	Liu Jingyun	Wang Shunli	Liao Yuan
	Lu Wenqin	Guo Peiyuan	Guan Rui	Yuan Tian
	Guo Sitong	An Guojun		

Material provided by: Monetary Policy Department, Financial Market Department, Statistics and Analysis Department, Technology Department, International Department, and Credit Reference Bureau of the People's Bank of China; Department of Resource Conservation and Environmental Protection and Department of Fiscal and Financial Affairs of the National Development and Reform Commission; Department of Finance of the Ministry of Finance; General Office and Climate Department of the Ministry of Ecology and Environment; Department of Standard and Quota, Center of Science, Technology and Industrial Development of the Ministry of Housing and Urban-Rural Development; Policy Research Bureau and Property and Casualty Insurance Supervision Department of China Banking and Insurance Regulatory Commission; Supervisory Department of Corporate Bonds and China Institute of Finance and Capital Markets of China Securities Regulatory Commission; National Association of Financial Market Institutional Investors; Asset Management Association of China; Insurance Asset Management Association of China; Green Finance Committee; Guangzhou Branch, Beijing Business Administration Department, Chongqing Business Administration Department, Nanchang Central Sub-branch, Guiyang Central Sub-branch, Lanzhou Central Sub-branch, Urumqi Central Sub-branch, Shenzhen Central Sub-branch, Taiyuan Central Sub-branch, Huzhou Central Sub-branch and Quzhou Central Sub-branch of the People's Bank of China; China Central Depository & Clearing Co., Ltd.; Export-Import Bank of China; Agricultural Development Bank of China; Industrial and Commercial Bank of China; Agricultural Bank of China; Bank of China; China Construction Bank; Industrial Bank; Huaxia Bank; Bank of Jiangsu; Bank of Huzhou; Silk Road Fund; China Reinsurance (Group) Corporation; China PICC Property & Casualty Co., Ltd.; China Beijing Green Exchange; China Emissions Exchange; CCX Green Finance; China Lianhe Equator Environmental Impact Assessment Co., Ltd.; CECEP Consulting Co., Ltd.; SynTao Green Finance; Avic Trust Co., Ltd.; UNEP; Institute of Finance & Banking, Chinese Academy of Social Sciences

CONTENTS

Chapter I	**Executive Summary**	**103**
Chapter II	**Continuous Improvement in Green Finance Systems**	**111**
	Section 1 Actively Responding to National Strategies	111
	Section 2 Continuously Improving the Systems and Mechanisms	114
	Section 3 From Pilot Zones to Regional Trials	119
	Section 4 Encouraging Innovation in Green Financial Products and Services	120
Chapter III	**Steady Development of Green Financial Markets**	**123**
	Section 1 Green Credit Market in Rapid Growth	123
	Section 2 The Green Securities Market in Steady Progress	129
	Section 3 Green Insurance Providing Greater Risk Protection	144
	Section 4 Innovation and Development of Green Funds and Green PPP	149
	Section 5 Development of Environmental Rights Markets Accelerated	152
	Section 6 Environmental Benefits of Green Trust Projects More Prominent	154
Chapter IV	**Significant Progress Made for Green Finance Practices in Local Economies**	**158**
	Section 1 Construction of Pilot Zones for Green Finance Reform and Innovation Going Deeper	159
	Section 2 Green Finance Reform and Innovation in Other Regions	172
	Section 3 Green Finance Supporting Pollution Prevention and Key Areas of People's Livelihood	176

CONTENTS

Chapter V	**In-depth Development of International Cooperation in Green Finance**	**188**
	Section 1 Progress Made in the Green Finance Cooperation under the Belt and Road	189
	Section 2 Engaging in and Leading Multilateral International Cooperation on Green Finance	193
	Section 3 New Progress Made in Biliteral Cooperation on Green Finance	203
	Section 4 More International Cooperation Practices of Market Institutions	206
Chapter VI	**Green Finance Remains an Arduous Task**	**210**
Appendix I	**Chronicle of Green Finance Events in 2020**	**214**
Appendix II	**List of 2020 Green Finance Policies and Regulations**	**219**
Appendix III	**List of Achievements in Building the System of Green Finance Standards in 2020**	**221**

CONTENTS

Column	Column 1-1	Green Recovery is Already a Global Consensus	105
	Column 3-1	Structural Analysis of Green Loans 2020	125
	Column 3-2	Innovation Cases of Green Credit Products and Services	126
	Column 3-3	Overview of Green Debt Financing Instruments 2020	131
	Column 3-4	Bonds for Pandemic Prevention and Control	138
	Column 3-5	Innovation in Green Insurance	146
	Column 3-6	Innovation in Nuclear Insurance	147
	Column 3-7	Innovation Cases of Green Funds	149
	Column 3-8	Innovation Cases of Green Trust	156
	Column 4-1	Huzhou Releasing China's First Regional Environmental Disclosure Report	166
	Column 4-2	Cases of Coordinated Development Between Green Finance and Green Buildings	179
	Column 4-3	Green Finance Supporting the Treatment of Black and Odorous Water Bodies: Guangdong Practice	186
	Column 5-1	Overview of CERAT	190
	Column 5-2	A Brief Introduction to the *Overview of Environmental Risk Analysis by Financial Institutions*	194
	Column 5-3	The Research on the Consistency between China and Other Countries in Green Finance Taxonomy is Making Progress	196
	Column 5-4	Sustainable Blue Economy Finance Principles	200
	Column 5-5	Leveraging the Advantages of On-lending to Promote International Sustainability	206

CHAPTER I
Executive Summary

The scientific establishment of the green financial system is an important measure to apply Xi Jinping Thought on Socialism with Chinese Characteristics for a New Era in a more purposeful and determined manner. It is a significant component of ecological civilization system reform as well as financial supply-side reform and a powerful endogenous driver in promoting the green, low-carbon, and high-quality development of China's economy and society. In 2020, China's green finance industry has seen severe challenges brought by the global spread of the COVID-19 pandemic as well as the huge opportunities arising from the goals of peak carbon dioxide emissions and carbon neutrality. With green, low-carbon, and high-quality development as its primary task and fundamental guideline, it strives to improve the policy framework and standard system; enrich products, tools and service models; and constantly deepen regional reform and international cooperation on green finance, which has been fruitful. While promoting the transformation of "lucid waters and lush mountains" into "invaluable assets", it has greatly contributed to enhancing the adaptability, competitiveness, and inclusiveness of China's financial industry and building a modern financial system with Chinese characteristics, starting a new chapter of the development of green finance.

I. New Challenges and New Opportunities for Global Green Development

In 2020, the ravage of the COVID-19 pandemic plunged the global economy into the most severe recession since World War II, and international financial markets were shaken violently. As a result, global green development and climate risk prevention are facing a series of new challenges and problems, and the development path is suffering from multi-dimensional impacts.

First, the international carbon emission process was distorted. The COVID-19 pandemic has led to a stagnation of international interactions and economic activities, and a significant decline in global carbon emission levels. The International Energy Agency (IEA) forecasts that global energy-related carbon dioxide emissions will fall by nearly 2 billion tons in 2020, a 5.8% year-on-year decline, the largest annual decrease since the World War II. This has led to an oversupply of carbon allowances, a fall in the price of carbon credits in the market, and a failure of the carbon price formation mechanism.

Second, the COVID-19 pandemic has been a drag on the introduction of green development policies. At the international level, the role of global green governance mechanisms was weakened by postponed meetings such as the 26th UN Climate Change Conference (COP26), the 15th Conference of the Parties (COP15) of the Convention on Biological Diversity (CBD), and the second United Nations Global Sustainable Transport Conference. The first global industry emissions reduction program, the Carbon Offsetting and Reduction Scheme for International Aviation (CORSIA)[①], has been disrupted, further driving up uncertainties about aviation emissions reductions. Nationally, the pandemic has led to a significant rise in public debt in various countries, which means that insufficient financial resources will slow down the green low-carbon transition process.

Third, stimulative economic policies may favor high-carbon industries and strengthen high-carbon lock-in. Most countries launched economic recovery plans focused on fighting the pandemic, protecting people's livelihood and reducing the risk of economic crisis, while lacking sufficient green elements. "*Are We Building Back Better?*"[②], a report led by the Oxford University Economic Recovery Project and the United Nations Environment Programme (UNEP), shows that in 2020, the 50 major global economies have announced a total of USD 14.6 trillion in spending to address the COVID-19 pandemic. Of the USD 14.6 trillion spent on COVID-19 response, only USD 341 billion will be spent on green recovery. The reason for this is that, on the one hand, coal, steel, and other high-carbon industries are mostly asset-heavy industries, with larger enterprises, higher industry shares and better credit ratings, which may receive more financial support in large-scale quantitative easing and asset purchase plans. On the other hand, in order to prevent continued and rapid economic decline, some countries have also relaxed environmental requirements for high-carbon industries, further increasing the high-carbon reliance of their economic development paths.

---

① The Carbon Offsetting and Reduction Scheme for International Aviation (CORSIA) is the first global industry emissions reduction scheme. By early 2020, 82 countries and regions have voluntarily joined the first control period, covering 77% of the global civil aviation industry's carbon emissions. The International Civil Aviation Organization (ICAO) originally planned to use 2019 and 2020 as the baseline years, which means airlines would use the average emissions level in 2019 and 2020 as a baseline and pay for increments above that baseline. The global aviation industry is expected to reduce carbon emissions by 37 percent in 2020 as many airlines sharply cut flights due to the coronavirus epidemic. On June 30, 2020, in response to the unusual decline in base-year emissions, the Council of the 36 member states of the International Civil Aviation Organization decided to adjust the baseline to 2019 emission levels, which was to effective for at least the first three years of CORSIA. The International Air Transport Association (IATA) expressed support for this adjustment, and in 2022, the ICAO Assembly will consider the need for further baseline amendments, adding to the uncertainty surrounding emissions reductions in aviation.

② Are We Building Back Better? Evidence from 2020 and Pathways to Inclusive Green Recovery Spending.

Fourth, the pandemic has increased the potential for climate change-related financial risks. Most economies around the world have adopted large-scale monetary stimulus policies that provide strong support in the short term to combat the pandemic, while also facing exit challenges. In the future, the low interest rate and negative interest rate environment may persist for a long time, and the response to climate change-related financial risks will face a more complicated situation. Issues such as pressure on insurance companies' balance sheets, increased asset depreciation and transition risks for energy companies, insufficient policy space for monetary policy authorities, and greater vulnerability to shocks in less developed countries and regions are of particular concern.

Opportunities always come along with challenges. In the face of a series of problems and challenges, green recovery has gradually become a global consensus and an important economic driver. Green finance has also ushered in new development opportunities and space. Globally, the International Energy Agency (IEA) pointed out in *Net Zero by 2050, A Roadmap for the Global Energy Sector* that in the net zero scenario, total annual energy investment surges to USD 5 trillion by 2030, adding an extra 0.4 percentage point a year to annual global GDP growth. According to estimates from the Intergovernmental Panel on Climate Change, if we are to limit the temperature rise within 2℃ by 2050, an annual investment of 3 trillion US dollars is required, and the annual investment in low-carbon energy technology and energy efficiency needs to be increased by about five times compared with the 2015 level. Domestically, there are many calculations in various sectors of the funding needs for achieving peaking carbon dioxide emissions and carbon neutrality, all of which have a scale level of over RMB 100 billion. Government funds can only cover a small part of such a huge capital demand, while the rest must be made up by market funds. This requires the establishment and improvement of a green financial policy system to guide and encourage the financial system to support green investment and financing activities in a market-oriented manner.

Column 1-1

Green Recovery is Already a Global Consensus

Since 2020, in response to the impact of the COVID-19 pandemic, the international community has emphasized the need to "Build Back Better" in the post-epidemic world, and "green recovery" has received great attention from countries around the world.

International organizations are actively urging countries to practice "Green Recovery." UN Secretary General António Guterres said that the current crisis is unprecedentedly alarming. Faced with such an opportunity for the economy to "turn from gray to green," governments should promote "green recovery." He also proposed six actions, such as "providing new jobs and business opportunities through cleaner production and green transformation" and "saving businesses must be linked to achieving green jobs and sustainable growth." The World Bank proposed a "Sustainability Checklist," which includes two major elements – climate adaptation and decarbonization, to provide guidance for governments to consider their economic recovery plans. The International Monetary Fund and the International Energy Agency have urged governments to take advantage of the economic reboot to move toward net zero emissions. Akinwumi Adesina, President of African Development Bank, said that the COVID-19 pandemic and the desert locust infestation are twin crises in Africa, and more resources must be spent on health, environmental protection and climate adaptation.

Many countries around the world are pushing for a "green recovery" plan. Following the "European Green Deal" announced in December 2019, which explicitly proposed to take the lead in achieving the global goal of "carbon neutrality" by 2050, the leaders of the EU-27 reached a historic agreement on July 21, 2020 on a post-pandemic economic recovery fund and budget for the next seven years. Highlighting green development and digital transformation, the agreement will provide a total of EUR 1.8243 trillion for post-pandemic reconstruction, of which 30% will be used to finance climate-related policies and projects, providing financial security for the EU's "green recovery". Germany announced an economic recovery package totaling EUR 130 billion, of which EUR 50 billion will be used in promoting the development of electric vehicles, building more charging stations, as well as supporting for German railroads and public transport companies. South Korea is the world's seventh-largest emitter of greenhouse gases, with coal-fired power generation accounting for about 40 percent of the country's energy. On July 14, President Moon Jae-in said he would invest USD 94.6 billion in a "Green New Deal" over the next five years to develop digital technology-driven environment-friendly industries, including electric and hydrogen-powered vehicles, smart grid and telemedicine, and to shift away from dependence on fossil fuels. On his first day in office, President Biden announced the return of the United States to the *Paris Agreement* with a plan for a "clean energy revolution and green justice" that commits the United States to achieving net zero emissions no later than 2050. With a widespread sense of a "COVID-climate crisis" in Africa, a May 25, 2020 report led by the President of the Gabonese Republic and supported by African leaders recommends that national stimulus plans focus on resilient infrastructure, food and water security. France, the United Kingdom, Denmark and other economies have also launched "green recovery" plans or higher emissions reduction targets.

Green finance is increasingly becoming an important driver of post-pandemic green development. The concepts of green investment and sustainable investment are increasingly mainstreamed in international capital markets. Deutsche Bank estimates that global environmental, social and governance (ESG) investments will reach USD 135 trillion by 2030, accounting for 95% of total assets. European and U.S. financial institutions are showing greater commitment to post-pandemic low-carbon development and are also seizing dominance of green finance rules and standards. On July 15, the UK Energy Minister said that the UK government plans to create a "Green Investment Bank 2.0" to ensure the achievement of the 2050 carbon neutrality target. On July 20, Morgan Stanley said it will officially join the Partnership for Carbon Accounting and Finance (PCAF)[1] organization, becoming the first major U.S. bank to publicly disclose carbon emissions from its lending and investment operations, and will help PCAF develop a global carbon accounting standard for all financial institutions.

Green production and lifestyle will become the "new normal" after the pandemic. Telecommuting, video conferencing, online education, Internet health care and other low-carbon production and lifestyle practices spread rapidly during the pandemic. On May 4, 92 French industrial leaders published an article pledging to "put the environment at the heart of economic recovery in the name of social justice". On July 21, Apple announced its plan to become carbon neutral across its business, manufacturing supply chain and product life cycle by 2030. Maersk, Microsoft and seven other multinational companies have also launched a net-zero carbon emissions alliance.

II. China's green finance development opens a new chapter

As an important engine of the global economy, China attaches great importance to green recovery and accelerates its low-carbon transformation. Both the "two new's and one major"[2] construction tasks proposed in the 2020 *Government Work Report* and the "six stability" tasks and "six security" objectives [3] have put forward new requirements for green recovery, green industrial upgrading

---

[1] Launched in 2019, PCAF's 66 full members include financial institutions from around the world with more than USD 5.3 trillion in assets. The agency will calculate and standardize greenhouse gas emissions from projects funded by asset managers, banks and other institutions.

[2] "Two new" refers to new infrastructure and new urbanization, and "one major" refers to major projects like transportation and water conservancy.

[3] The "six fronts" refer to employment, financial operations, foreign trade, foreign investment, domestic investment, and expectations, and "six areas" refer to job, basic living needs, operations of market entities, food and energy security, stable industrial and supply chains, and the normal functioning of primary-level governments.

and optimal resource allocation, and have provided new space and opportunities for green finance development. In particular, at the 75th session of the United Nations General Assembly in September 2020, General Secretary Xi Jinping solemnly promised that China will "have CO_2 emissions peak before 2030 and achieve carbon neutrality before 2060." Since then, China's climate and environmental constraints have been further strengthened. Green finance has been accelerated to generate new development opportunities and make a series of new achievements and breakthroughs. Domestically, we rolled up our sleeves and worked hard to get things done. Green finance has gradually made the leap from blueprint and concept to choice and action in the whole society, and has increasingly become the choice of local governments and market players. Internationally, we uphold the responsibility of a great nation and actively promote the construction of a community of shared future for all mankind by developing green finance. At present, the five pillars of China's green financial system have basically taken shape.

First, the construction of green financial standards system was accelerated. The key to green finance does not lie in the statistics, but in the guiding rules. In 2018, after establishing the Working Group on Green Financial Standards under National Financial Standardization Technical Committee, the People's Bank of China focused on climate change, pollution control and energy conservation and emission reduction. Following the principle of "domestic unification and international convergence", it promoted the establishment and improvement of a cross-sector, market-oriented, and authoritative green financial standard system embedded in the whole business process of financial institutions. By the end of 2020, one international standard has been voted and published by the International Organization for Standardization Technical Committee on Sustainable Finance (ISO/TC 322); one national standard has been approved by the National Standardization Management Commission of the P.R.C. for formal establishment; five industry standard drafts have been submitted for review; and four draft standards have been submitted for approval in the green finance reform and innovation zones.

Second, information disclosure requirements and regulation of financial institutions have been strengthened. Regulators continue to enhance the mandatory and standardized environmental information disclosure of financial institutions, securities issuers and the public sector, and strive to improve the transparency of the green finance market. The UK-China Climate and Environmental Information Disclosure Pilot continues to make progress, with the number of Chinese participating institutions expanding to 15 and the pilot experience demonstrating preliminary replication value. We also organized financial institutions and some regional organizations to carry out environmental risk stress tests on a pilot basis, so as to explore the integration of climate and environment-related risks into the regulatory framework.

Third, incentives and regulations were gradually improved. On the basis of Green Credit Performance Evaluation Scheme, the green finance evaluation mechanism has been improved to guide financial institutions to increase green asset allocation, thus leaving more policy space for the central bank to address climate change. The active information collection mechanism of environmental law enforcement has been gradually improved, and the construction of the social credit system of "praising integrity and punishing breach of trust" has been accelerated. In the pilot zone of green finance reform and innovation, there are a number of innovations in financial support and supervision policies. Investment in green project increased, measurement standards became more accurate, and a series of policies have been put in place to promote green finance reform and innovation. By the end of 2020, the balance of green loans in the pilot zone was RMB 236.833 billion, accounting for 15.14% of all loans, 8.22 percentage points higher than national average.

Fourth, green financial products as well as market systems continue to be enriched. Green financial products and services are the most direct path to the real economy and they carry the intentions of a policy. By encouraging product innovation, improving the issuance system, regulating the transaction process and enhancing transparency, China has formed a multi-level green financial product and market system including green loans, green bonds, green insurance, green funds, green trusts, carbon financial products, etc. This has helped providing diversified financing channels for green projects and increasing the efficiency of identifying and serving green low-carbon development. By the end of 2020, the balance of China's green loans in domestic and foreign currencies was RMB 11.95 trillion, ranking first in the world in terms of stock size; the stock size of green bonds was RMB 813.2 billion, ranking second in the world. Th green financial assets is of good quality. As of the end of 2020, the non-performing rate of green loans was 0.33%, 1.65 percentage points lower than the non-performing rate of corporate loans in the same period, and there were no default cases of green bonds.

Fifth, international cooperation in green finance has been deepening. China is making use of various multilateral and bilateral platforms and cooperation mechanisms to promote international exchanges in green finance and enhance international recognition and participation in China's green finance policies, standards, products and markets. By telling China's stories, we improved China's international discourse on green finance and took the lead in promoting the industry to become an international mainstream. Central Banks and Supervisors Network for Greening the Financial System (NGFS), initiated by the People's Bank of China, has expanded to 84 full members and 13 observer institutions. The Sustainable Banking Network (SBN), launched by the China Banking and Insurance Regulatory Commission (CBIRC), plays an increasingly important role in facilitating cooperation and exchanges in the field of green finance among developing countries. The International Platform on Sustainable Finance (IPSF), jointly launched by China, Europe and other economies, focuses on promoting global convergence of green finance standards and other efforts. Green finance continues to be a key topic in the China-UK and China-French high-level financial dialogues and the "Belt and Road" construction.

III. Green finance has broad space for development

The construction of an ecological civilization is a long way off, and the development space of green finance is broad. At present, China is in the critical period of accelerating economic and social recovery and building a moderately prosperous society. This year also marks the start of the 14th Five-Year Plan and the new journey of building a comprehensive socialist modern country. In accordance with new development concept, it is of great significance to take the initiative to explore a new green recovery path and lead the way to healthy development of the world economy in the post-pandemic era. From a domestic perspective, in the short term, this is an effective way to to advance stability on the six fronts and security in the six areas and fight against the epidemic. In the medium and long term, it is in line with China's need to cultivate new growth points for China's economy, enhance the resilience and sustainability of economic development, and move toward high-quality and modern development. A green development path is also a necessary choice for improving the adaptability, competitiveness and universality of the financial system and building a strong financial industry. From a global perspective, green recovery will help promote China's international cooperation in sustainable development and build our image of a responsible major country. In terms of key tasks, in 2021, we should focus on promoting a mandatory climate and environmental information disclosure system, improve the green financial performance evaluation system, launch new carbon emission reduction support tools, further improve the green financial standard system based on peaking carbon dioxide emissions and carbon neutrality, and promote local green financial pilots and international cooperation.

Looking ahead, the financial industry will continue to improve its political stance, focus on the vision of carbon peak and carbon neutral targets and promote green financial reform and innovation, thus contributing to the national strategy of green low-carbon development and the construction of a community with a shared future for mankind.

CHAPTER II
Continuous Improvement in Green Finance Systems

In 2020, the green finance policy system was improved, the construction of the green finance standard system was accelerated, and the incentive and restraint mechanisms were optimized. They set an important cornerstone for the rapid development of China's green finance and the continuous expansion of the market.

Section 1 Actively Responding to National Strategies

I. Establishing a Modern Environmental Governance System

In February 2020, the General Office of the Communist Party of China (CPC) Central Committee and the General Office of the State Council issued the *Guiding Opinions on Building a Modern Environmental Governance System*. It is proposed to (1) establish a national green development fund; (2) promote the development of the liability insurance for environmental pollution, and study and establish a compulsory liability insurance system for environmental pollution in areas of high environmental risk; (3) carry out pollutant discharge rights trading, research and explore collateral financing of such trading; (4) encourage the development of financial leases for major environmental protection equipment; (5) speed up the establishment of provincial soil pollution prevention funds; and (6) uniform domestic green bond standards.

II. Establishing a Sound Economic System for Green, Low-carbon and Circular Development

In December, the Central Economic Work Conference was held in Beijing. The meeting outlined policy priorities in eight specific area in 2021, including to conduct work to peak carbon dioxide emissions by 2030 and achieve carbon neutrality by 2060. According to the meeting, (1) China will seize the time to formulate an action plan for peaking carbon dioxide emissions before 2030. The country will support areas with favorable conditions to peak the emissions ahead of the schedule. (2) China will accelerate the adjustment and optimization of the industrial structure and energy structure and promote coal consumption to peak carbon dioxide emissions as soon as possible. The country will also vigorously develop new energy, speed up the construction of national trading markets for energy use quota and carbon emissions, and improve the dual control system of total energy consumption and energy intensity. (3) China will continue to promoting triumph in the uphill battle for prevention and control of pollution and achieve synergistic effects of pollution control and carbon reduction. (4) China will promote afforestation and improve the carbon sink capacity of the ecological system.

On December 30, the 17th meeting of the Central Comprehensively Deepening Reforms Commission deliberated and approved the *Guiding Opinions on Accelerating the Establishment of a Sound Economic System for Green, Low-carbon and Circular Development*. It proposes to vigorously develop green finance, green credit and green direct financing; strengthen the evaluation and assessment of green financial performance of financial institutions; unify green bond standards and establish green bond rating standards; develop green insurance and give play to the role of insurance premium as an adjustment mechanism; support eligible green enterprises to go public; encourage financial institutions and related enterprises to carry out green financing in the international market; promote the convergence of international green financial standards; promote the two-way opening of green financial markets; and facilitate climate investment and financing.

III. Establishing a National Green Development Fund and Promoting the PPP Model

In July, the Ministry of Finance, the Ministry of Ecology and Environment, and the Shanghai Municipal Government formally established the National Green Development Fund, which is based in Shanghai. The first phase of the fund is RMB 88.5 billion, jointly funded by the Central Government and the local governments of 11 provinces (cities) along the Yangtze River Economic Belt, as well as the private sector. It operates as a company in a market-oriented manner. During the first term of its existence, it takes Yangtze River Economic Belt as the key investment destination, focuses on the restoration and conservation of the ecological environment and the development of green industries, and promotes economic restructuring and green transformation.

Moreover, the Ministry of Finance and stakeholders in this regard continue to regulate and promote the public-private partnership (PPP) model to encourage social capital to participate in the investment, construction, and operation of green and low-carbon projects. This move has played a positive role in alleviating the financial pressure on green development and improving the ecological environment in urban and rural areas.

IV. Enhancing the Green Finance Support in Responding to Climate Change

In October, the Ministry of Ecology and Environment, the National Development and Reform Commission, the People's Bank of China, the China Banking and Insurance Regulatory Commission, and the other ministry issued the *Guiding Opinions on Promoting the Investment and Financing in Response to Climate Change* (MEE [2020] No. 57). With the goal facilitate peaking carbon dioxide emissions and carbon neutrality, the ministries and commissions will vigorously promote the development of investment and financing in response to climate change. They encourage banks and insurers to develop climate-friendly green financial products while maintaining risk control and business sustainability, provide effective financial support for major climate projects, and promote low-carbon and green transformation of the economy and society.

V. Improving Policies for Finance Sector to Support the Growth of Green and Environmental Protection Industries

In May, the National Development and Reform Commission, the Ministry of Science and Technology, the Ministry of Industry and Information Technology, and other three ministries issued the *Implementation Opinions to Support the Healthy Development of Private Energy-Saving and Environmental Protection Enterprises* (NDRC [2020] No. 790). The ministries and commissions encourage financial institutions to incorporate environmental, social, and governance requirements into their business processes; improve professional green finance services for private energy-saving and environmental protection enterprises; and vigorously develop green financing. They will develop green credit, strengthen communication on major national energy-saving and environmental protection projects, and increase financing support for eligible projects. They support the issuance of green bonds by qualified private energy-saving and environmental protection enterprises, unifying domestic definition standards for green bonds, and releasing the *Catalogue of Projects Backed by Green Bonds* in accordance with the *Green Industry Guidance Catalogue* (2019). They will increase the credit enhancement methods for energy-saving and environmental protection industries and explore the inclusion of energy use quota, carbon emission quota, pollutant discharge rights, future return from contractual energy management, and franchise royalties in the pledge guarantee for financing. In July and December, NDRC worked with relevant departments to issue two documents, namely, the *Notice on Organizing the Construction of Green Industry Demonstration Zones* (NDRC [2020] No. 519) and the *Notice on Printing and Distributing the List of Green Industry Demonstration Zones* (NDRC [2020] No. 979). They aimed to provide greater policy support, shored up the support of green credit and green bonds, and encouraged the green industry demonstration zones to engage in green finance innovations.

Section 2   Continuously Improving the Systems and Mechanisms

I. Consolidating the Green Finance Standard System

Green finance standards are an important guarantee for better exerting the service function of the market and enhancing the services of finance for the real economy. In 2020, the development of China's green finance standards advanced in accordance with the principles of "domestic unification, geared to international standards, clear and enforceable" . A work pattern that features government guidance, market drive, social engagement, and coordinated advancement has come into shape. Significant progress has been made in various tasks.

(I) Steady Advancement in Development and Implementing Domestic Green Finance Standards

Relying on the Working Group on Green Finance Standards of China Financial Standardization Technical Committee, the People's Bank of China works with competent departments and market institutions to effectively promote the preparation of some important green finance standards under the principle of "demand orientation and prioritizing urgent use". By the end of 2020, the national standard *Green Finance Terminology* was formally approved for preparation, which will become the basic general standard for defining the connotation and denotation of green finance. The *Green Bond Credit Rating Standards*, the *Guidelines for Environmental Information Disclosure of Financial Institutions*, the *Environmental Equity Financing Tools*, the *Basic Requirements for Green Private Equity Investment Funds*, and the *Carbon Financial Products* have been submitted for review. The industry standard *Environmental Information Disclosure of Listed Companies* is applying for project approval, which will provide strong support for the regulated development of green financial products and services.

In February, the General Office of the People's Bank of China issued the *Notice on the Trial Implementation of Some Green Finance Standards in Green Finance Reform and Innovation Pilot Zones* (CBIRC [2020] No. 15). Drafts of four standards including the *Green Finance Terminology* were put into trial implementation in green finance reform and innovation pilot zones.

(II) Successful Concluding Acceptance of Trials of Financial Standard Innovation

At the end of 2020, trials of financial standard innovation in Chongqing and Zhejiang, which were carried out by the People's Bank of China, China Banking and Insurance Regulatory Commission, China Securities Regulatory Commission, and the Standardization Administration of China, completed the concluding acceptance. As an important part in the trials, the innovation and implementation of green finance standards achieved remarkable results. Relying on Chongqing Financial Society, Chongqing established a Professional Committee for Green Finance and a Financial Standardization Committee. They prepared the group standard *Fundamental Data Element of Green Credit* and implemented it in Changjiang Lvrongtong, an integrated service system for green finance based on big data. They also promoted the Bank of Chongqing to develop corporate standards such as the *Business Process Specification of Green Credit* and the *Information Disclosure Specification of Green Bonds* to guide financial institutions to provide green financial services in an orderly manner.

(III) Progress in Green Finance Standards' being Geared to International Standards

China and the EU promote the convergence of green taxonomy. In October 2020, the People's Bank of China and relevant departments of the EU established a task force under the International Platform on Sustainable Finance (IPSF). It is dedicated to studying and comparing the similarities and differences of green taxonomy between China and the EU to propose a path for the convergence of standards. It also studies the establishment of a common taxonomy for green finance/sustainable finance recognized by both sides to lay a foundation for promoting the coordinated development of the Chinese and European green finance markets.

The People's Bank of China has continued to engage in the work of the International Organization for Standardization Technical Committee on Sustainable Finance (ISO/TC 322). The *Sustainable Finance – Basic Concepts and Key Initiatives* compiled by Chinese experts is to be released, which will provide an internationally recognized basic reference for sustainable finance activities. In December, the Third Plenary Meeting of ISO/TC 322 was held. At the meeting, Chinese experts proposed to develop two international standards, including the *Basic Requirements for Sustainable*

Private Equity Investment Funds, which were established as preliminary work items (PWIs) by the Technical Committee. Chinese experts also participated in the development of international standards such as the *Framework for Sustainable Finance: Principles and Guidelines*. In addition, to better coordinate the standardization of green and sustainable finance at home and abroad, experts from various institutions for this regard in China formed a working group dedicated to ISO/TC 322 to support engagement in the development of international standards for sustainable finance.

II. Improving the Green Financing Statistical Rules

In June 2020, the General Office of the China Banking Regulatory Commission issued the *Notice on the Work Concerning the Green Financing Statistical Rules* (CBIRC [2020] No. 739). Based on the *Green Industry Guidance Catalogue* (2019) issued by the National Development and Reform Commission, the People's Bank of China, and other agencies, it redefines the scope and statistical methods of green financing. According to the *Notice*, green financing includes not only on-balance sheet loans and green bond investments but also off-balance sheet financing such as green bank acceptance bills and green credit balances. The *Notice* provides data for comprehensively reflecting the effectiveness of green finance practice by banks and institutional support for them to better bolster the development of green industries.

III. Optimizing Business Rules Concerning the Issuance of Green Bonds

In May, NDRC issued the *Notice from the General Office of the National Development and Reform Commission on Evaluating the Credit of the Lead Underwriter of Corporate Bonds and Credit Rating Agencies in 2020* (NDRC [2021] No. 409), and entrusted a third-party agency to publish the evaluation plan. The participation of securities companies in innovative varieties of corporate bonds such as green bonds is scored as an important operational capability indicator.

In November, the Shanghai Stock Exchange revised the supporting rules for its registration system, and issued *No. 2 Guidelines of Shanghai Stock Exchange for the Approval of Corporate Bond Issuance and Listing: Specific Types of Corporate Bonds*. The *Guidelines* set up a chapter for *Green Corporate Bonds* to regulate the use of funds raised by green bonds, information disclosure, and evaluation and certification arrangements.

In November, the Shenzhen Stock Exchange issued the *No. 1 Guidelines of Shenzhen Stock Exchange for Innovations of Corporate Bonds: Green Corporate Bonds*. The *Guidelines* optimize and integrate business rules and documents concerning the green corporate bond business such as notices, guidelines, and Q & A. It upgrades the content of long-term guiding and regulatory significance and applicable for the actual conditions into business rules of the Exchange. In this way, it establishes a concise and clear system of rules on the innovation product sequence of corporate bonds. The *Guidelines* clearly stipulate the definition of green corporate bonds, verification criteria for green industry, third-party evaluation and certification, requirements for application materials and information disclosure for issuance of green corporate bonds, and inspection criteria for intermediary agencies.

IV. Further Improving Information Disclosure and Sharing Policies

(I) Establishing a Legal Disclosure System of Environmental Information

In December, the 17th meeting of the Central Comprehensively Deepening Reforms Commission deliberated and approved the *Plan for the Reform of the Legal Disclosure System of Environmental Information*. The meeting pointed out that the legal disclosure of environmental information is an important system for corporate environmental management and a basic part of the ecological civilization system. It is necessary address outstanding issues and focus on corporate environmental behaviors that have a significant impact on the ecological environment, public health, and citizens' interests, and are highly concerned by the market and society. We should enforce the legal obligations of companies, improve the disclosure requirements, establish a coordinated management mechanism, improve the supervision mechanism, and strengthen the rule of law. The goal is to form a mandatory disclosure system of environmental information with self-discipline of companies, effective management, stringent supervision, and strong support.

(II) Enhancing the Supervision of Environmental Information Disclosure of Listed Companies and Bond Issuers

The Shenzhen Stock Exchange issued the *Guidelines of the Shenzhen Stock Exchange for Standardized Operation of Listed Companies (Revised in 2020)* (SZSE [2020] No. 125, applicable to companies listed on the main board and the small and medium-sized enterprise board) and the *Guidelines of the Shenzhen Stock Exchange for Standardized Operation of Companies Listed on the Growth Enterprise Board (Revised in 2020)* (SZSE [2020] No. 499, applicable to listed companies on the Growth Enterprise Board) in March and June, respectively. The two *Guidelines* optimize the requirements for social responsibility and environmental information disclosure. They emphasize that listed companies shall develop overall environmental protection policies based on their environmental impact; assign specific personnel to be responsible for the establishment, implementation, maintenance, and follow-up of the company's environmental protection system; and provide necessary human, material, technical, and financial support for environmental protection. The latter even has a new code of conduct for technology research and development of listed companies in ecological environment and other areas.

In September, the Shenzhen Stock Exchange revised the *Measures of the Shenzhen Stock Exchange for the Evaluation of Information Disclosure of Listed Companies* and included the performance of social responsibility of listed companies in the evaluation. The revised *Measures* focus on whether listed companies (1) disclose social responsibility reports, (2) disclose their environmental, social, and governance (ESG) conditions, and (3) disclose their conformation to major national strategic guidelines, (4) provide detailed and complete information in their reports.

In September, to implement the new *Securities Law*, encourage and regulate companies listed on the Shanghai Stock Exchange Sci-Tech Innovation Board (STAR) to carry out voluntary information disclosure, improve the effectiveness of the disclosure, and prevent misconduct in the disclosure, the Shanghai Stock Exchange released *No. 2 Guidelines of the Shanghai Stock Exchange for the Application of the Self-Regulatory Rules for STAR Listed Companies: Voluntary Information Disclosure* (SHSE [2020] No. 70). According to Article 14 "Environmental, Social and Corporate Governance," sci-tech innovation companies may disclose additional information based on their industry, business characteristics, and governance structure, besides the general environmental, social and corporate governance information in accordance with laws and regulations.

(III) Inputting Environmental Law Enforcement Information in to the Basic Financial Credit Information Database

The Credit Reference Center of the People's Bank of China regularly inputs the environmental law enforcement information publicized online by provincial departments of environmental protection into the basic financial credit information database. Such information will also be presented in the credit report to provide reference for financial institutions. By the end of 2020, the credit reference system had collected 127,200 pieces of environmental penalty information, involving 96,700 enterprises, as well as 208,800 pieces of environmental license information, involving 134,400 enterprises. In 2020, the environmental penalty information of 8,947 enterprises in China was queried 1.9 million times by 1,484 financial institutions. The searches had helped them avoid 43,000 contracts with corporate credit risk, involving an amount of about 560 million yuan. Moreover, 1,565 enterprises with credit risks were alerted to financial institutions, involving a financing amount of 17.1 billion yuan.

Section 3 From Pilot Zones to Regional Trials

I. The Construction System for Green Finance Reform and Innovation Pilot Zones

In 2020, green finance reform and innovation pilot zones in nine cities in six provinces (autonomous regions) across China strengthened policy making, improved standards, increased incentives, and promoted experience, further improving the construction of pilot zones. For example, Jiangxi Province issued the *Guidelines of Jiangxi Province for the Verification and Management of Green Bills (for Trial Implementation)*, which is the first to implement the standard for green bills in China. Guangzhou issued the *Detailed Rules for the Implementation of Policies and Measures to Promote Green Finance in Huangpu District and Guangzhou Development Zone in Guangzhou* (HP [2020] No. 11) for the purpose to promote the green finance reform and innovation experience of Huadu District to all jurisdictions. Zhejiang Province's Huzhou City issued and implemented the *Implementation Measures of Huzhou City for Special Loans for Major Projects and Special Green Fiscal Interest Subsidy Funds* for the purpose to increase financial incentives and promote the green recovery of the economy within its jurisdiction.

II. Some Localities Imposing Cross-regional Joint Punishment on Environmentally Dishonest Enterprises

In October, competent departments of Shanghai, Jiangsu, Zhejiang, and Anhui in the Yangtze River Delta jointly issued the *Memorandum of Cooperation in the Implementation of Joint Credit Reward and Punishment in Ecological Environment in the Yangtze River Delta (2020)*. The memorandum requires that, in accordance with the joint reward and punishment measures established by the Central Government and the above provinces and city, the environmental credit status of enterprises will be taken as an important basis for enterprises in the Yangtze River Delta to enjoy preferential policies and institutional convenience. According to the memorandum, full-process credit management and joint reward and punishment will be implemented in administrative approval, comprehensive supervision, financial services, industry self-discipline, and market cooperation.

III. Green Finance Providing Support for Regional Economic Growth

In February, the People's Bank of China, the China Banking and Insurance Regulatory Commission, the China Securities Regulatory Commission, the State Administration of Foreign Exchange, and the Shanghai Municipal People's Government jointly issued the *Opinions on Further Accelerating the Construction of Shanghai as an International Financial Center and Providing Financial Support for the Integrated Development of the Yangtze River Delta Region* (PBC [2020] No. 46). They put forward 30 measures for actively promoting the implementation of the pilot program first in the Lin-gang Special Area, accelerating the opening up of Shanghai's financial industry at a higher level, and providing financial support for the integrated development of the Yangtze River Delta. In the opinions, Article 25 is about promoting the integrated construction of a green financial service platform of the Yangtze River Delta. It includes promoting the application of the management system for green financial information of the Yangtze River Delta, boosting the linkage and coordination of regional environmental quota trading markets, and accelerate the establishment of a green project database of the Yangtze River Delta.

In May, the People's Bank of China, the China Banking and Insurance Regulatory Commission, the China Securities Regulatory Commission, and the State Administration of Foreign Exchange jointly issued the *Opinions on Financial Support for the Development of the Guangdong-Hong Kong-Macao Greater Bay Area* (PBC [2020] No. 95). They proposed to launch a pilot zone for carbon emissions trading using foreign exchange, study the establishment of the Guangzhou Futures Exchange, and establish a uniform standard for green finance. They also encourage more companies in the Greater Bay Area to finance and certify green projects on platforms based in Hong Kong and Macao and support Guangdong-based financial institutions to issue green finance bonds in the two SARs. This policy will enhance the supporting and leading role of the Guangdong-Hong Kong-Macao Greater Bay Area in China's economic growth and opening up and provide strong financial support for the construction of a first-class bay area and world-class city clusters with vigor and international competitiveness.

Section 4　Encouraging Innovation in Green Financial Products and Services

I. Supporting Green Enterprises to Leverage the Capital Market for Direct Financing

In March, to implement of the requirement in the *Implementation Opinions on Setting up the Science and Technology Innovation Board and Launching the Pilot Program of the Registration System on the Shanghai Stock Exchange* to provided key support for industries such as new energy, energy conservation, and environmental protection, the Shanghai Stock Exchange issued the *Interim Provisions of the Shanghai Stock Exchange on Application and Recommendation for Issuance and Listing of Enterprises on the STAR Market*. The *Provisions* support issuers in the energy conservation, environmental protection, and new energy industries to apply for the STAR Market and get listed on the Shanghai Stock Exchange.

In June, the Shenzhen Stock Exchange issued the *Interim Provisions on Application and Recommendation for Issuance and Listing of Enterprises on the GEM Market*, which clearly stipulates that innovative start-ups such as new energy companies that belong to the domain of high-tech industries and strategic emerging industries would be supported in the process of going public.

II. Establishing a Sound Liability Insurance System for Environmental Pollution

In February, the General Office of the CPC Central Committee and the General Office of the State Council issued the *Guiding Opinions on Building a Modern Environmental Governance System*. The *Guiding Opinions* clearly requires to "promote the development of liability insurance for environmental pollution and study the establishment of a system of compulsory liability insurance for environmental pollution in areas with high environmental risks".

In September, the *Law of the People's Republic of China on the Prevention and Control of Environmental Pollution by Solid Wastes* took effect. Its Article 99 clearly states that "entities that collect, store, transport, utilize, and dispose of hazardous wastes shall, in accordance with relevant regulations of the State, purchase liability insurance for environmental pollution".

III. Guiding Funds to Support Green Development

In March, the China Securities Regulatory Commission issued the revised *Special Provisions on Shareholding Reduction by Venture Capital Fund Shareholders of Listed Companies*. It improved the reverse linkage policy[1] to guide venture capital funds to invest early, in a small amount, and for the long run, and relax the eligibility criteria for the differentiated shareholding reduction policy. It also simplifies relevant application procedures, facilitate the exit of venture capital funds, and realizes a virtuous circle of investment-exit-reinvestment. In this way, it promotes venture capital

---

[1] Under the "reverse linkage" policy, the lock-up period of the shares invested by venture capital funds is inversely proportional to the investment period before the IPO, that is, the longer the initial investment period, the shorter the lock-up period.

funds to support small and medium-sized green enterprises with development potential, thus bolstering the development of green finance.

IV. Accelerating the Development of Environmental Equity Financial Products

The report of the 18th National Congress of the CPC ordered to launch pilot zones for carbon emission trading and establish a carbon emission trading market. The report of the 19th National Congress of the CPC noted that China should speed up reform of the system for developing an ecological civilization, develop a green and low-carbon circular economic development system, initiate a national carbon emission trading system, and steadily advance the construction of a national carbon emission trading market. In October 2020, the Ministry of Ecology and Environment and other four ministries and commissions jointly issued the *Guiding Opinions on Promoting the Investment and Financing in Response to Climate Change*. They stated that under the premise of risk control, they will support institutions and capital to actively develop financial products and services related to carbon emission equity and orderly explore and operate carbon futures and other derivative products and businesses. On October 9 of the same year, the preparation group for the Guangzhou Futures Exchange was established with the approval of the State Council. The preparation group is also exploring the development and application of carbon futures products.

In 2015, according to the *Guiding Opinions of the General Office of the State Council on Further Advancing the Pilot Work for the Paid Use and Trading of Emission Rights*, the Ministry of Finance and competent ministries issued the *Interim Measures for the Management of Revenues from the Assignment of Pollutant Discharge Rights*. Under the above policies, the Ministry of Finance promotes the establishment of a paid use and trading system for pollutant discharge rights and regulates the collection, use, and management of pollutant discharge rights revenue. It also guides 28 provinces (autonomous regions and municipalities) such as Zhejiang and Jiangsu to carry out trials and leverage the market mechanism to promote pollution reduction. The pilot zones steadily advance the paid use and trading of pollutant discharge rights, and carry out a lot of practices in system establishment, platform construction, and policy innovation. They have also invented methods such as registered pollutant discharge and pollutant discharge rights-pledged loans, and achieved positive demonstration effects.

CHAPTER III
Steady Development of Green Financial Markets

In 2020, China gave full play to the market mechanism as the foundation of the allocation of financial resources; supported market participants in innovating green financial products, tools and business models; and promoted the integration of environmental and climate change risks into the financial pricing system. The country's environmental risk management saw improvement. The green financial markets maintained rapid growth; environmental benefits emerged; and green financial products and services have become more diversified.

Section 1 Green Credit Market in Rapid Growth

China's financial system is dominated by indirect finance. As a pivotal part in the green financial system, green loans are an important source of funds for the green and low-carbon development of the real economy. The priority of China's green financial system construction has always been to vigorously develop green credit and focus on improving the fundamentals of green loans, including standard setting, statistics, and evaluation. In 2020, faced with the unexpected COVID-19 pandemic, China sized up the situation and took a coordinated approach to push forward relevant work. China had become the first major economy in the world with a positive growth rate since the pandemic. The green loans enjoyed constant growth, which indicated the country's strong resilience and vitality.

I. Status Quo of Green Loan Business

(I) Overview of National Green Loans

In 2020, green loans continued to grow. According to the People's Bank of China, as of the end of

2020, China's green loan balance stood at RMB 11.95 trillion[1], accounting for 6.7% of the loan balance in RMB and foreign currencies. The balance increased by 20.3% over the beginning of the year, registering an increase of 2.02 trillion yuan for the whole year. Among them, the unit green loan balance was 11.91 trillion yuan, accounting for 10.8% of the loan balance of enterprises and institutions in the same period. An annual increase of 2 trillion yuan was recorded throughout the year, accounting for 16.5% of the loan increment to enterprises and institutions in the same period.

The asset quality of green loans is generally high. As of the end of 2020, the balance of green non-performing loans was RMB 39 billion, with a non-performing rate of 0.33%, 1.65 percentage points lower than that of corporate loans in the same period and down by 0.24 percentage points from the beginning of the year. Specifically, the non-performing rate of green loans for the green upgrade of infrastructure was 0.16%. The non-performing rate in eastern China was 0.2%. The non-performing rates of green loans for large and medium-sized banks were 0.19% and 0.39%, respectively, down by 0.37 and 0.14 percentage points from the beginning of the year.

(II) Green Loans from 24 Major Banks[2]

As of the end of 2020, the green loan balance of 24 major banking institutions was RMB 10.33 trillion, registering a year-on-year increase of 21.89%. The green loan balance accounted for 7.79% of the total balance of all types of loans in the 24 banks. The balance of green non-performing loans was RMB 25.316 billion, with a non-performing rate of 0.25%.

In terms of green loan balance, among the 24 banks by the end of 2020, the highest was RMB 2,268.2 billion while the lowest was RMB 10.6 billion, with an average of RMB 430.253 billion and a median of RMB 184.568 billion.

---

[1] As the statistical methods and scope of targets are not exactly the same, the green loan data of the People's Bank of China is different from that of the China Banking and Insurance Regulatory Commission. The latter one collected information about 21 major banks across China, including China Development Bank, Export-Import Bank, Agricultural Development Bank, Industrial and Commercial Bank, Agricultural Bank, Bank of China, Construction Bank, Bank of Communications, Postal Savings Bank, China Merchants Bank, Shanghai Pudong Development Bank, China CITIC Bank, Industrial Bank, Minsheng Bank, China Everbright Bank, Huaxia Bank, China Guangfa Bank, Ping An Bank, Hengfeng Bank, Zheshang Bank, and Bohai Bank. As of the end of 2020, the green credit balance of these 21 major banks was RMB 11.5 trillion.

[2] Source of data: People's Bank of China. 24 major banks include China Development Bank, Export-Import Bank, Agricultural Development Bank, Industrial and Commercial Bank, Agricultural Bank, Bank of China, Construction Bank, Bank of Communications, Postal Savings Bank, China Merchants Bank, Shanghai Pudong Development Bank, China CITIC Bank, Industrial Bank, Minsheng Bank , China Everbright Bank, Hua Xia Bank, China Guangfa Bank, Ping An Bank, Hengfeng Bank, Zheshang Bank, Bohai Bank, Bank of Beijing, Bank of Shanghai and Bank of Jiangsu.

In terms of the proportion of green loan balance of all types of loans, among the 24 banks, the highest rate was 18.79% while the lowest was 0.84%, with an average of 5.77% and a median of 5.72%. Only two of the 24 banks accounted for more than 10% of the balance of green loans. On the whole, there is still much room for improvement in their green loan business.

In terms of the growth rate of loan balance, the 24 banks witnessed the highest year-on-year growth rate of 60.84% and the lowest rate of −5.12%, with an average of 22.62% and a median of 19.99%.

In terms of the non-performing rate of green loans, among the 24 banks, the highest was 1.82% while the lowest was 0.07%, with an average of 0.57% and a median of 0.405%.

Column 3-1

Structural Analysis of Green Loans 2020

According to statistics from the People's Bank of China, as of the end of 2020, China's green loan balance was RMB 11.95 trillion. In light of use purpose, the loan balance of green infrastructure[1] upgrading sectors and clean energy sectors stood at RMB 5.76 trillion and RMB 3.2 trillion, an increase of 21.3% and 13.4% throughout the year. Altogether they accounted for 74.9% of the total green loan balance. In light of sectors, the green loan balance in infrastructure industries[2] was RMB 8.86 trillion, an increase of 15.9% throughout the year. The figure accounted for 74.1% of the total balance.

From the view of regions, green loans in the eastern and central regions grew faster, while the western and northeastern regions saw slower growth. As of the end of 2020, the green loan

---

[1] According to the *Green Industry Guidance Catalogue (2019)* (FGHZ [2019] No. 293), the green upgrade of infrastructure includes building energy efficiency and green buildings, green transportation, environmental infrastructure, urban energy infrastructure, sponge cities, and landscaping; the clean energy industry includes the manufacturing of new energy and clean energy equipment, the construction and operation of clean energy facilities, the clean and efficient use of traditional energy, and the efficient operation of energy systems.

[2] Infrastructure industries in this report refers to the transportation, storage, and postal industries; the production (or generation) and supply of electricity, heat, gas, and water; and the management of water conservancy, environmental, and public facilities.

balance in China's eastern region[①] was RMB 5.91 trillion, an increase of RMB 1.12 trillion or 23.5% over the beginning of the year (which was 3.2 percentage points higher than the national average). In China's central region, the figure was RMB 1.97 trillion, an increase of RMB 414.4 billion or 26.6% throughout the year (which was 6.3 percentage points higher than the national average). In China's western region, the amount was RMB 3 trillion, an increase of RMB 380.2 billion or 14.5% throughout the year. In China's northeastern region, the figure was RMB 533.5 billion, an increase of RMB 58.9 billion or 12.4% throughout the year.

From the view of institutions, green loans from small and medium-sized banks grew rapidly, and green loans from large banks were concentrated. As of the end of 2020, the green loan balance of major Chinese banks was RMB 7.75 trillion, an increase of RMB 1.33 trillion or 20.6% throughout the year. The green loan balance of mid-sized Chinese banks was RMB 2.46 trillion, an increase of RMB 500.5 billion or 25.5% throughout the year. The green loan balance of small Chinese banks was RMB 942.1 billion, an increase of RMB 172.3 billion or 22.4% throughout the year.

The environmental benefits of green credit have emerged. According to the statistics of the China Banking and Insurance Regulatory Commission, based on the proportion of credit funds in the total investment of relevant green projects, as of the end of 2020, green credit of 21 major Chinese banks was expected to support saving 320 million tons of standard coal and reducing carbon dioxide equivalent by 730 million tons, which was a great contribution to achieving the goals of peaking carbon dioxide emissions and carbon neutrality.

Column 3-2

Innovation Cases of Green Credit Products and Services

Carbon Sink Loan. Zhongtai Sub-district in Hangzhou's Yuhang District is famous for producing

---

[①] The eastern region covers 10 provinces (municipalities), namely, Beijing, Tianjin, Hebei, Shanghai, Jiangsu, Zhejiang, Fujian, Shandong, Guangdong, and Hainan. The central region covers 6 provinces, namely, Shanxi, Anhui, Jiangxi, Henan, Hubei, and Hunan. The western region covers 12 provinces (regions and municipalities), namely, Inner Mongolia, Guangxi, Chongqing, Sichuan, Guizhou, Yunnan, Tibet, Shaanxi, Gansu, Qinghai, Ningxia, and Xinjiang. The northeastern region covers 3 provinces, namely, Heilongjiang, Jilin, and Liaoning.

bamboo flute with the local bitter bamboo. It has a bitter bamboo plantation of over 10,000 mu (appx. 6.67 km^2), the only one in China. The Postal Savings Bank of China innovatively launched the Carbon Sink Loan and issue targeted operating loans to the operating entities of the bamboo flute industry chain in Zhongtai. The use of loans is not limited to bamboo tending. It can be used for all production and operation segments in the bamboo flute industry chain, including bamboo planting, bamboo raising, flute making, flute sales, and cultural promotion. The bank gives a special preferential interest rate based on the annual carbon sinking of the project, which can be as low as 3.95%, lower than the local market operating loan interest rate (5%+) by more than 105 BP. As of the end of 2020, the Postal Savings Bank of China had issued a "carbon sink loan" worth of RMB 300,000 to the company for its daily operation and capital turnover.

Water Saving Loan. In May 2020, the Jiangsu Provincial Departments of Finance and Water Resources cooperated with Industrial Bank to launch the Water Saving Loan. They set a special loan limit of RMB 1 billion to provide special financing services for the resumption of work and production and high-quality development of water-saving enterprises along the Yangtze River Economic Belt. The Jiangsu Provincial Government has built a platform for projects funded by Water Saving Loans to screen qualified companies and transfer them to cooperative banks. The platform focuses on supporting projects such as water-saving technology transformation, water supply network transformation, and unconventional water source utilization. The Industrial Bank facilitates enterprises that meet the Water Saving Loan access in mortgage and pledge rate, approval channels, and financing costs. In 2020, the Industrial Bank issued Water Saving Loans to four projects, with a financing amount of RMB 43 million.

Financing services under the EOD model. The Bank of Jiangsu focuses on the financing challenge of public welfare projects such as ecological protection and restoration along the Yangtze river, explores the Ecology-Oriented Development (EOD) model featuring coordinated development of ecological governance and industries, and provides targeted financing schemes for major projects such as the protection of the Yangtze River and the treatment of cave-in land in coal mines. Under the EOD model, the Bank of Jiangsu generates its revenue from land premium, land transfer income and industrial dividends. The former is easier to achieve but lacks sustainability. The latter has fewer successful cases due to the long cycle of industrial development and much uncertainty. The Bank of Jiangsu was creative to organically combine operating projects with cash flow and public projects without cash flow and properly solved the financing difficulties of a shoreline relocation and green restoration project in Nanjing.

II. Evaluation of Green Finance

After the *Notice on Conducting Green Credit Performance Evaluation of Banking Depository Financial Institutions* was issued in July 2018, the People's Bank of China conducted green credit performance evaluation on the first batch of 24 major banks. In the first quarter of 2019, the evaluation was extended to all banking institutions around China. The evaluation results of 24 major banks in 2020 are as follows.

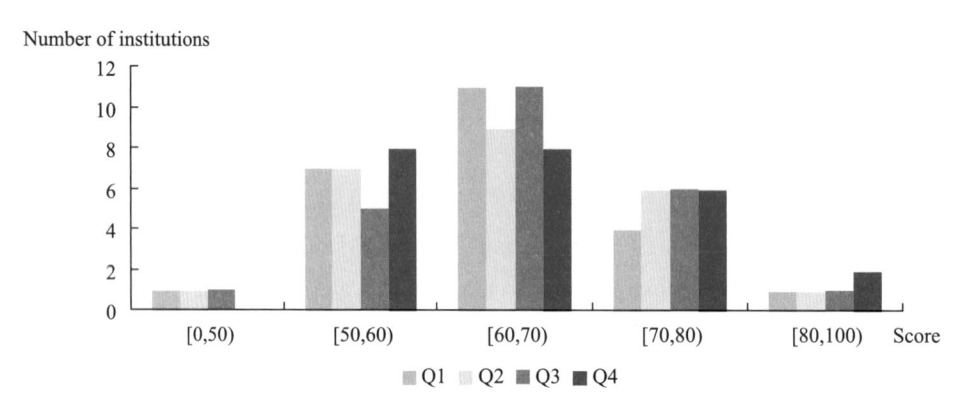

Figure 3-1 Results of the performance evaluation of the green credit of 24 major banks in 2020

According to the results of the performance evaluation, the 24 banks are generally on the rise in green credit, with the results increasingly concentrated. This shows that the performance evaluation has effectively motivated banking institutions to put more emphasis on the green loan business and created a good incentive and restraint mechanism for promoting the development of green loans. While some major banks (such as National Development Bank, Agricultural Development Bank of China, Industrial and Commercial Bank of China, and China Construction Bank) and green financial banks (such as China Industrial Bank and Huaxia Bank) perform outstandingly in the evaluation, some urban commercial banks still get a persistently low score. They need to put more emphasis on green financial services such as green loans in the future.

After the goals of peaking carbon dioxide emissions and carbon neutrality were introduced, the green and low-carbon transition of China's economy faces a more urgent situation, and there is a huge investment demand in the green and low-carbon area. In the foreseeable future, the demand for green loans in the real economy will further increase. In the near future, we will continue to remove the constraints in the way of green loans, improve the incentive and restraint mechanism for the green loan business, and create a more favorable system and market environment for the development of green loans.

Section 2   The Green Securities Market in Steady Progress

I. The Green Bond Market More Adaptable to Green Financing Needs

In 2020, China's green bonds took on new features. Market participants became diversified, and issuance maturities grew longer. Innovative products kept emerging. The green bond market adapted better to the green financing needs of the real economy. The goals of peaking carbon emissions and carbon neutrality injected fresh impetus into the innovative development of green bonds. More policy incentives for green bonds were rolled out. In addition, the ratings of green bonds and facilities maintained high, as they became more cost-competitive. This landscape proved positive for corporate green financing. The raised funds continued to focus on green industries such as green services and the green upgrade of infrastructure.

(I) Overview of Issuance

In 2020, domestic entities in China issued green bonds totaling about RMB 258 billion. Among them, 155 issuers issued 220 green bonds of various types in the domestic market, with a total scale of RMB 216.582 billion. 10 issuers issued 17 green bonds offshore, with a total scale of RMB 41.42 billion. As of the end of 2020, green bonds worth of RMB 1,413.4 billion were issued in China, and the stock was RMB 813.2 billion. Throughout the year, various bonds worth of RMB 57.3 trillion were issued in the Chinese bond market, a year-on-year increase of 26.5%. Among them, green bonds accounted for 0.3%, half of the 0.6% in 2019.

(II) Green Bonds More Adaptable to the Real Economy

1. Market Participants More Diversified

In 2020, participants in the domestic green bond market became more diversified. Issuance, underwriting, and trading remained active.

In terms of the sectoral distribution of issuers, the industrial sector has become an important force in the issuance of green bonds. Throughout the year, the industrial sector issued green bonds of RMB 108.708 billion, accounting for 50.19% of the total amount, an increase of 18.47 percentage points from 2019. The issuance of the public utility sector accounted for 24.38%, ranking second, an increase of 2.19 percentage points year-on-year. The issuance scale of the financial industry ranked third, accounting for 17.84%, a year-on-year decrease of 17.91 percentage points. The proportion of financial green bonds has declined since 2016, when it accounted for more than 90% of green bonds. This indicates that green bond issuers continue to be diversified, and entity companies have an increasing demand for green bonds.

Table 3-1　　Domestic Green Bonds in 2020 by First-class Categories of the Wind Industry Classification Standard

Sector	Bond scale (RMB 100 million)	Proportion of issuance scale (%)	Number of bonds	Proportion of issuance count (%)
Industry	1,087.08	50.19	119	54.09
Public utility	527.98	24.38	55	25.00
Finance	386.36	17.84	26	11.82
Materials	51.9	2.40	8	3.64
Optional consumption	46	2.12	7	3.18
Energy	30	1.39	1	0.45
Real estate	27	1.25	3	1.36
IT	9.5	0.44	1	0.45
Total	2,165.82	100	220	100

From the view of the nature of issuers, the issuers of green bonds are mainly local state-owned enterprises, state-controlled enterprises, and central enterprises, and the proportion of financial institutions has dropped significantly. In 2020, green corporate bonds dominated the green bond issuance, with a total of 91 bonds issued at a scale of RMB 73.21 billion, a year-on-year decrease of 13.85%. 47 green enterprise bonds were issued, at a scale of RMB 48.54 billion, focusing on supporting green transportation, sewage treatment, sponge city construction, clean energy, and the construction of energy ecological parks. 30 green medium-term notes were issued, at a scale of RMB 33.85 billion, which generally remained stable. The issuance scale of financial green bonds continued to decline. Throughout the year, 9 financial institutions issued 11 financial green bonds at a scale of RMB 27.2 billion, a year-on-year decrease of 67.3%. 30 green asset-backed securities were issued at a scale of RMB 24.632 billion, which effectively lowered the threshold and cost of corporate financing and, to a certain extent, alleviated the difficulty and high cost of financing in the private sector.

Table 3-2　　Domestic Issuance of Green Bonds in 2020

Type	Number of bonds	Scale (RMB 100 million)
Corporate bond	91	732.1
Enterprise bond	47	485.4
Medium term note	30	338.5
Financial bond	11	272

Chapter III Steady Development of Green Financial Markets

continued

Type	Number of bonds	Scale (RMB 100 million)
Asset-backed securities	30	246.32
Short-term financing bill	6	36.5
Local government bond	1	27
Placement note	3	16
Project revenue note	1	12
Total	220	2,165.82

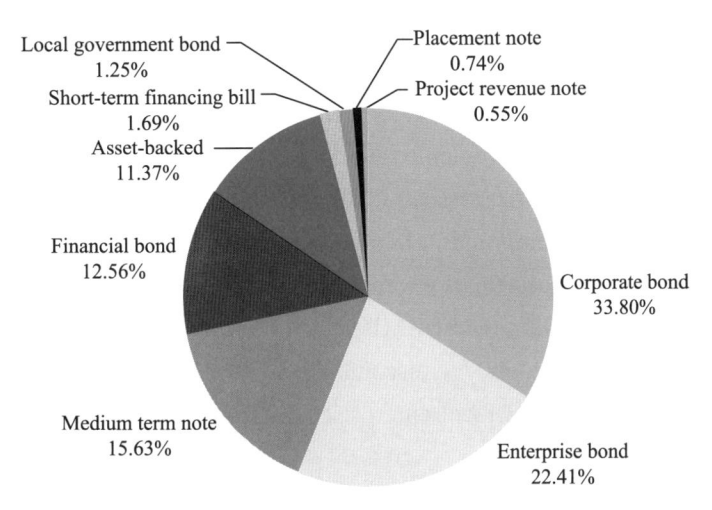

Figure 3-2 Domestic Issuance of Green Bonds in 2020
Source of data: China Central Depository & Clearing Co., Ltd. and Wind

- Local government bond 1.25%
- Short-term financing bill 1.69%
- Asset-backed 11.37%
- Financial bond 12.56%
- Medium term note 15.63%
- Enterprise bond 22.41%
- Corporate bond 33.80%
- Placement note 0.74%
- Project revenue note 0.55%

Column 3-3

Overview of Green Debt Financing Instruments 2020

In 2020, green debt financing instruments became more popular and their environmental benefits were obvious. Altogether 53 green debt financing instruments, including green ABN, registered RMB 54.37 billion, a year-on-year increase of 19%. The proportion of these financing instruments increased from 19.8% in 2019 to 23.8% in 2020. The market share kept growing. As of the end of 2020, green debt financing instruments worth of RMB 149.82 billion had been issued, which were quite effective in energy conservation and emissions reduction. According to the data disclosed in green assessment and certification reports, it is estimated that the green projects backed by those funds will save more than 180 million tons of standard coal each year, equivalent to 3.7% of the total energy consumption in 2019. That means 450 million tons of carbon emssions will be saved.

The product variety continued to expand, and the product mix was richer. Since 2020, innovative products such as blue bonds, green asset-backed commercial paper (ABCP), and green merger and acquisition notes were launched to meet the diversified green financing needs of issuers. In 2020, a total of 13 green asset-backed notes (ABN) worth of RMB 14.12 billion were issued. More green assets in stock were put to use.

Market entities covered a wide range of areas and various industries. First, the scale of issuance in key provinces and regions continued to grow. As of the end of 2020, enterprises in the Yangtze River Economic Belt had issued green debt financing instruments of RMB 61.5 billion, those in the Beijing-Tianjin-Hebei region issued RMB 49 billion, and those in the Guangdong-Hong Kong-Macao Greater Bay Area issued RMB 16.7 billion. Second, the regional distribution was directly related to the emphasis of local governments and the incentive measures introduced. Provinces with green finance reform and innovation pilot zones, such as Zhejiang and Guangdong, issued green bonds of RMB 29 billion, accounting for 20% of the market. Jiangsu introduced an incentive policy to discount the interest rate of 30% for enterprises issuing green bonds in the province, and local enterprises issued green bonds of RMB 16.2 billion, accounting for 11% of the total.

The issuers had high credit ratings, and the maturity most products was in the medium and long term. In terms of credit ratings, the issuers of green debt financing instruments were well qualified. As of the end of 2020, issuers of AAA green debt financing instruments accounted for 61%, and AA+ accounted for 19%. In terms of product maturity, given that the use of funds raised by green debt financing instruments needs to match green projects, the maturity of most products is in the medium and long term. Among the 131 new green bonds issued throughout the year, 119 projects had a maturity of 3 years or more, accounting for 91% of the total.

Market entities were increasingly active and their participation grew deeper. First, the enthusiasm of issuers to participate continued to increase. In 2020, 42 issuers engaged in the issuance of green debt financing instruments. They were distributed in more regions, at different credit levels, and of different types. Among them, 10 issuers have issued green debt financing instruments multiple times throughout the year; in addition, in 2020, 11 companies that have registered debt financing instruments for the first time were introduced through green debt financing instruments, including Fujian Strait Environmental Protection, Luneng New Energy, China Development Bank New Energy, Wuhan Bishui, Hangzhou Youxing, Xuzhou Bus,

Nanjing Bus, Guangzhou Bus, Shanghai Shenneng Financial Leasing, Datang Commercial Factoring, and Yichun State-owned Assets.

Table 3-3 Multiple Issuance Factsheet of Green Debt Financing Instruments in 2020

Number	Issuer	Issuance count	Issuance scale (RMB 100 million)	Purpose of raised funds	Major underwriter
1	Chongqing Rail Transit (Group) Co., Ltd.	2	30	Clean transport	Bank of China
2	Ningbo Rail Transit Group Co., Ltd.	2	30	Clean transport	National Development Bank, China Construction Bank
3	Nanjing Financial City Construction Development Co., Ltd.	2	24	Green building	Bank of Communications, Bank of Nanjing, Haitong Securities, Bank of Ningbo
4	Huaneng Tiancheng Financing Leasing Co., Ltd.	3	20	Wind power	Bank of China, Bank of Beijing, Orient Securities, Huaxia Bank
5	Chengdu Rail Transit Group Co., Ltd.	2	20	Clean transport	China CITIC Bank
6	Datang Commercial Factoring Co., Ltd.	2	11	Photovoltaic and wind power (underlying assets)	Industrial Bank
7	CPI Ronghe Financial Leasing Co., Ltd.	2	19.9	New energy vehicles, photovoltaic and wind power (underlying assets)	Industrial Bank, Hengfeng Bank
8	GD Power Development Co., Ltd.	2	17.68	Wind power	Huatai Securities, China Zheshang Bank, Bank of Communications, Industrial and Commercial Bank of China

continued

Number	Issuer	Issuance count	Issuance scale (RMB 100 million)	Purpose of raised funds	Major underwriter
9	Huaneng Lancang River Hydropower Inc.	2	15	Hydro power	National Development Bank, Industrial and Commercial Bank of China
10	Shenyang Metro Group Co., Ltd.	2	15	Clean transport	China Merchants Bank

Source of information: National Association of Financial Market Institutional Investors.

Second, more investors engaged in the activity. In terms of the denomination of green bond positions, as of the end of September 2020, Industrial Bank, Agricultural Bank of China, and Bank of China ranked top among national commercial banks and policy banks. Guangzhou Rural Commercial Bank, Bank of Jiangsu, and Bank of Changsha performed prominently among urban commercial banks and rural financial institutions. CITIC Securities, E Fund and National Social Security Fund were active among securities institutions and investment funds. Taikang Asset Management, Yangtze River Pension Insurance, and Dajia Assets were the top three insurance financial institutions. Overseas investment institutions such as the Hong Kong Monetary Authority and Bank of China (Hong Kong) Limited were also active participants in the domestic green bond market.

Third, lead underwriters were more enthusiastic. In 2020, 25 financial institutions participated in the underwriting of green debt financing instruments. In terms of underwriting amount, the Bank of China registered a total underwriting amount of RMB 7.94 billion and secured a market share of 15.7%. Industrial Bank and China Merchants Bank followed closely, underwriting RMB 6.14 billion and RMB 5.4 billion, respectively. China CITIC Bank, Agricultural Bank of China, China Development Bank, Industrial and Commercial Bank of China, China Construction Bank, Shanghai Pudong Development Bank, and CITIC Securities also performed outstandingly in the underwriting of green debt financing instruments.

In 2020, 82 financial institutions participated in the underwriting of domestic green bonds (except the first green REITs). Among them, 24 were banks, underwriting a total of RMB 58.268 billion. The top three banks in undertaking amount were Bank of China, Industrial Bank, and China Merchants Bank, with RMB 8.751 billion, 7.505 billion, and 5.6 billion respectively. 58 were securities companies, a year-on-year increase of 7, underwriting RMB 157.39 billion in total. The top three securities companies were CITIC Construction Investment, CITIC Securities, and Guotai Junan Securities, with RMB 16.852 billion, 12.104 billion, and 9.836 billion, respectively.

The trading volume of the secondary market of green bonds continued to grow. In 2020, 480 green bonds were traded, with a scale of RMB 725.089 billion, a year-on-year increase of 19.86%. Among them, green financial bonds saw brisk trading, accounting for about 60% of the total trading volume.

2. Maturities in a Wider Range

In 2020, the maturities of green bonds were mainly 3 years, 5 years, and 7 years. The proportion of long-term bonds increased. Among them, the scale of 3-year green bonds accounted for 37.23%, a year-on-year decrease of 9.24%; 5-year accounted for 23.97%, a year-on-year decrease of 9.51%; and 7-year accounted for 12.83%, a year-on-year increase of 9.33%. In 2020, short-term green bonds with maturities of 21 days, 60 days, 90 days, and 180 days were issued for the first time, which better met the issuers' short-term liquidity needs under the influence of the COVID-19 pandemic.

Table 3-4 Distribution of Maturities of Domestic Green Bonds in 2020

Maturity	Total offer amount (RMB 100 million)	Proportion of issuance scale (%)	Number of bonds
1 year	147.28	6.80	23
2 years	60.23	2.78	7
3 years	806.33	37.23	71
4 years	40.89	1.89	4
5 years	519.23	23.97	55
6 years	47	2.17	3
7 years	277.8	12.83	33
8 years	8.7	0.40	1
9 years	27.06	1.25	2
10 years	132	6.09	15
15 years	20.5	0.95	2
18 years	6.8	0.31	1
20 years	72	3.32	3
Total	2,165.82	100	220

3. Innovative Products Emerging

2020 witnessed the emergence of various innovative green bond products. In terms of variety, asset-backed securities make active innovations; in terms of theme, pandemic prevention and control represents the new, widely released theme.

In January, Longyuan Power issued a special program of 713 million yuan to support green assets for the establishment of corporate renewable energy tariff supplementary subsidy on the Shenzhen Stock Exchange. This marked the first renewable energy subsidy green ABS across the entire market for a central government-owned enterprise.

In February, Datang Financial Leasing Co., Ltd. issued China's first green bond on pandemic prevention and control on the Shanghai Stock Exchange. The raised funds were mainly used to ensure the power supply in key areas. Huadian International Power Co., Ltd. issued China's first green bond on pandemic prevention and control and green asset securitized product on pandemic control, i.e. targeted green asset-backed notes (pandemic prevention and control bonds). The basic asset is a renewable energy tariff supplementary subsidy with a term of 2.5 years. The funds raised totaled 1.551 billion yuan, which were allocated to ensure the power supply for green infrastructure construction in Hubei, Ningxia, Shandong, Inner Mongolia and pandemic-hit areas in China and the emergency repair of the power supply system for pandemic control.

In March, the first green corporate bond featuring innovation, entrepreneurship and pandemic control, i.e. one-year Kailun shares worth of 50 million yuan was issued on the Shenzhen Stock Exchange.

In April, the first innovative variety of corporate bond supporting pandemic prevention, i.e. Wuhan Chedu Sishui Gongzhi Project Management Co., Ltd. green proceeds corporate bond was issued on the Shenzhen Stock Exchange. This was the first innovative corporate bond program approved in Hubei Province after the coronavirus outbreak.

In April, the Agricultural Development Bank issued an RMB-2-billion three-year financial bond for environmental protection to global investors for the first time, with an interest rate of 1.649%. The funds raised were mainly used to support key areas of ecological progress, including ecological conservation and restoration, water resources conservation and utilization, water environment management in key river basins, urban and rural environmental governance, and pollution prevention and control.

In July, the China Development Bank issued the first Bond Connect green financial bond for responding to climate change to global investors in multiple markets, with a total scale of RMB 10 billion and an issuance rate of 2.4984%. The raised funds were used for green projects such as low-carbon transportation, for the purpose to effectively mitigate and restrain climate change and reduce pollutant discharge.

In October, the first new energy power generation infrastructure REITs product and green REITs product, the ICBCCS CEEIC Wind Farm Green Asset Backed Securities Prime, was issued. The underlying sponsor was China Energy Engineering Investment Co., Ltd. The issuance scale was RMB 725 million.

In November, China Power Investment Ronghe Financial Leasing Co., Ltd. issued 1.05 billion yuan of green asset-backed commercial paper (ABCP), which was the first of its kind in the inter-bank market. This green asset-backed commercial paper integrates ABCP and green bonds. The issuance period is 30 days and the corporate rating is AAA. The project will provide financing support for 16 small and micro enterprises. The basic assets involve 17 projects, including central heating, pollution control, new energy vehicles, and photovoltaic and wind power. They have generated satisfactory results in energy conservation, emission reduction, resource recycling, and sustainable energy development.

In November, ChinaBond Pricing Center Co., Ltd. issued the world's first ChinaBond ESG Select Credit Bond Index. The constituents of the index were credit bonds issued by top-ranking issuers in ChinaBond's ESG evaluation with a maturity period of not less than 1 month, a ChinaBond market implied rating of not lower than AA, and domestic public offering and listing. The index was the world's first wide-based renminbi credit bond ESG factor index compiled based on the ChinaBond ESG evaluation system.

In November, Qingdao Water Group issued the first series of green medium-term notes of 2020, with a scale of RMB 300 million and a maturity of 3 years. The raised funds were used for the construction of seawater desalination projects. The bonds not only met the standard of green bonds but also were qualified as blue bonds. It was the first blue bond issued by a global non-financial company. Blue bonds are a type of green bonds. The raised funds are specifically used for sustainable marine economy, which can play an important role in promoting marine conservation and sustainable use of marine resources.

Column 3-4

Bonds for Pandemic Prevention and Control

On February 1, 2020, the People's Bank of China, Ministry of Finance, the China Banking Regulatory Commission, the China Securities Regulatory Commission, and the State Administration of Foreign Exchange jointly issued the *Notice on Further Strengthening Financial Support for the Prevention and Control of the Epidemic of Novel Coronavirus Pneumonia* (PBOC [2020] No. 29). The notice emphasized the need to improve the efficiency of services such as bond issuance. According to the notice, a "green channel" should be established for the registration and issuance of financial bonds, asset-backed securities, and corporate credit bonds raising funds mainly for pandemic prevention and control or issued by financial institutions and companies in areas severely hit by the pandemic. After that, bond regulators issued specific arrangements for the "green channel" for bond business during the pandemic prevention and control. According to the arrangements, "in the case that all or part of the raised funds are used for pandemic prevention and control, '(Pandemic Prevention and Control Bond)' can be added after the full name of the bond during declaration or issuance".

In 2020, a total of 10 green bonds were issued for pandemic prevention and control, totaling 6.406 billion yuan. The funds raised went to the "Four Waters Governance" project of Wuhan Economic and Technological Development Zone (Hannan District), the project of polymer waterproof material, and the repayment of loans from targeted poverty alleviation programs. They also helped support targeted poverty alleviation programs, build more high-standard vegetable greenhouses, supplement the issuer's liquidity, and repay interest-bearing liabilities.

Table 3-5 Issuance of Some Pandemic Prevention and Control Bonds in 2020

Name	Issuer	Nature of issuer	Scale (RMB 100 million)
Huadian Power International Corporation Limited 2020 Asset Backed Note Series 1 (Pandemic Prevention and Control Bond)	Huadian Power International Corporation Limited	Central enterprise	15.51
Hangzhou Youxing Technology Co., Ltd. 2020 Asset Backed Note Series 1 (Pandemic Prevention and Control Bond)	Hangzhou Youxing Technology Co., Ltd.	Other	10

continued

Name	Issuer	Nature of issuer	Scale (RMB 100 million)
20 Shouguang G1(Pandemic Prevention and Control Bond)	Shouguang Huinong New Rural Construction Investment Development Co., Ltd.	State-owned holding	5
G20 Datang Leasing 1 (Pandemic Prevention and Control Bond)	Datang Financial Leasing Company Limited	State-owned holding	10
20 Canlon SG (Pandemic Prevention and Control Bond)	Jiangsu Canlon Building Materials Co., Ltd.	Private enterprise	0.5
Yangtze River Chuyue-Optical Valley Flue Gas Desulfurization Service Charging Right, Green Asset- Backed Plan (Pandemic Prevention and Control Bond)	Wuhan Optical Valley Environmental Science and Technology Co., Ltd.	State-owned holding	4.4
G20 Yongrong (Pandemic Prevention and Control Bond)	Fujian Eversun Holdings Group Co., Ltd.	Private enterprise	3
20 Sishui G1 (Pandemic Prevention and Control Bond)	Wuhan Chedu Sishui Gongzhi Project Management Co., Ltd.	State-owned holding	10
G20 Golden Gun (Pandemic Prevention and Control Bond)	Suzhou Golden Gun New Material Co., Ltd.	Private enterprise	0.2
20 China Resources Leasing (Pandemic Prevention and Control Bond)	China Resources Financial Leasing Co., Ltd.	Central enterprise	5.45

(III) Green Bonds Maintaining High Ratings, with Significant Cost Advantages

Most green bond issuers had the credit rating of AA. As approval agencies opened green channels for green bonds, issuers with lower ratings were more willing to issue green bonds. Nonetheless, the green bonds and facilities maintained high ratings, with AAA accounting for the largest proportion, 72.93% of the total issuance. The facility rating is higher than the entity rating, which means that investors have much confidence in the debt repayment capability of green projects.

Table 3-6   Rating of Domestic Green Bonds in 2020[1]

Rate	Scale (RMB 100 million)	Proportion of issuance scale (%)	Issurance number
AAA	1,246.81	72.93	97
AA+	354.68	20.75	45
AA	95.2	5.57	17
AA-	3	0.18	1
A-1	10	0.58	1
Total	1,709.69	100	161

The issuance rates domestic green bonds continued to decline. As a result, the financing cost of green projects was further reduced. In 2020, the average issuance rate of AAA 1-to-3-year bonds was 3.27%, 95 basis points lower than that in 2019. That of 3-to-5-year bonds was 3.93%, 49 basis points lower than that in 2019.

Table 3-7   Issuance Rate of Domestic Green Bonds in 2020 (%)

Rate	Within 1 year	1 to 3 years (included)	3 to 5 years (included)	5 to 10 years (included)	Above 10 years
AAA	3.63	3.27	3.93	4.54	3.55
AA+	4.91	4.18	4.70	5.30	5.45
AA	—	3.82	6.96	6.66	6.09
AA-	—	4.50	—	—	—
A-1	2.54	—	—	—	—

Among the 190 domestic green bonds issued in 2020 (excluding green asset-backed securities), 106 green bonds[2] are comparable in issuance costs[3]. Compared with similar bonds (of the same type, the same maturity, and the same rating, issued in the same month), 68.87% of the green bonds have

---

[1] Among the domestic green bonds issued in 2020, 59 had no facility ratings, with a total scale of approximately RMB 45.613 billion. This table only includes those with facility ratings.

[2] Among the 190 green bonds (not including ABS) issued in 2020, after excluding green bonds issued by private placement, green policy bank bonds, and green ultra-short-term financing bonds, a total of 106 green bond are selected as samples.

[3] The issuance cost analysis aims to compare and analyze the issuance costs of green bonds with the average issuance interest rate of bonds of the same maturity, type, and credit rating issued in the current month to determine whether green bonds have an issuance cost advantage. Some bonds are not included in the analysis sample because there were no similar bonds in the month of issuance.

a lower coupon rate, which brings them advantages in issuance costs. According to statistics, from 2016 to 2020, there were 389 green bonds as samples for the research on issuance costs. Comparing by types, more than 70% of the green corporate bonds and green medium-term notes publicly issued in the past three years have an advantage in issuance costs. The proportion of advantageous green corporate bonds basically maintains at more than 60%. The financing cost of green bond is lower.

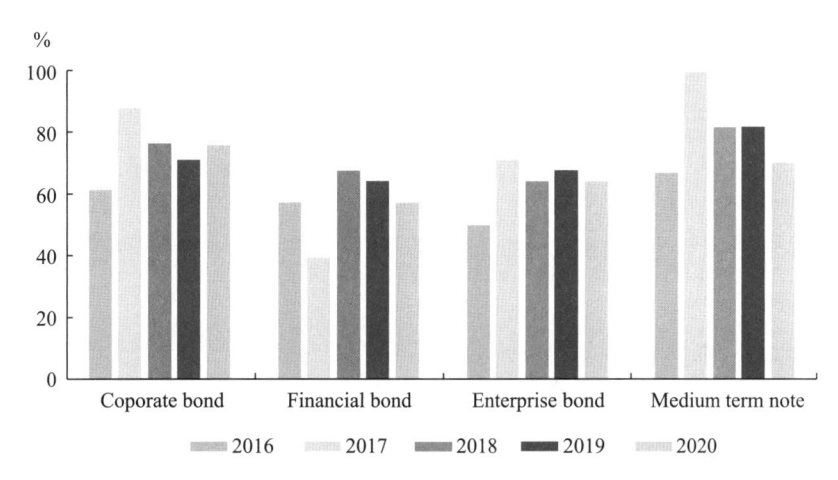

Figure 3-3 Proportion of Cost Advantages of Green Bonds in 2016 – 2020
Source of data: China Chengxin International Credit Rating Co. Ltd.

(IV) The Raised Funds Mainly Invested in Green Services and Two Other Areas

Funds raised from green bonds in 2020 were mainly invested in green services, energy conservation and environmental protection, and green upgrade of infrastructure, accounting for 30.13%, 28.07%, and 19.98%, respectively.

Table 3-8 Investment of Funds Raised from Domestic Green Bonds in 2020

Area	Scale (RMB 100 million)	Issuance number
Green services	652.64	59
Energy conservation and environmental protection	607.92	72
Infrastructure	432.83	37
Clean energy	349.53	37
Ecological environment	67.4	10
Clean production	55.5	5
Total	2,165.82	220

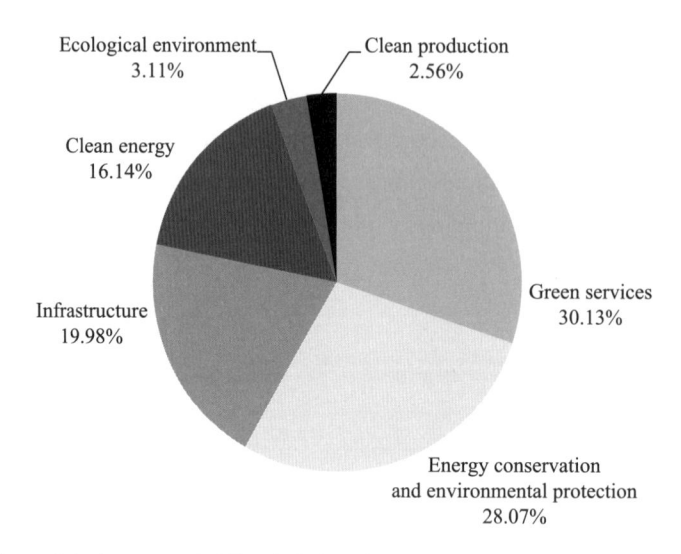

Figure 3-4 Investment of Funds Raised from Domestic Green Bonds in 2020
Source of data: China Central Depository & Clearing Co., Ltd. and Wind.

II. The Capital Market Offers Greater Support for Green Development

(I) Supporting Green Companies in Their IPO Endeavor on Domestic and Foreign Stockmarkets

In 2020, 20 enterprises applied for "ecological protection and environmental governance sector" on the GEM, expecting to raise a total of RMB 17.978 billion (12.997 billion in IPO and 4.981 billion in refinancing). The SSE STAR Market declared 26 energy-saving and environmental protection enterprises and 14 new energy enterprises. They expected to raise RMB 37.7 billion and 16.1 billion, respectively. As of the end of 2020, among the 329 companies declared by the SSE STAR Market, there were a total of 40 energy-saving, environmental protection, and new energy companies, accounting for 12%. Compared with 2019, the absolute and relative scales of green corporate financing grew by 155.0% and 1.2%.

In 2020, five green companies applied for overseas IPO, including the H-share IPO and "Full Circulation" Guangdong EFOR Environmental Group Company Limited, the H-share IPO of Liaoning Clean Energy Group Co., Ltd., the H-share IPO of Fujian Lanshen Environmental Technology Co., Ltd., and H-share IPO and "Full Circulation" of Tianjin Tianbao Energy Co., Ltd. There applications were approved by the China Securities Regulatory Commission. The IPO application of IRICO Group New Energy Company Limited was approved by the China Securities Regulatory Commission, which raised approximately HKD 1.5 billion. Tianbao Energy's H-share

"Full Circulation" was completed.

(II) The Applied Research of Green Index Compilation Makes Headway

On December 3, 2020, China Securities Index Co., Ltd. officially released its ESG evaluation method that takes into consideration the sectoral characteristics and information quality of a public company. The method focuses on the three dimensions of Environmental, Social and Governance performance. With 180 underlying indicators, it is comprised of 14 themes and 22 modules. The assessment approach is rooted in actual market conditions and reflects the ESG fundamentals of a company objectively. Arguably it is a powerful tool for better business operations and investment management.

In 2020, China Securities Index Co., Ltd. published 12 green indexes. Among them, there were 9 stock indexes and 3 bond indexes. As of the end of 2020, it had released 58 green indexes, covering ESG, sustainable development, environmental protection industries, new energy, social responsibility and governance. There were 46 stock indexes and 12 bond indexes.

New progress has been made in the research on green governance indexes. In 2020, Shenzhen Securities Information Co., Ltd., a wholly-owned subsidiary of the Shenzhen Stock Exchange, released the innovative CACG Green Governance Index, which was the first green governance index in China. It rolled out the CNI Xiangmi Lake Green Finance Index. As of the end of 2020, the Shenzhen Stock Exchange and its affiliated information companies had launched a total of 24 green indexes, covering such ESG topics as environmental protection, corporate responsibility, and governance. They have formed a green index system with wide coverage and strong representation, which plays a positive role in guiding market investment in green industries.

Table 3-9   Shenzhen Stock Exchange Green Index List

Index code	Index name	ESG area	Market coverage
399378	CNI ESG 300 Index	E+S+G	Shenzhen+Shanghai
980058	CACG Green Governance Index	E+S+G	Shenzhen
399358	CNI EP Index	E	Shenzhen+Shanghai
399412	CNI New Energy Index	E	Shenzhen+Shanghai
399417	CNI New Energy Vehicles Index	E	Shenzhen+Shanghai
399556	CCTV Ecology Industry Index	E	Shenzhen+Shanghai
399638	SZSE Environmental Protection Index	E	Shenzhen
399695	SZSE Energy Conservation Index	E	Shenzhen
980032	CNI NEVehicle Battery Index	E	Shenzhen+Shanghai

continued

Index code	Index name	ESG area	Market coverage
CNB00013	CUFE-CNI High Grade Green Bond Total Return Index	E	Domestic bonds
CNB00014	CUFE-CNI High Grade Unlabeled Green Bond Total Return Index	E	Domestic bonds
CNB00015	CUFE-CNI Labeled Green Bond Total Return Index	E	Domestic bonds
G10013	CUFE-CNI SZ-HK Connect Green Selection Index	E	Shenzhen+HK
G10165	CNI SZ-HK Connect Energy Conservation Index	E	Shenzhen+HK
G10169	CNI SZ-HK Connect Alternative-energy Cars Index	E	Shenzhen+HK
399322	CNI Corporate Governance Index	G	Shenzhen+Shanghai
399328	SZSE Corporate Governance Index	G	Shenzhen
399554	CCTV 50 Corporate Governance Index	G	Shenzhen+Shanghai
399550	CCTV 50 Index	S+G	Shenzhen+Shanghai
399341	Shenzhen Responsibility Index	S	Shenzhen
399369	CNI Social Responsibility Index	S	Shenzhen+Shanghai
399555	CCTV 50 CSR Index	S	Shenzhen+Shanghai
399651	SZSE SME CSR Index	S	Shenzhen
399650	SZSE SME Corporate Governance Index	G	Shenzhen

Section 3　Green Insurance Providing Greater Risk Protection

I. Positive Progress Made in Environmental Pollution Liability Insurance

In 2020, liability insurance for environmental pollution was introduced in 31 provinces (autonomous regions and municipalities) across China, covering such high risk industries as metallurgy, pharmaceuticals, papermaking, and thermal power. A total of of 64.661 billion yuan in risk guarantee was offered, registering a year-on-year increase of 21.75%.

II. Catastrophe Insurance Providing Effective Protection for Green Development

In 2020, China's catastrophe insurance products and services were further enriched. China Reinsurance (Group) Corporation launched the heavy rainfall catastrophe index-based insurance in multiple cities of Guangdong and Wuhan City in Hubei Province. The product provided risk protection of more than RMB 6 billion. Moreover, Zhejiang and Fujian incubated catastrophe insurance at all levels. The Index-based Insurance of Ningbo for Public Health Emergencies, the Innovation Insurance Project of Ningbo for Embankment Disaster, and the Insurance Project of Ningde for Marine Plastic Fishing Raft Upgrade were successfully launched.

The catastrophe risk management platform is an important digital infrastructure for the innovation and development of catastrophe insurance. On November 11, 2020, the International Catastrophe Portfolio Risk Management Platform (Phase I) developed by China Reinsurance (Group) Corporation was launched for trial operation. The platform adopts cloud native architecture. Resources and services can be dynamically expanded horizontally, ensuring the high performance and stability of the platform. It marks a zero-to-one breakthrough in China's reinsurance industry in terms of platforms for the real-time accumulation of catastrophe risks and single and portfolio risk assessment and management.

III. Innovation in Agriculture-related Green Insurance Going Deeper

The innovation in index-based insurance for local agricultural products continued to advance. In 2020, China Continent Property & Casualty Insurance successfully implemented the meteorological index-based insurance for hybrid rice seed production in Jiangxi Province, providing insured farmers with risk protection of RMB 4,899,800. It has effectively avoided the decline in yield or seed quality caused by abnormal climate changes such as abnormal rainfall, high temperature and low temperature, and supported the healthy development of the seed production industry. China Property & Casualty Reinsurance Co., Ltd. innovated a number of insurance products for local agricultural specialties. It launched more than 10 innovative products, including the Low-temperature Weather Index-based Insurance for Citrus in Chongqing, the Drought Index-based Insurance for Honeysuckle in Shandong's Linyi, and the Typhoon Index-based Insurance for Sugarcane in Zhejiang's Wenling. These products have effectively promoted the development of the local agricultural industry and agricultural economy.

Qinghai Province launched a pilot project for increasing the efficiency of fertilizers and pesticides. To improve farmers' ability to withstand the risk of yield reduction of crops in the pilot project, China Continent Insurance launched an innovative product, the yield insurance for crops in the project for increasing the efficiency of fertilizers and pesticides in Qinghai Province. It provided risk protection of RMB 48.81 million for 325,900 acres of barley, wheat, rape, and other crops of 1,514 households of insured farmers in Hainan Prefecture, Qinghai Province.

IV. Green Building Insurance Contributing to the Healthy Development of the Green Building Market

Many localities carried out application trials of green building performance insurance and ultra-low energy building performance insurance. An "insurance + service + technology + credit" model has formed to provide credit enhancement, risk control services, and loss compensation for green building projects.

Column 3-5

Innovation in Green Insurance

Qingdao issued China's first green building insurance policy in the Passive House Promotion and Demonstration Community Project (Phase II) of the Sino-German Ecological Park. As the applicant and the insured, the owner insures the ultra-low energy consumption buildings. The insurer commissions third-party risk control agencies to supervise the entire construction process of the ultra-low energy consumption buildings. If the insured buildings fail to meet the performance index and requirements for ultra-low energy consumption buildings in terms of annual heat consumption for heating, annual heat consumption for cooling, and air tightness, the insurer shall compensate for the energy saving rectification costs of the project or the excessive energy consumption as agreed in the insurance contract. It shall also bear the appraisal costs and legal costs incurred thereby.

Qingdao is also exploring the energy-saving insurance for buildings. If a renovation project fails to meet the energy-saving index specified in the insurance contract (the comprehensive energy-saving rate of public buildings must reach 20%), the insurer shall bear the responsibility for the rectification or economic compensation of the energy-saving project and compensate as agreed in the insurance contract.

V. Clean Energy Insurance Boosting the Development of the Energy Industry

Offshore wind power insurance has developed rapidly. In 2020, China Property & Casualty Reinsurance undertook 16 offshore wind power projects, including SPI Binhai, Dafeng Offshore Wind Power, Zhoushan Putuo No. 6 Offshore Wind Power, and CGN Rudong Offshore Wind Power, with premium income of approximately RMB 5.67 million. China Continent Insurance undertook 34 offshore wind power engineering projects and 9 offshore wind power operation projects, with coverage of RMB 14.2 billion and 2.7 billion, respectively.

Nuclear energy insurance has developed steadily. In 2020, the Chinese Nuclear Insurance Community (CNIC) provided insurance for nuclear property worth about RMB 900 billion in China. It also provided insurance for more than 20,000 front-line workers with a cumulative coverage of up to RMB 13 billion. In its overseas nuclear insurance business, CNIC has participated in the reinsurance of more than 400 nuclear facilities in 27 countries or regions around the world. It underwrites about 90% of the world's nuclear power units.

Column 3-6

Innovation in Nuclear Insurance

The nuclear insurance for the operation period of the first reactor of HPR1000 (Hua-long Pressurized Reactor) in the world. Nuclear insurance is a typical catastrophe insurance with the characteristics of low frequency and high loss. It is also the most representative type of professional reinsurance in the globalized context. In September 2020, the nuclear insurance policy issued by CNIC for the operation period of HPR1000's first reactor in the world came into effect. The insurance policy contains the clauses that combine to cover the most extensive areas in the global nuclear insurance market. In the underwriting process, CNIC cooperated closely with Fujian Fuqing Nuclear Power Co., Ltd. and successfully implemented the best insurance guarantee scheme, which was widely supported and participated by reinsurance entities at home and abroad.

The Emergency Response Platform for Nuclear Damage Compensation 2.0. In 2020, CNIC launched the Emergency Response Platform for Nuclear Damage Compensation 2.0. On the basis of Version 1.0, Version 2.0 comprehensively upgrades the functions of the platform. It can perform simulation evaluation and visual display of the impact range and compensation amount of the existing 45 operating nuclear power units in different accident scenarios. It can also provide full-process protection against nuclear accidents, including plan preparation, emergency response, and compensation management. It fills the gap of nuclear damage compensation by commercial insurance in China's emergency response mechanism for nuclear accidents.

The intelligent risk control management platform for nuclear insurance. In 2020, CNIC launched the development of an intelligent risk control management platform for nuclear insurance. The platform applies big data analysis and data mining technology for the digital transformation of the risk management of nuclear insurance. It will further enhance the company's professional capabilities and risk management, and improve risk prevention, disaster prevention, and loss reduction services.

The Nuclear Star blockchain-based operation service platform for nuclear insurance. Nuclear Star, CNIC's blockchain-based operation service platform for nuclear insurance, is the world's first of its kind. The platform performs trustworthy evidence preservation relying on the traceable and non-tamperable blockchain, which greatly enhances data security. It is also constructed flexibly in a service-oriented manner to optimize service processes and functions, effectively improving the efficiency and level of operational services. In 2020, CNIC launched the Nuclear Star blockchain platform 3.0, with new functional modules such as overseas inbound business. It is a one-stop solution for CNIC business operations and provides permanent, transparent, and traceable services to member companies.

VI. Green Investment of Insurance Funds Facilitating the Development of Green Industry

Insurance companies have rolled out innovative products of insurance debt investment and equity investment funds, and invested in green projects such as wind power generation, clean energy and green transportation. Their efforts produce sound environmental and economic benefits. By the end of 2020, the registered scale of debt investment plans involving green industries in insurance fund entity investment projects had reached 1,027.762 billion yuan. Among them, 311.322 billion yuan was invested in the transportation sector, 314.505 billion yuan in the energy sector and 68.804 billion yuan in the water conservancy sector.

In 2020, China Life provided capital in the form of sustainable debt for the 225MW wind power project of Energy China in Xilin Gol Aqi. It also offered working capital support worth of RMB 2 billion for Energy China. The project would promote the growth of local industries such as building material and transportation, create more jobs, and boost the tertiary industry. After the completion of the project, it could supply 580 million kWh of clean electricity every year, save 188,000 tons of standard coal, as well as reduce the emission of 1,598 tons of sulfur dioxide, 1,391.2 tons of nitrogen oxides and 508,500 tons of carbon dioxide. Good environmental benefits are achieved.

In 2020, Huatai Insurance Group provided 3 billion yuan in the form of debt investment plan for seven wind power projects, including China Energy Conservation Group (CECEP) Wind Power Project in Changlianggou, Yuanping City, CECEP Wind Power Project in Weishi County, and Wind Farm Project in Yunfeizhang, Bobai County. The total installed capacity reaches 469.6 MW, and the annual on-grid power is estimated to exceed 1 million MWh. That means about 2 billion tons of coal reserves would be saved. The projects help promote employment and increase local fiscal revenues. After the completion of the project, about 400,000 tons of standard coal can be saved every year, representing an emission reduction of carbon dioxide, sulfur dioxide, carbon monoxide and nitrogen oxides. Moreover, there will be less lime-ash and a large amount of fresh water will be saved.

Section 4　Innovation and Development of Green Funds and Green PPP

The green investment philosophy has taken root in the fund industry. As of the end of 2020, there were 80 green public funds in the market with a scale of RMB 169.411 billion. Among them, there were 6 social responsibility investment funds[1] with a management scale of RMB 10.614 billion; 7 ESG investment funds[2] with a management scale of RMB 3.788 billion[3]; 67 funds focusing on ecology, low-carbon, environmental protection, green, environmental governance, new energy, and Beautiful China[4], with a management scale of RMB 155.009 billion[5].

Column 3-7

Innovation Cases of Green Funds

I. Green Investment Practice of China AMC

China Asset Management Co., Ltd. (China AMC) is the first public fund company in China

---

[1] The name of the fund contains "social responsibility".
[2] The name of the fund contains "ESG".
[3] One of the funds was newly established at the end of December 2020, whose scale is to be disclosed.
[4] The name of the fund contains "ecology, low-carbon, environmental protection, green, environmental governance, new energy, and Beautiful China".
[5] Three of the funds were newly established in December 2020, whose scale is yet to be disclosed.

to sign the United Nations Principles for Responsible Investment (PRI). It is China's first fund company to establish a company-wide ESG business committee led by CEO. It also implements the *China AMC Responsible Investment Policy* and a three-tier ESG integration strategy within the company. In the "Strategy and Governance" module of the evaluation report of PRI signatories in 2020, PRI rated this practice as A+, the highest level in the world. China AMC incorporates ESG considerations in the process of international portfolio investment, which include investment policy making, fundamental research, portfolio management, risk management, engagement in listed company governance, and post-investment supervision and reporting.

In March 2020, China AMC and its Dutch partner NNIP jointly issued the world's first cross-border responsible investment product that invests in the Chinese equity market, NN(L) International China A-Share Equity Fund. This is the world's first Undertakings for Collective Investment in Transferable Securities (UCITS) product managed by a Chinese fund company. As of the end of 2020, the fund's return since its establishment was 87.92%, which exceeded the benchmark index by 31.87%. The MSCI ESG rating of the fund portfolio was BB, which was one grade higher than the benchmark index.

II. Green Investment Practice of Yuhong Capital

In 2020, Shanghai Yuhong Capital Co., Ltd. (Yuhong Capital), guided by the UN's 17 Sustainable Development Goals, launched China's first impact investment theme map. In green investment, it set 8 primary themes and 27 secondary themes, including clean energy, waste management, and circular economy.

III. SSE Deepening the Innovation of Green Financial Products

The Shanghai Stock Exchange promotes the listing of green index products. It promoted 8 products to be submitted to the China Securities Regulatory Commission for examination and approval, named Beixin Ruifeng CSI ESG 120 ETF, ICBC CS 180 ESG ETF, PY AXA CSI 120 ESG ETF, CIB MSCI China A-Share ESG ETF, Jiashi CSI 300 Index ESG ETF, Fullgoal CSI 300 ESG ETF, China Merchants Fund CSI 300 ESG ETF, and Fullgoal China Securities ESG 120 ETF. The number of ESG products submitted hit a record high.

IV. China Securities Index Releasing a Number of Green Indexes

As of the end of 2020, China Securities Index Co., Ltd. released 58 ESG-related indexes, covering ESG, sustainable development, environmental protection industries, new energy, social responsibility and governance. Among them, 46 are stock indexes and 12 are bond indexes. They serve as diversified tools for guiding funds to support the development of green industries and promoting capital markets to serve the real economy.

V. Shenzhen Stock Exchange Remaining Committed to Building a Distinctive Green Fund Market

Under the overall national plan of energy conservation and emission reduction, energy transformation, environmental protection, as well as low-carbon and green development, Shenzhen Stock Exchange plans to roll out a wide array of green-themed funds focusing on green and low-carbon development, carbon neutrality, new energy, environmental protection industry, environmental governance, and ESG. By the end of 2020, more than 20 funds were ready to be issued. The goal is to realize the demonstration effect and cluster effect of green funds in the multi-level capital market of Shenzhen Stock Exchange. Going forward, Shenzhen Stock Exchange will continue to follow the concept of green development, introduce diversified green-themed funds and better serve the green finance development strategy.

Green and low-carbon PPP projects making remarkable results. Green and low-carbon PPP projects play an active role in alleviating insufficient investment in green development, improving the urban and rural ecological environment, and promoting the development of green and low-carbon markets. As of the end of 2020, in the project management database of the national comprehensive PPP information platform, there were 5,826 pollution prevention and green, low-carbon projects with an investment of RMB 5.6 trillion. These projects cover 31 provinces (autonomous regions and municipalities directly under the Central Government) and Xinjiang Corps. It involves more than 10 industries, including public transportation, water supply and drainage, ecological construction and environmental protection, water conservancy construction, renewable energy, education, science and technology, culture, pension, medical and health, forestry, tourism. Among them, 3,954 projects had signed contracts and kicked off, with an investment of RMB 3.8 trillion. 2,396 projects had started construction, with an investment of RMB 2.2 trillion.

Section 5 Development of Environmental Rights Markets Accelerated

I. Major Opportunities for the Carbon Emission Trading Market

As of the end of 2020, the pilot carbon markets in Beijing, Tianjin, Shanghai, Chongqing, Hubei, Guangdong, and Shenzhen covered more than 20 industries, including electric power, steel, and cement, and nearly 3,000 key emission companies. The cumulative trading volume of quotas was 445 million tons, which was worth RMB 10.279 billion. They have contributed to carbon control and emission reduction in the pilot zones. China Certified Emission Reduction (CCER) plays an important role in the pilot carbon market compliance offset. As of December 31, 2020, CCER's cumulative transaction volume reached 269 million tons, which were worth of RMB 2.314 billion.

In December 2020, the Central Economic Work Conference called for faster establishment of a national carbon emission trading market. On December 30, the Ministry of Ecology and Environment issued the *Notice on Issuing the Implementation Plan for Quota Setting and Allocation for the National Carbon Emissions Trading 2019 – 2020 (Power Generation Industry), the List of Key Emissions Entities in the Quota Management of National Carbon Emission Trading 2019 – 2020, and Effectively Completing the Pre-allocation of Quotas for the Power Generation Industry* (MEE [2020] No. 3). On the 31st, the *Measures for the Administration of Carbon Emissions Trading (for Trial Implementation)* was officially issued, marking a breakthrough in the construction of the national carbon emission trading market.

II. A National Energy Use Quota Trading Market to be Launched

Since 2017, Zhejiang, Henan, Fujian, and Sichuan launched energy use quota trading pilot projects. In January 2020, Fujian issued the *Interim Measures of Fujian Province for the Administration of Energy Use Quota Transactions* (Order 212 of the People's Government of Fujian Province). So far, the energy use quota trading systems in the four pilot zones has been completed. Among them, those in Henan, Fujian, and Sichuan adopt the trading model of inter-enterprise total quota, and that in Zhejiang adopts the trading model of incremental between the government and enterprises. In addition to the pilot zones, other localities have independently launched energy use quota trading trials. Since the 13th Five-Year Plan, the energy use quota transactions in Hubei Province have totaled more than 1.9 million tons of standard coal, with a transaction amount of more than RMB 100 million. In December 2020, the Central Economic Work Conference requested that the construction of the national energy use quota trading market be accelerated.

III. Trading and Mortgage Financing of Pollutant Discharge Rights Carried Out in Many Provinces

Nearly 30 provinces, autonomous regions, and municipalities directly under the Central Government across China have launched pollutant discharge rights trading trials. Among them, Jiangsu, Zhejiang, Tianjin, Hubei, Hunan, Inner Mongolia, Shanxi, Chongqing, Shaanxi, Hebei, Henan, and Qingdao are national pilot zones. Some other provinces (municipalities) have carried out pollutant discharge rights transactions independently. In 2020, China's pollution discharge permits covered all fixed sources. As of the end of 2020, a total of 337,700 pollutant discharge permits were issued nationwide, and there were 2,365,200 registered pollutant discharge companies. In 2020, the transaction volume of pollutant discharge rights in Zhejiang Province was 11,500 tons, and the transaction volume was about RMB 300 million. On September 21, Shaanxi Province launched the secondary market of pollutant discharge rights trading. The total transaction volume of two indicators of pollutant discharge rights, sulfur dioxide and nitrogen oxide, was 1,746.81 tons, and the transaction volume was RMB 16.7384 million.

On March 3, 2020, the General Office of the CPC Central Committee and the General Office of the State Council issued the *Guiding Opinions on Building a Modern Environmental Governance System*. The *Opinions* proposed to study and explore the implementation of mortgage financing for pollutant discharge rights trading. At the end of March, Shanxi's first mortgage loan for pollutant discharge rights was implemented, providing financing of RMB 20 million. In June, the first batch of mortgage financing for pollutant discharge rights in Guangdong Province was implemented, providing RMB 40 million in loan for two companies. In August, the Jiangsu Provincial Department of Ecology and Environment, headquarters of the Bank of Jiangsu, the Jiangsu Provincial Department of Finance, and the People's Bank of China Nanjing Branch held the launch ceremony of mortgage loans for pollutant discharge rights. They granted a comprehensive credit of RMB 20 million to an enterprise.

IV. Other Environmental Rights Markets in Steady Progress

As of the end of 2020, the accumulated water volume of the national water rights trading market was approximately 3.188 billion cubic meters. Among them, the volume of regional water rights/intake right trading was 3.167 billion cubic meters, and that of irrigation water users' water rights trading was 21 million cubic meters. For regional water rights/water rights trading, the volume of a single transaction is larger, the transaction price per unit is higher, and the transaction period is longer. On the contrary, the volume and price of a single transaction of the irrigation water users' water rights trading are lower; the transaction period is mainly one year, and there are more types of transaction entities. In December 2020, China's first transaction of rainwater use right was concluded. The market entity transferred the right to use the collected and stored rainwater to a sanitation company to replace the tap water for greening and cleaning operations. This marked that the marketization of the ecological value of China's unconventional water resources came into practice.

Since July 1, 2017, China has implemented a voluntary purchase and trading for renewable energy green power certificates (green certificate trading). As of the end of 2020, the cumulative trading volume of wind power green certificates was 41,618 MWh, with an average daily price of RMB 174 per certificate. The cumulative trading volume of photovoltaic green certificates was 166 MWh, with an average daily price of RMB 668 per certificate.

Section 6   Environmental Benefits of Green Trust Projects More Prominent

In 2020, under the guidance of the *Green Trust Guidelines*, trust companies practiced the concept of green development. In terms of the scale of green trust assets, the scale of existing assets was RMB 359.282 billion, a year-on-year increase of 7.1%, and the scale of new assets was RMB 119.993 billion. The number of existing projects was 888, an increase of 6.73% year-on-year. The number of new projects was 360.

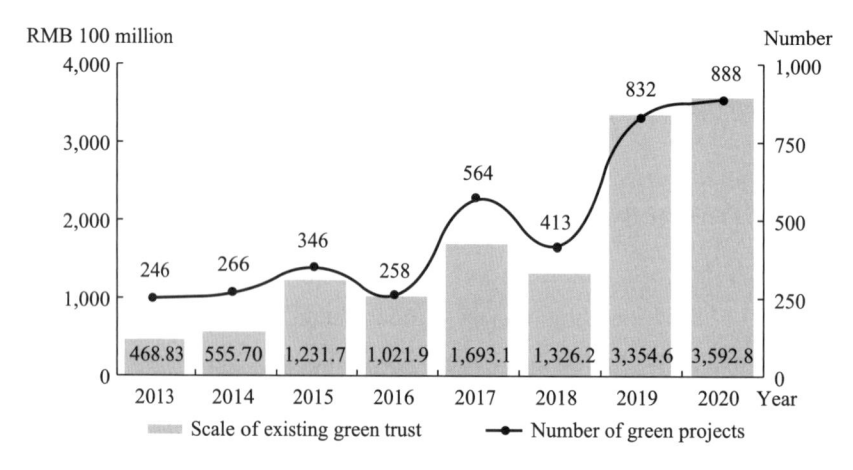

Figure 3-5   Asset Scale and Number of Projects of Green Trust from 2013 to 2020
Source of data: China Trust Industry Corporate Social Responsibility Report by China Trustee Association.

Trust companies innovated products and service modes based on the characteristics of the green, energy-saving, and environmental protection industries. They carried out fruitful explorations in broadening green industry investment and financing channels and filling gaps in traditional banking services. Among them, green trust loans are still the main green financial instrument used by trust companies, with an existing scale of RMB 190.912 billion. Among the innovative businesses, green asset securitization has made prominent performance.

Table 3-10   Green Financial Instruments of Trust Companies in 2020

Green financial instruments	Existing scale (RMB 100 million)
Green trust loan	1,909.12
Green equity investment	184.44
Green bond investment	44.82
Green asset securitization	641.84
Green industry fund	217.51
Green supply chain	17.30
Carbon finance	24.05
Charitable green trust	15.88
Other	537.86

The environmental benefits of green trust projects have grown more prominent. In 2020, the projects saved 2.5612 million tons of standard coal and 265.7381 million tons of water. They also reduced the discharge of 7,988,900 tons of CO_2 equivalent in GHG emissions, chemical oxygen demand by 87,000 tons, ammonia nitrogen by 377,800 tons, sulfur dioxide by 51,500 tons, and ammonia nitrogen compounds by 20,900 tons.

Green trust supports the development of green industries with more precision. In 2020, green trust funds were mainly invested in clean energy industries and industries in relation to the green upgrade of infrastructure, accounting for 33.94% and 25.76%, respectively. The proportion of funds invested in energy-saving and environmental protection industries and ecological environment industries was 17.51% and 10.01%. Funds supporting clean production industries and green services accounted for 3.56% and 3%. 6.36% of green trust funds supported diversified green industries.

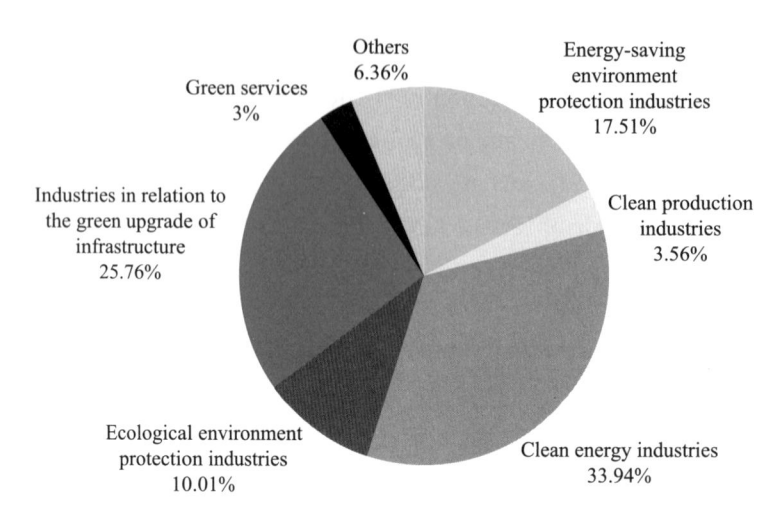

Figure 3-6   Proportion of Investment Orientation of Green Trust in 2020

Column 3-8

Innovation Cases of Green Trust

GreenGold No. 1 Property Trust Plan Series 1of Guangdong Yuecai Intrust & Investment Company. Its underlying asset is the financial leasing accounts receivable held by the principal, Canton GreenGold Financial Leasing Ltd. It is China's first green debt financing plan for leasing issued at Beijing Financial Assets and the first green debt financing plan in the Guangdong-Hong Kong-Macao Greater Bay Area. Its underlying assets include the environmental protection projects in civil engineering projects, such as municipal sewage sludge, waste-to-energy, landfill, and biogas power generation. It is estimated that every year, its sewage treatment projects can reduce the emission or discharge of biochemical oxygen demand by about 438 tons, chemical oxygen demand by about 2,321.40 tons, suspended solids by about 620.50 tons, ammonia nitrogen by about 397.12 tons, total nitrogen by about 638.75 tons, and total phosphorus by about 46.94 tons. In 2020, its waste-to-energy projects achieved 13,200 tons of fossil energy replacement and coordinated emission reduction of 35,300 tons of carbon dioxide, 346.90 tons of sulfur dioxide, 298.08 tons of nitrogen oxide, and 144.72 tons of dust. Its environmental protection benefits were remarkable.

China Industrial International Trust - Green Finance Select Collective Capital Trust Plan. It is the industry's first open net standardized green asset investment trust, which is actively managed by China Industrial International Trust. It selects standardized green financial assets for allocation and makes timely adjustments based on the dynamic changes of various factors. The trust plan is a fixed-income product with a trust scale of RMB 10 billion. The first series will be RMB 21 million and the period will be 5 years. It is open for investment every month.

The innovative "Equity + Debt" Investment-loan Coordinated Financial Solution of AVIC Trust. It provides medium and short-term necessary funds for the development of Ningbo Nuoke Environmental Technology Co., Ltd., which mainly deals with hazardous wastes and pollutants in cement kilns. The solution helps the company accelerate the formation of core assets from a professional perspective and enhance its core competitiveness in sub-sectors. Since the establishment of the partnership, Nuoke Environmental Technology has collected 106,800 tons of hazardous waste and disposed of 89,200 tons. In 2020, 84,800 tons of hazardous waste were collected and 67,700 tons were treated. As such, the partnership has achieved good results and delivered extensive social benefits.

CHAPTER IV
Significant Progress Made for Green Finance Practices in Local Economies

The development, reform, and innovation of green finance in China need the enthusiasm and creativity of local economies. Reform policies also need to be tested, enriched, and improved with primary practices. In 2020, the construction of pilot zones for green finance reform and innovation achieved new results in continuous reflection, reform, and innovation.

The construction of pilot zones for green finance reform and innovation has been further advanced. Based on the local ecological and environmental resource endowments, the nine pilot zones in six provinces (regions) have explored and formed their unique reform and innovation of green finance. They have accumulated a lot of useful experience that can be replicated and promoted, thus strongly supporting the development of green industries and the low-carbon transformation of the economy. Among them, Zhejiang Province's Huzhou, the birthplace of General Secretary Xi Jinping's Theory (lucid waters and lush mountains are invaluable assets), has practiced this theory. Through the regulated development of green finance and the effective transformation of ecological environment resources and supported by strong technological empowerment and the coordinated efforts of Central Government's policies, it has shaped the Huzhou Experience of green finance reform.

Furthermore, the non-pilot zones have followed the philosophy of green development. Based on the best practices of the pilot zones, they have guided the reform and development of regional green finance into the "fast track" and effectively promoted the low-carbon and green transition of the economy and society. For example, in advancing major national development and strategic plans such as the integrated development of the Yangtze River Delta and the building of the Greater Bay Area linking Guangdong, Hong Kong and Macao, we have vigorously promoted the reform and innovation of green finance and integrated green financial development and regional economic development.

In addition, to practice the Two Mountains Theory, some areas have also carried out key infrastructure and pollution prevention projects, such as green finance for clean heating, disposal and recycling of waste in livestock and poultry breeding, and green buildings. In this way, they have explored sustainable financial support models that conform to market principles.

Section 1 Construction of Pilot Zones for Green Finance Reform and Innovation Going Deeper

2020 was the concluding year of the 13th Five-Year Plan and a crucial year for the construction of pilot zones for green finance reform and innovation. Over the past three years, nine areas in six provinces (regions), namely, Huzhou and Quzhou in Zhejiang, Ganjiang New Area in Jiangxi, Huadu in Guangdong's Guangzhou, Gui'an New Area in Guizhou, Lanzhou New Area in Gansu, and Changji, Hami, and Karamay in Xinjiang, gave full play to the advantages of the green finance reform and innovation. They have focused on promoting the green and low-carbon transformation of the economy with financial innovation and drawn force from the establishment of a sound mechanism to support the green and high-quality development of the regional economy.

I. Implementation of the Mechanisms for Green Finance Reform and Innovation

First, relevant mechanisms and systems have been established and improved and green finance standards have been promoted to be implemented. In 2020, the pilot zones strengthened their organization and coordination, optimized the policy environment, and prepared development plans and assessment and incentive mechanisms. They vigorously promoted the establishment of institutional mechanisms and the implementation of policies and rules and introduced more than 20 policies concerning green finance.

Table 4-1 Key Policies and Systems Introduced in the Pilot Zones in 2020

Region	Policy and System
Zhejiang	*Guiding Opinions on Financial Support for the Green and High-quality Development of the Live Pig Industry in Quzhou* (QZ of PBC [2020] No. 34)
	Measures of Huzhou Municipality for the Implementation of Special Loans for Major Projects and Special Interest Subsidy Funds for Green Finance
	2020 Promotion Plan of Huzhou Municipality for the Construction of the National Pilot Zone for Green Finance Reform and Innovation (HZ [2020] No. 6)

continued

Region	Policy and System
Jiangxi	*Guidelines of Jiangxi Province for the Verification and Management of Green Notes (for Trial Implementation)*
	Notice on the Use of Rediscount Instruments to Support the Development of Green Notes
	Notice on Effectively Completing the Financing and Coordination of Green Projects in Jiangxi Province in 2020
Guangdong	*Notice of Guangzhou Financial Supervisory Authority on Issuing the 2020 Work Plan for Promoting the Construction of the Guangzhou Pilot Zone for Green Finance Reform and Innovation*
	Implementation Rules of Huadu District to Support the Innovation and Development of Green Finance (HD [2020] No. 1)
	Detailed Rules of Huangpu District and Guangzhou Development Zone of Guangzhou Municipality for the Implementation of Policies and Measures to Promote the Development of Green Finance (HZ [2020] No. 11)
	Notice on the Implementation Rules (for Trial Implementation) for the Management of the Green Enterprise and Project Library of the Guangzhou Pilot Zone for Green Finance Reform and Innovation (HZ [2020] No. 5)
	Measures for the Administration of the Verification of Green Projects and Green Enterprises in Guangzhou Development Zone, Huangpu District, Guangzhou (for Trial Implementation) (HZ [2020] No. 4)
	Opinions on Financial Support for the Development of the Guangdong-Hong Kong-Macao Greater Bay Area (PBC [2020] No. 95)
Guizhou	*Reply on Agreeing to Establish a Leading Group for Green Finance Reform and Innovation in Gui'an New District of Guiyang City* (ZWBHZ [2020] No. 34)
	Notice on Printing and Distributing the Work Plan of Offering Financial Support for High-quality Development of Gui'an New District (QJJF [2020] No. 11)
Xinjiang	*Trial Work Plan for Green Finance Standards*
	Implementation Plan of Hami Municipality for Green Finance Standards in the Pilot Zone for Green Finance Reform and Innovation (for Trial Implementation) (HN [2020] No. 11)
	Implementation Plan of Karamay for Standards in the Pilot Zone for Green Finance Reform
	Work Promotion Plan of the Autonomous Prefecture for the Construction of the Pilot Zone for Green Finance Reform and Innovation in the Last Two and a Half Year
Gansu	*Implementation Plan of Lanzhou New Area for the Construction of a Pilot Zone for Green Finance Reform and Innovation* (GZBF [2020] No. 60)
	Five-Year Development Plan of Lanzhou New Area for Green Finance (2020 – 2024)
	Incentive Policy of Lanzhou New Area for Green Finance Development (for Trial Implementation)

Second, the monetary policy support has been strengthened. Monetary policy instruments such as refinancing and rediscounting have been used to expand the supply of green credit. In 2020, Huzhou launched the Online Loan model of refinancing and the innovative online service of Loan Supported by Central Bank Policies. It issued RMB 15.046 billion for refinancing throughout the year, with a weighted average interest rate of 4.62%. It included 90 deals of online financing, totaling RMB 175 million. This has effectively promoted the central bank's low-cost funds to efficiently reach the real economy. Ganjiang New Area rediscounted RMB 500,000 for standard green notes, which was the first green bill rediscount in Jiangxi. Guangzhou allocated another special support quota for green rediscount, supporting financial institutions in Guangzhou to handle the green bill rediscounting business totaling RMB 2.3 billion throughout the year. It also guided Dongguan, Foshan, and other municipalities to innovate their green bill business, which issued more than RMB 1.9 billion for green notes and rediscounting. Changji Prefecture achieved a zero-to-one breakthrough in the rediscount business, issuing RMB 36 million in green rediscounts. In addition, in all localities, the results of the green credit performance evaluation of deposit legal-person banking institutions have been incorporated into the central bank's ratings of financial institutions.

II. Quality of Green Financial Services in Steady Improvement

(I) Sound Development of the System of Green Financial Organizations

First, green specialized banking institutions have grown rapidly, and the concept of green development and the awareness of green financial services has become stronger. As of the end of 2020, Huzhou established 16 green specialized branches and 23 green finance business units. Quzhou established 54 green specialized branches and green finance business units. Ganjiang New Area established 7 green specialized branches and 3 green finance business units. Guangzhou established 12 green specialized banking institutions, including 5 green branches, 3 green sub-branches, 1 green finance innovation center, and 3 green finance business units. Gui'an New Area established 15 green banking institutions. Among them, the Bank of Guizhou announced to adopt the Equator Principles, becoming the sixth Equator Bank in China. In Hami, Changji, and Karamay, all banking institutions now have green specialized institutions, with a total number of 59. Among them, 14 are in Hami Municipality, 25 are in Changji Prefecture, and 20 are in Karamay Municipality. 3 green sub-branches were established in Lanzhou New Area. As the number of green financial organizations continued to grow, the quality of green financial services has also improved.

Second, non-banking green specialized institutions have developed at different levels and in a diversified manner. As of the end of 2020, Huzhou established 2 innovation laboratories for green insurance products. Among them, Zheshang Property and Casualty Insurance established a Yangtze River Delta Innovation Laboratory for Green Insurance. Insurance institutions in Quzhou established 10 green finance business units. Among them, PICC P&C Quzhou Branch established the first green insurance office in Zhejiang Province. Ganjiang New Area established 4 green insurance laboratories (business units). Guangzhou established 13 non-banking green specialized institutions, including 1 green finance business unit, 3 green finance laboratories, 3 green funds, 2 trading venues, and 4 other non-banking green specialized institutions. Gui'an New Area established 8 non-banking green financial institutions, including 3 green guarantee business units and 1 green securities business unit. Xinjiang established 6 green finance business units and 1 green guarantee business unit. Among them, PICC P&C Hami, Shenwan Hongyuan Securities, and Galaxy Securities established a green finance business unit each. Karamay Municipality established 1 green finance business unit for insurance, 1 green finance business unit for green convertible bond issuance, and 1 green guarantee business unit.

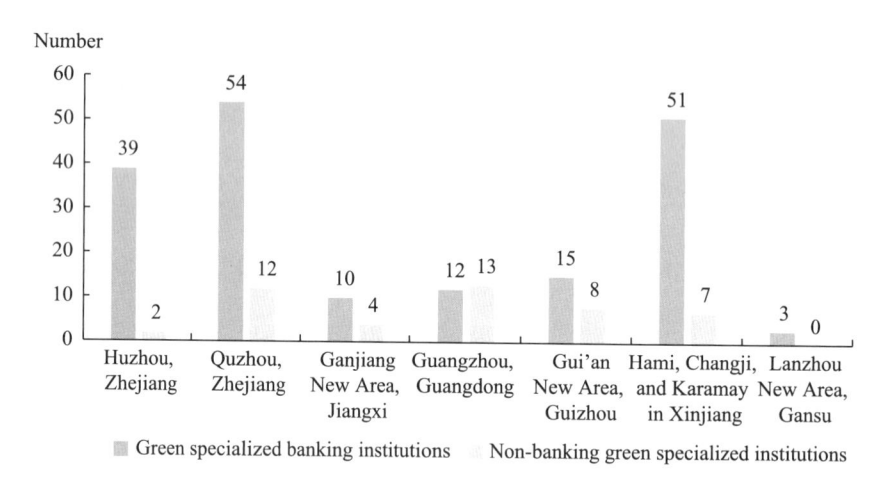

Figure 4-1 Number of Green Finance Bbusiness Uunits or Specialized Institutions in the Pilot Zones by the End of 2020

(II) Quality of Green Financial Products and Services Continuously Improved

First, the green credit supply capacity has been significantly improved, the assets has maintained high quality, and product and service innovation has continued to advance. As of the end of 2020, the green loan balance in the pilot zones was RMB 606.65 billion, an increase of 36.04% over the beginning of the year. Among them, Guangzhou had the highest green loan balance, reaching up to RMB 382.068 billion. Ganjiang New Area and Lanzhou New Area saw the fastest growth in green loans, with year-on-year growth rates of 96.25% and 81.64%, respectively. The balance of green loans in the pilot zones accounted for 8.83% of the local domestic and foreign currency loans, higher than the national average. Among them, Hami had the highest proportion, up to 34.5%. Six pilot zones, including Lanzhou New Area, Huzhou, and Karamay, had a proportion more than 10%. The green credit assets in the pilot zones were of high quality and stable, with an average non-performing rate of only 0.16%, far lower than the national average. Among them, the non-performing

Chapter IV   Significant Progress Made for Green Finance Practices in Local Economies

rate of green loans in three pilot zones in Xinjiang and Lanzhou New Area was 0. In addition, the pilot zones actively met market demand and comprehensively improved the quality of their products and services. For example, Quzhou Changshan Rural Commercial Bank launched an innovative Golden Grapefruit Loan based on the local hu grapefruit industry. As of the end of 2020, it issued 143 Golden Grapefruit Loan with a total amount of RMB 21.15 million. Guangzhou launched China's first green financial service for the automotive supply chain to provide green supply chain financing for car makers and meet their financing needs for energy conservation and environmental protection. Karamay introduced the innovative models of "account receivable pledge + special equipment" and "charging rights pledge + photovoltaic equipment," and issued green loans of RMB 1.12 billion to support projects of natural gas purification and photovoltaic power generation.

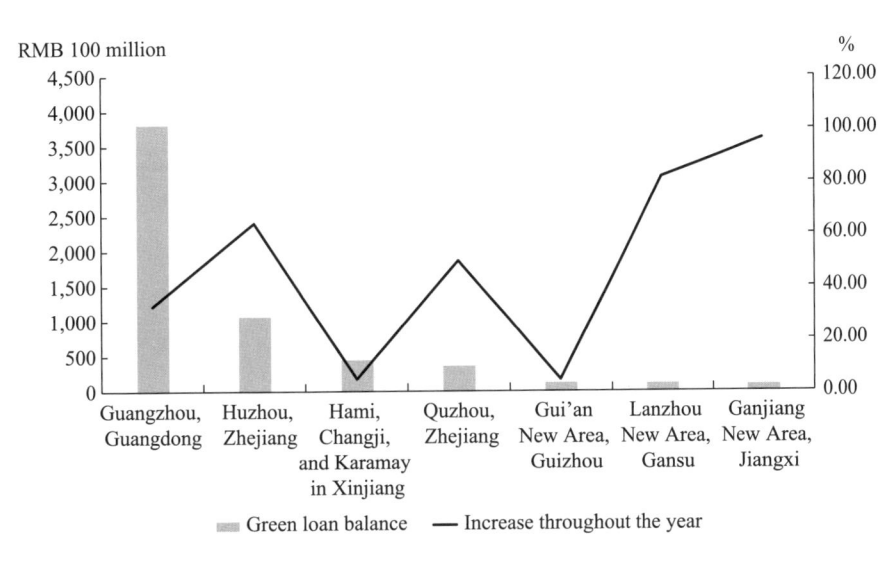

Figure 4-2   Green Loans in the Pilot Zones in 2020

Second, green financing has been supported in the securities market. The pilot zones have encouraged enterprises and financial institutions to issue green bonds and supported eligible green enterprises to go public and raise funds. In this way, financing channels have been more diversified. As of the end of 2020, nine green enterprises of the pilot areas were listed on NEEQ, and they raised a total of RMB 14.6126 million in the whole year. The balance of labelled green bonds issued by the pilot zones was RMB 88.776 billion, a year-on-year increase of 34.5%. In 2020, Quzhou issued green bonds of RMB 500 million. Six companies in Guangzhou issued green bonds of RMB 12.35 billion. Lanzhou New Area issued RMB 2.204 billion, mainly to support rainwater storage projects, agricultural exhibitions, and other green projects. In addition, the pilot zones actively supported the listing and financing of companies whose main business income mainly comes from green industries and areas. By late 2020, nine green companies of the experimental zone had been listed on the New

OTC Market, raising a total of RMB 14.6126 million throughout the year. In 2020, Guangzhou promoted 7 companies, including Qiaoyin Environmental Tech, Guangzhou Jet Biofiltration, and Xiaopeng Motors, to be listed on the SME Board, ChiNext, and the New York Stock Exchange, raising RMB 5.5 billion. Among these listed companies, green equity financing accounted for 87%.

Third, the development of green funds has been accelerated. The pilot zones attach great importance to the development of green funds and continue to expand the scale of green funds. This has effectively encouraged more financial institutions and social capital to carry out green investment and financing, thus resolving the shortage of funds in financial innovation. As of the end of 2020, Huzhou established 65 green industry funds with a total scale of RMB 48.649 billion. The actually amount received was RMB 12.04 billion, and the actual amount used was RMB 10.813 billion, which was invested in 175 projects. Quzhou established a variety of green industry investment funds with a scale of RMB 18.993 billion. RMB 7.589 billion of it has been in place. In 2020, Guangzhou established 6 green industry funds, with more than RMB 27 billion under management. Changji established 4 governmental guidance funds for green industries with a total scale of RMB 8.71 billion. Hami established the Hami Equity Investment Fund for STI Industries, providing RMB 30 million to support the green development of high-tech small and medium-sized enterprises. Karamay established 2 governmental industry guidance funds, raising RMB 170 million. Lanzhou New Area established a development fund of the pilot zone for green finance reform and innovation with a total scale of RMB 3 billion.

Fourth, the innovation of green insurance products and services has been deepened. The pilot zones have promoted green insurance products, such as the liability insurance for environmental pollution, the liability insurance for work safety, and agricultural insurance. They have also carried out trials on green building insurance. In the area of green buildings, Huzhou has explored the performance insurance for green building projects and work safety liability insurance for green buildings. It has also launched innovative insurance for green energy efficiency, green renovation projects, and potential quality defects in green construction projects. As of the end of 2020, Changji Prefecture launched an environmental pollution liability insurance business. It updated and optimized the directory list of 365 key enterprises in high-risk industries, and achieved 100% coverage of Liability Insurance of Workplace Safety. In addition, relying on the "cotton insurance + futures" pilot program, it explored and carried out the reform and innovation of green agricultural insurance, with a premium income of RMB 297 million. Hami Property Insurance Company underwrote 23,864 green insurance policies, with a premium income of RMB 144 million and coverage amount of RMB 14.737 billion.

Fifth, personal green financial products have further developed. Relying on the Smart Payment projects, Huzhou has used financial technology to explore green financial products for individuals. Anji Rural Commercial Bank has issued China's first green certificate of deposit and launched the innovative online product Green Save. The deposits it accepted have been used to support the green development of the county. The interests of the green deposits in Anji Rural Commercial Bank have been used to encourage residents to lead a green lifestyle, such as encouraging waste sorting, low-carbon travel, and green payment among residents. Quzhou has conducted big data analysis on the data of "personal carbon accounts," and launched the inquiry and application functions with restrictions for different subjects. It also has encouraged financial institutions to offer incentives such as preferential green financial services, to promote citizens to form green payment habits.

Sixth, green finance has supported the resumption of work and production. Huzhou has made full use of the re-lending support policy and expanded the functions of the Green Loan Connect platform. It has added the module of Loans Backed by Central Bank Policies and launched the loan backed by the Central Bank's support policies for agriculture, small enterprises, and pandemic prevention. Through standardized customization and systematic display of target customers, interest rates, and conditions, it has effectively improved the availability of corporate financing. In 2020, Karamay allocated a special quota of RMB 300 million for the resumption of work and production. It also investigated the needs of green, small and medium-sized enterprises for bill discounting, and offered a price discount of 30 Bp.

III. Green Finance Infrastructure Further Improved

First, the construction of green project libraries has been accelerated. Huzhou has launched a green financing entity identification and evaluation system (Green Info Connect) and an ESG evaluation system, realizing intelligent, comprehensive, and value-based green evaluation. As of the end of 2020, 763 green financing companies and 98 green financing projects were identified. Changji Prefecture issued the *Measures of Changji Prefecture for Green Enterprise Identification (for Trial Implementation)* and the *Measures of Changji Prefecture for Green Project Identification (for Trial Implementation)*. Lanzhou New Area formulated the *Measures of Lanzhou New Area for Green Enterprise Identification and Evaluation* and the *Measures of Lanzhou New Area for Green Project Identification and Evaluation*. They provide a policy basis for the scientific construction of green project libraries and break the bottleneck in the implementation of green finance. As of the end of 2020, the total number of green project library projects in all pilot zones exceeded 2,900, a year-on-year increase of nearly 30%, and the cumulative investment was about RMB 1.75 trillion. The pilot zones selected 2,299 projects to be listed on the Beijing Green Exchange (formerly Beijing Environment Exchange), a year-on-year increase of 407.51%.

Second, the information disclosure and sharing mechanisms have been improved. The governments and financial institutions in the pilot zones have reached consensus on green finance practices and environmental information disclosure. The quality of their environmental information disclosure has been improved. In terms of environmental information disclosure, in February 2020, the People's Bank of China organized the pilot zones to implement the *Guidelines for Environmental Information Disclosure of Financial Institutions (for Trial Implementation)*. Huzhou has released China's first regional environmental information disclosure report, which included 1 regional environmental information disclosure report and environmental information disclosure reports of 19 major banking institutions. In this way, it has effectively acted as the "window" for display of green finance reform. 4 legal-person urban commercial banks in Jiangxi Province has carries out the environmental information disclosure of financial institutions, making Jiangxi the first province in China where all legal-person urban commercial banks disclose environmental information. In terms of environmental information sharing, Changji Prefecture has opened the green project library to financial institutions and social investment entities. It also poses the publicity information, implementation of laws and regulations, administrative approval, water environment quality, air quality, and other information of construction projects on the website of the Prefecture People's Government. Lanzhou New Area has incorporated the information about environmental administrative punishment over companies into the credit information system to provide information for financial institutions in supporting the development of green industries. By the end of 2020, the information about environmental administrative punishment over 1,487 companies and the results of "1 examination and 2 evaluations" for environmental protection of 1,297 companies were released.

Column 4-1

Huzhou Releasing China's First Regional Environmental Disclosure Report

In 2020, Huzhou City took the lead in implementing the *Guidelines for Environmental Information Disclosure of Financial Institutions (for Trial Implementation)* (the *Guidelines*) in China. It released China's first regional environmental information disclosure report, which included 1 regional environmental information disclosure report and environmental information disclosure reports of 19 major banking institutions[1].

---

[1] The major banking financial institutions in Huzhou City with assets of more than RMB 10 billion in the year.

Chapter IV Significant Progress Made for Green Finance Practices in Local Economies

I. Main practices

The first is unifying standards and enhance the credibility of information disclosure. Huzhou developed the *Framework of Huzhou Municipality for Environmental Information Disclosure of Banking Institutions (2020)* in accordance with the *Guidelines*. The *Framework* quotes documents and financial terms and definitions in a clear and normative manner, and determines 8 major items and 19 minor items for disclosure, including the overview, strategies and objectives, and the governance structure.

The second is emphasizing details and enhancing the authenticity of information disclosure. First, legal entities shall have a clear design of the environmental mechanism in corporate governance. The board of directors of legal entities must analyze and judge environmental risks and opportunities. Second, entities shall strengthen the analysis and management of environmental risks and opportunities. They must improve their ability to analyze and measure environmental risks. Third, infrastructure construction shall be strengthened. Entities, especially legal entities, must ensure the accuracy of green credit data and strengthen the protection of the privacy data of green credit customers.

The third is increasing guidance and intensifying the responsibility of banking institutions. Huzhou delivers virtual courses on environmental information disclosure to provide targeted guidance and training on relevant policies, statistical methods, and regulatory requirements for banking institutions. It also emphasizes that banking institutions shall disclose the total amount, per capita, and varieties of greenhouse gas emissions.

II. Major outcomes

As of the end of 2019, the green credit balance of 19 major banking institutions was RMB 54.967 billion[1]. The green loans issued that year helped reduce carbon dioxide emissions by 2,665,200 tons[2]. As of the end of 2020, 16 banks in Huzhou set environmental risk management procedures and measures, which improved the prevention mechanism for green credit risks.

---

[1] Calculated with the statistical method of China Banking and Insurance Regulatory Commission.
[2] Calculated according to the Guidelines of the China Banking and Insurance Regulatory Commission for Energy Conservation and Emission Reduction in Green Credit Projects.

Third, financial technology boosts green and sustainable development. As of the end of 2020, 17 systems or platforms for green finance were developed or launched in the pilot zones (see Table 4-2). New breakthroughs were achieved in system building, information technology, and standardization of green finance.

Table 4-2   Development of Green Finance Systems (Platforms) with Financial Technology by the Pilot Zones

Pilot zone	Name of the system (platform)	Main functions	Host
Huzhou	Green Finance Information Management System	A supervision platform for green financial information that integrates real-time data collection, processing, analysis, and application	Research Bureau and Huzhou Central Branch of the People's Bank of China
	Green Finance Integrated Service Platform	Green Financing Subject Identification (Lvxintong); the Bank-Enterprise Matching Service (Lvdaitong); and Project Capital Matching (Lvrongtong)	Huzhou Municipal Financing Office
	Integrated System for the Supervisory Rating and Information Analysis of Green Banks (Lvyin System)	Quantify the degree of greening of banks with information systems to provide reference for regulatory policies	China Banking and Insurance Regulatory Commission Huzhou Branch
	Green Credit Management System	Green credit identification and environmental risk management	Bank of Huzhou
Quzhou	Special Statistical Information Management System for Green Loans	Generate various types of green credit statistics, results of environmental benefit measurement, and evaluations of green credit performance	Quzhou Central Branch of the People's Bank of China
	Credit Information Platform for Financial Services	Government-bank-enterprise interaction; identification, evaluation, and incubation of green enterprises (projects); risk warning and monitoring; credit enhancement and financing for credit and insurance funds; and visual statistical analysis	Quzhou Municipal Government
Ganjiang New Area	Financing Service Platform for Micro and Small Customers	Promote green projects to match financial institutions for financing	Nanchang Central Branch of the People's Bank of China
	Information Platform for Green Enterprises	Display the information and financing needs of green enterprises	Jiangxi Joint Equity Exchange

Chapter IV Significant Progress Made for Green Finance Practices in Local Economies

continued

Pilot zone	Name of the system (platform)	Main functions	Host
Guangzhou	Financing Matching System of Guangzhou Pilot Zone for Green Finance Reform and Innovation (Lvsuitong)	An integrated platform for policy support, financing matching, project management, and incubation and cultivation	The People's Government of Huadu District and the People's Bank of China Guangzhou Branch
	Online Platform for Green Financial Leasing (Green Yinlintong)	Credit overlay of financial leasing companies and banks; support green industries	Bank of Jiujiang Guangdong Pilot Free Trade Zone Nansha Sub-branch
	Ecological Compensation Platform of the Green Finance System (Ecological Compensation Platform)	Provide online trading and matching of ecological compensation products and projects with financial technology	China Emissions Exchange
	Supply Chain Financing Platform for Green Enterprises	Facilitate supply chain financing for new energy vehicles	China Construction Bank Guangzhou Branch and Industrial and Commercial Bank Guangzhou Branch
Gui'an New Area	Integrated Green Financial Services Platform of Guizhou Province	Publicize green finance projects, display green financial institutions, and release green finance policies and developments	Provincial Financial Supervisory Authority and the Administrative Committee of Gui'an New Area
Xinjiang	Green Financial Services Platform	Display the information of green projects and share it with financial institutions and social investors	Green Finance Office of Xinjiang Autonomous Region
	Management System of Changji for Green Micro Loans for Farmers	Trace the flow of green credit funds and prevent green loan risks	Changji Rural Commercial Bank
	Information Sharing Platform of Karamay for the Government, Financial Institutions, and Enterprises	Release the information of the green project library	Karamay Municipal Office of Finance
Lanzhou New Area	Integrated Green Financial Services Platform of Lanzhou New Area	Bank-enterprise financing matching, professional green services, and integration of some social information data of enterprises	Administrative Committee of Lanzhou New Area

Fourth, the environmental rights trading market has grown. As of the end of 2020, the pilot zones completed a variety of environmental equity transactions worth RMB 5.8 billion in total, a year-on-year increase of 22.61%. A multi-level carbon trading market system has taken shape, including carbon emission quota trading market, greenhouse gas voluntary emission reduction trading market and carbon inclusive market. The cumulative trading volume of carbon emission quota in Guangdong pilot carbon market reached 172 million tons, with a turnover of RMB 3.545 billion, ranking the first in China. It represents the first pilot carbon market in China with a quota turnover of more than RMB 3 billion. Changji and Karamay issued pollutant discharge permits to 205 enterprises under their jurisdiction and completed pollutant discharge registrations for 1,809 enterprises.

Table 4-3   Volume of Trading of the Environment Rights Markets in the Pilot Zones

Region	Volume of trading (RMB 100 million)
Huzhou	6.02
Quzhou	9.49
Ganjiang New Area	0
Guangzhou	40.02
Guizhou Province	1.2
Hami, Changji, and Karamay in Xinjiang	1.3
Lanzhou New Area	0

Fifth, the construction of green finance think tank platforms has been strengthened. The pilot zones have established professional committees and institutes for green finance to accelerate the training of green finance professionals and continuously improve green finance research capacity. In July 2020, Guangzhou Institute for Green Finance was established. In September, the 2020 annual meeting of Green Finance Committee of Guangdong Society for Finance and Banking (GFC GSFB) was organized and held in Guangdong. The meeting adjusted and improved the organizational structure of GFC GSFB, formed a number of special working groups, and strengthened the government-industry-university-research coordination on green finance in Guangdong. In December, the People's Government of Huzhou Municipality signed the *Cooperation Framework Agreement on the Joint Establishment of the "Two Mountains Academy for Green Finance"* with the Bank of China and the Beijing Institute of Green Finance and Sustainable Development.

IV. Support Measures for the Reform and Innovation Further Improved

First, the judicial support and the dispute mediation mechanism for green finance have been improved. The pilot zones have promoted the rule of law. They have strengthened the finance-justice collaboration, established a dispute mediation mechanism, and improved legal support. Huzhou Intermediate People's Court, Huzhou Municipality Finance Office, Huzhou Central Branch of PBOC, and another party signed a framework agreement on finance-justice collaboration. Huzhou Intermediate People's Court, Eas China University of Political Science and Law, Huzhou Central Branch of PBOC, and other two parties signed the *Cooperation Agreement on Rule of law and Risk Governance for Green Finance*. Huzhou has established China's first mediation center for green finance disputes and the Judges' Office of Huzhou Mediation Division for Green Finance Disputes under the brand of Farun Lvjin. As of the end of 2020, the local government successfully mediated 88 bank-enterprise disputes, involving subject matter of RMB 149 million.

Second, the construction of incentive mechanisms such as fiscal rewards and subsidies has been promoted. The pilot zones have innovated the policy guidance mechanisms and clarified the mechanisms for risk compensation and guarantees for green financing and subsidies for green insurance premium. In this way, they have strengthened the support for green finance reforms and leveraged financial resources to help the development of green industries. In 2020, the financial and fiscal departments of Quzhou Municipality incorporated the development performance of green finance into the evaluation index system for the competitive deposit of fiscal funds with a weight of 30%. They introduced special interest discount policies for green enterprises (projects), and provided 15%, 10%, and 5% discounts to "dark green," "medium green," and "light green" enterprises (projects), respectively. Among the 6 competitive deposits of fiscal funds (total of RMB 8.733 billion) they carried out, 5 banking institutions with better green finance development received 51.2% of the funds. Changji Prefecture issued the Management Measures of Changji Prefecture for the Use of Special Funds for Green Finance Development (for Trial Implementation). It clearly states that the government will arrange special funds of at least RMB 20 million each year as subsidies, risk compensation, and rewards for green finance. Karamay Municipality focused on supporting the resumption of work and production of green enterprises, saving a total of RMB 313 million in costs for green enterprises, a year-on-year increase of 2.4 times. Lanzhou New Area issued the *Incentive Policy of Lanzhou New Area for Green Finance Development (for Trial Implementation)*. During the pilot period, special fiscal funds of RMB 1 billion was arranged to concentrate financial resources to green industries and green projects in Lanzhou New Area.

Third, guarantee and credit enhancement mechanisms for green loans have been implemented.

In response to the difficulties in financing and guaranteeing green projects, the pilot zones have innovated green credit guarantee products and provided differentiated guarantee support based on the green level. Huzhou has created three green guarantee models, namely the Policy-guaranteed Targeted Support, the Insurance for Green Micro-loan, and the Green Credit Guarantee. These models have subsidized up to 75% and 50% of guarantee costs for "dark green" and "medium green" enterprises, respectively. As of the end of 2020, Huzhou provided guarantee credit of RMB 256 million for 153 green small and micro enterprises, and policy financing guarantees of RMB 1.454 billion for 1,009 households. Guiyang Rural Commercial Bank introduced an innovative "4321" guarantee method (guarantee companies at the current level undertake 40%; provincial funds for financial risk compensation, 30%; banks or insurance institutions, 20%; and the compensation funds for fiscal risks of municipal or county guarantee institutions at the current level, 10%). It provided loans of RMB 740 million for the construction of the integrated industrial park for Shandong maple planting and processing in Qingzhen City. The project is expected to help 1,600 registered impoverished households in Qingzhen to shake off poverty.

V. International Cooperation on Green Finance Further Expanded

The pilot areas have participated in international exchange activities to promote the quality and efficiency of green finance. In April 2020, the Bank of Jiujiang from Ganjiang New Area joined the United Nations Environment Programme Financial Initiative (UNEP FI), becoming the first urban commercial bank in China to sign the *Principles for Responsible Banking* (*PRB*). In December, the Bank of Huzhou signed a memorandum of cooperation with the Asian Development Bank (ADB), becoming the first banking institution in China to do so with ADB.

Section 2　Green Finance Reform and Innovation in Other Regions

Besides the nine pilot zones in six provinces (regions), major national development regions such as the Yangtze River Delta (Shanghai, Jiangsu, and Zhejiang), the Guangdong-Hong Kong-Macao Greater Bay Area (Guangdong, Hong Kong, and Macao), and the Chengdu-Chongqing Economic Circle (Chongqing and Sichuan), as well as some other provinces (autonomous regions and municipalities), have also vigorously promoted the reform and innovation of green finance. They have explored new paths for green finance to support regional development, aiming to achieve an organic combination of green finance and economic transformation and development.

Chapter IV Significant Progress Made for Green Finance Practices in Local Economies

I. National Major Regional Development Strategies Vigorously Promoting the Development of Green Finance

(I) Green Finance Bringing New Opportunities for the Development of the Guangdong-Hong Kong-Macao Greater Bay Area

In September 2020, the Green Finance Committee of Shenzhen Society for Finance and Banking, the Green Finance Committee of Guangdong Society for Finance and Banking, the Hong Kong Green Finance Association, and the Macau Association of Banks jointly established the Guangdong-Hong Kong-Macao Greater Bay Area Green Finance Alliance. The secretariat of the alliance is permanently based in Shenzhen. As China's first regional green finance alliance, it is an important measure to implement the *Opinions on Financial Support for the Development of the Guangdong-Hong Kong-Macao Greater Bay Area* (PBC [2020] NO.95) and Guangdong-Hong Kong-Macao cooperation in green finance. It will bring new impetus to the deepening of Guangdong-Hong Kong-Macao financial cooperation. The alliance will launch innovative explorations in green supply chain finance (automotive manufacturing), solid waste disposal, green building projects, and blockchain photovoltaic projects. It will establish the Working Group on Guangdong-Hong Kong-Macao Unified Carbon Market Research, the Working Group on Green Asset Trading Research, and three other working groups.

(II) Green Finance Serving the Integrated Development of the Yangtze River Delta

To implement the decision and deployment of the CPC Central Committee and the State Council, with the approval of the State Council, on February 14, 2020, the People's Bank of China, the China Banking Regulatory Commission, the China Securities Regulatory Commission, the State Administration of Foreign Exchange, and the Shanghai Municipal Government jointly issued the *Opinions on Further Accelerating the Construction of Shanghai as an International Financial Center and Providing Financial Support for the Integrated Development of the Yangtze River Delta Region* (PBOC [2020] No. 46). It put forward 30 measures for actively promoting the implementation of the pilot program first in the Lingang Special Area, accelerating the opening up of Shanghai's financial industry at a higher level, and providing financial support for the integrated development of the Yangtze River Delta. They aim to further accelerate the construction of Shanghai as an international financial center and the integrated development of the Yangtze River Delta.

The Yangtze River Delta region has actively promoted the implementation of financial pilot programs and explored the establishment of a financial system that meets the requirements of integrated green development. In April 2020, Shanghai Pudong Development Bank established the Management Headquarters of the Demonstration Zone of the Integrated Development of the Yangtze River Delta in Shanghai. It focused on serving the innovation platform of free trade, scientific innovation, and green ecology. It accelerated the development of green finance and product innovation and fully supports the construction of Shanghai as an international financial center. In August, Shanghai Rural Commercial Bank established the Yangtze River Delta Financial Headquarters, with a plan to provide customers in the Yangtze River Delta region (excluding Shanghai) with loans of no less than RMB 120 billion in the next three years. By the end of 2020, the balance of green loans of all banking deposit financial institutions in the Yangtze River Delta was RMB 2.79 trillion.

(III) Green Finance Supporting the Green Development of the Yangtze River Economic Belt

In November 2020, General Secretary Xi Jinping hosted a symposium on comprehensively promoting the development of the Yangtze River Economic Belt in Nanjing. He called on turning the Yangtze River Economic Belt into the country's main focus for green development. He ordered the Yangtze River Economic Belt to work hard to build a demonstration belt of green development in which man and nature coexist harmoniously. He stressed again the need to strengthen the conservation and restoration of the ecological environment system. The restoration of the ecological environment of the Yangtze River should be a major priority, he said.

Financial institutions have actively supported the ecological priorities and green development of the 11 provinces (cities) in the Yangtze River Economic Belt. They have become an important force in promoting the overall green transformation of economic and social development. On December 8, 2020, the China Development Bank issued the Bond Connect green financial bonds on the topic of "coordinated conservation of the Yangtze River" to global investors, with an issuance scale of RMB 3.5 billion. The funds raised will be used for green industry projects in the Yangtze River Economic Belt, such as pollution prevention, resource conservation and recycling, ecological conservation, and response to climate change.

II. Green Finance Reform and Innovation in Other Regions

(I) Beijing: Green Finance Reform and Innovation Supporting the Capital's green, Low-carbon, and Circular Development

In 2020, Beijing included the establishment of a pilot zone for green finance reform in the 14th

Five-Year Plan. It coordinated the city's efforts to promote the application and establishment of the pilot zone and other preparations for implementation. The first is to promote targeted financial support for the high-quality development of green industries. Beijing's green technological innovation leads in China, with 115 key laboratories and 51 engineering technology centers for relevant discipline. In Beijing, green buildings are developed in a large scale. The city has approved a total of 531 certified green building projects, and the building area of two-star and above accounted for 93.9%. The scale of green bond issuance in Beijing ranks first in China. The city supports the listing and financing of many green companies, and cooperates with the implementation of the national goals of peaking carbon dioxide emissions and carbon neutrality. It is also the first to issue carbon neutrality bonds. Nearly 90% of all green loans in Beijing are used for energy conservation and environmental protection, clean energy, green buildings, and green transportation. The second is to promote Beijing Municipal Administrative Center to concentrate more green financial resources from a high starting point. Around the construction of green finance pilot sites, the administrative center attracts green and low-carbon funds, investment institutions that uphold the ESG concept, and green finance think tanks to establish offices. The third is to carry out international exchanges and cooperation on green finance with high standards. Beijing held the second plenary meeting of the *Green Investment Principles (GIP) for the Belt and Road*, the EU-China Green Finance Forum, the second ESG Investing Forum for Asset Management in China, and other major events. The fourth is to deepen the construction of a carbon emission trading market at a high level. In 2020, the transaction price of carbon quotas was four times the national average. The Beijing Environment Exchange was renamed as the Beijing Green Exchange. The construction of green financial infrastructure continued to accelerate.

(II) Chongqing: Accelerating the Application and Establishment of a Pilot Zone for Green Finance Reform and Innovation

In 2020, Chongqing carried out strategic deployment in accordance with the goals of peaking carbon dioxide emissions and carbon neutrality and accelerated the establishment of a pilot zone for green finance reform and innovation. First, it effectively completed the top-level design. Chongqing clarified the carbon emission reduction target for the construction of the pilot zone and established a preliminary "1 + N" development mechanism that integrates green finance and green industry. Second, it has observed high standards. In accordance with the national unified green finance standards, Chongqing formulated specifications for green project evaluation and built a database of carbon emission reduction projects. Third, it has improved the infrastructure. Chongqing launched the Yangtze River Green Finance system, which has functions such as statistical monitoring and intelligent identification of green projects. Fourth, it has improved incentives and restraints. Chongqing encouraged some districts and counties to introduce green finance awards and supplementary rules and realized the intelligent one-key generation of green credit performance evaluation in the city. Fifth, it has strengthened innovation. Financial institutions in Chongqing launched 140 green financial products. Their green loans and green bond balances totaled more than RMB 300 billion, an increase of more than 30% throughout the year. Chongqing Rural Commercial Bank became the first Equator Bank in mid-western China and the first banking institution that took part in UK-China Climate and Environmental Disclosure Pilot.

(III) Shenzhen: Green Finance Supporting the Opening up and Innovation of the Guangdong-Hong Kong-Macao Greater Bay Area

To implement the *Outline Development Plan for the Guangdong-Hong Kong-Macao Greater Bay Area* issued by the CPC Central Committee and the State Council, Shenzhen has taken green development as an opportunity, explored for green finance reform and practice, and further promoted the construction of a green finance system. In 2020, Shenzhen introduced China's first green finance regulation, the *Regulation of Shenzhen Special Economic Zone on Green Finance*, which won the Global Green Finance Innovation Award of the International Finance Forum (IFF). Shenzhen actively develops regional cooperation and exchanges. It initiated the establishment of the Guangdong-Hong Kong-Macao Greater Bay Area Green Finance Alliance with Guangzhou, Hong Kong, and Macao. The secretariat of the alliance is permanently based in Shenzhen. Besides, the Green Finance Committee of Shenzhen Society for Finance and Banking and the UNEP International Network of Financial Centres for Sustainability (C4S) jointly proposed a Laboratory for Green Financial Services for the Real Economy, which has been officially established. The lab has carried out the research project of "Research and Practice Exploration on Solid Waste Disposal" in the Greater Bay Area, aiming to give play to the supporting role of green finance in the construction of a "zero-waste city".

Section 3　Green Finance Supporting Pollution Prevention and Key Areas of People's Livelihood

In 2020, green finance continued to increase support for key projects of pollution prevention and control and key areas of people's livelihood, including ecological value compensation, "zero-waste cities", green buildings, garbage classification, clean heating, disposal and recycling of waste in livestock and poultry breeding, and the treatment of black and odorous water bodies. The exploration for sustainable financial support approaches continued. The goal is to continuously satisfy the low-carbon and circular development and the people's growing demand for a beautiful ecological environment.

I. Green Finance Making Progress in Promoting Ecological Value Compensation

Establishing mechanisms for realizing the value of ecological products is an important strategic focus for implementing the green development requirements of the CPC Central Committee and the State Council. To realize the value of ecological products at the national level, the mainly approach is financial transfer payments, including vertical ecological conservation compensation and horizontal ecological conservation compensation. For example, in the natural forest conservation and conversion of farmland to forests, the average compensation standard for national public welfare forests is RMB 5 per mu per year, and the compensation standard for national public welfare forests owned by collectives and individuals is RMB 15 per mu per year. Every year, the Central Government allocates part of the funds for water pollution prevention and control as guidance and reward funds to support 19 provinces (autonomous regions and municipalities) in the Yangtze River basin. In this way, the Central Government has improved the compensation mechanism for horizontal ecological conservation in the river basin. In addition, China has been conducting trials of carbon emission trading for more than 10 years, which has further enriched the channels for realizing the value of ecological products.

The realization of the value of ecological products at the local level includes government-oriented ecological conservation compensation and market-oriented industrial operation. For example, since 2019, the Office of the Leading Group for Promoting the Development of the Yangtze River Economic Belt has approved Zhejiang's Lishui, and Jiangxi's Fuzhou to carry out pilot projects of the mechanism for realizing the value of ecological products. The two places have formed the Ecological Loan model in which ecological products transform into ecological capital. Zhejiang's Anji has formed the Two Mountains Bank model for the industrial operation of ecological products. Lishui established a linkage incentive mechanism that connects ecological behaviors and financial credit. It has also launched the innovative Two Mountains Credit Loan and the Ecological Theme Card. Guangzhou established a market-oriented ecological compensation mechanism that combines the carbon market and carbon inclusiveness. Based on the deployment of the fight against poverty, Chongqing has carried out "carbon sink +" pilot projects for realizing the value of ecological products in the aspects of carbon compliance, carbon neutrality, and carbon inclusiveness. The forestry carbon sink projects in Wanzhou, Youyang, and Zhongxian generated about 1.9 million tons of carbon sinks.

II. Green Finance Supporting the Continuous Advancement of the Construction of "zero-waste cities"

In 2020, with the support of green finance, the "11+5" pilot cities and regions[①] continued to promote the construction of "zero-waste cities" and have achieved positive results. Among them, China Emissions Exchange exerted the role of green finance in supporting the construction of a "zero-waste city" relying on the Laboratory for Green Financial Services for the Real Economy. The lab has carried out the research project of "Research and Practice Exploration on Solid Waste Disposal" in the Greater Bay Area. The city built four synergistic networks for solid waste treatment, namely, the communication and coordination mechanism among governments for solid waste treatment in the Greater Bay Area; the layout, supervision, and coordination mechanism for solid waste treatment facilities; the solid waste treatment technology synergistic network; and the Guangdong (Shenzhen) solid waste trading platform. By the end of 2020, the system design and function development of the Shenzhen Hazardous Waste Trading Platform have been completed. The platform will cover more than 10,000 companies engaging in hazardous waste in Shenzhen. It can provide enterprises with "one-stop" online services for contract signing, testing, and payment. Shaoxing City in Zhejiang Province has established a business model of "insurance + credit evaluation + platform supervision" through the cooperation of insurance institutions, environmental regulators, and enterprises. An integrated environmental risk prevention and control system enabled by green finance for waste-related enterprises has been formed to minimize the environmental risks of solid waste, especially hazardous waste. As of the end of 2020, more than 150 potential environmental risks were investigated for 20 companies covered by the insurance. The total premiums were RMB 929,600, and the insurance coverage was RMB 135 million.

III. Coordinated Development of Green Finance and Green Buildings

In July 2020, the Ministry of Housing and Urban-Rural Development, the Development and Reform Commission, Ministry of Education, Ministry of Industry and Information Technology, the People's Bank of China, State Administration, China Banking and Insurance Regulatory Commission jointly

---

① The "zero-waste city" construction pilot zones are Shenzhen City in Guangdong Province, Baotou City in Inner Mongolia Autonomous Region, Tongling City in Anhui Province, Weihai City in Shandong Province, Chongqing City (central area), Shaoxing City in Zhejiang Province, Sanya City in Hainan Province, Xuchang City in Henan Province, Xuzhou City in Jiangsu Province, Panjin City in Liaoning Province, and Xining City in Qinghai Province. Besides, Hebei Xiong'an New Area, Beijing Economic and Technological Development Zone, Sino-Singapore Tianjin Eco-City, Guangze County in Fujian Province, and Ruijin City in Jiangxi Province as special cases, promote the construction against the standard of the "waste-free city" pilot zones.

issued the *Action Plan for the Creation of Green Buildings* (MoHURD [2020] No. 65). The Plan clearly states that in 2022, green buildings should account for 70% of the newly built buildings in cities and towns that year. It also calls on strengthening fiscal and financial support and improving the policy environment for green finance to support green buildings. In August, the Ministry of Housing and Urban-Rural Development, Ministry of Education, Ministry of Science and Technology, the Ministry of Industry and Information Technology, Department of Ecology and Environment, Ministry of Natural Resources, the People's Bank of China, Market Supervision Administration, and China Banking and Insurance Regulatory Commission jointly issued the *Opinions on Accelerating the Industrialization of New Buildings* (MoHURD [2020] No. 8). It proposes to increase financial assistance and support new construction industrialization enterprises to finance by issuing enterprise bonds and corporate bonds. Green financial support should be given to new construction industrialization projects that meet the star-level standard of green buildings. It also proposes to encourage localities to set up special funds to support the development of construction industrialization without adding new hidden debts.

In terms of credit, information about building energy efficiency and green buildings is included in the special statistical system of the People's Bank of China for green loans and the green credit statistical system of the China Banking and Insurance Regulatory Commission. In terms of insurance, trials of green insurance application are carried out, including green building performance insurance and ultra-low energy building performance insurance. An "insurance + service + technology + credit" model is created to provide credit enhancement, risk control services, and loss compensation for green building projects. In August 2020, PICC P&C signed the first green building performance insurance agreement under the new model of "insurance + service + technology + credit". In terms of bonds, real estate and urban investment companies support the open construction of green buildings by issuing corporate bonds, publicly offered corporate bonds, private placement bonds, and medium-term notes.

Column 4-2

Cases of Coordinated Development Between Green Finance and Green Buildings

I. Huzhou Experience

In March 2020, the Ministry of Housing and Urban-Rural Development, the People's Bank of China, and the China Banking and Insurance Regulatory Commission jointly approved

Huzhou to implement the coordinated development of green buildings and green finance under the framework of the pilot zone for green finance reform and innovation. Its practice focuses on setting an implementation system for the green building standard, the innovation of green financial support methods, and the development of supporting incentives. Huzhou became China's first pilot city for the coordinated development of green buildings and green finance, with remarkable results in the past year.

First, the implementation of pilot policies has accelerated. Huzhou issued the *Promotion Plan of Huzhou Municipality for the Coordinated Development of Green Buildings and Green Finance*. The *Plan* clearly indicates that by 2021, urban green buildings will account for more than 99% of new buildings in the city. Huzhou also issued the *Opinions on Accelerating the Quality and Development of Green Buildings*, which includes 16 supporting measures covering industry, fiscal, finance, and government investment management. The floor area ratio of green prefabricated buildings is approved to increase from 4% to 7%. The loan limit of the green building provident fund is lifted by 10%.

Second, Huzhou has tried out some standard systems. Huzhou has improved the local standards for green building evaluation and developed China's first set of green building loan identification rules. It clearly stipulates that for green building projects that meet 5 conditions, their loans issued by financial institutions can be counted as green credit. (The 5 conditions: 1. obtaining green building pre-certification; 2. the land transfer contract or project filed as green building; 3. purchasing green building performance insurance; 4. relevant entities with good credit records; and 5. with access to the self-discipline mechanism for information disclosure.) This move has effectively solved the mismatch between the green finance support and green building deadlines and information asymmetry. In addition, the Municipal Bureau of Housing and Urban-Rural Development and the Municipal Finance Office jointly organized the setting of standards for green building project identification, green building development loans, and consumer loans.

Third, a variety of financial products have been developed. 36 banking institutions in Huzhou developed 114 innovative products, including the Greenfield Loan, the Green Purchase and Construction Loan, and the Mortgage Loan for Green Constructors. An RMB-1.5-billion coordinated special fund for green investment loans was established. Green industry funds with a total scale of RMB 30.4 billion were established. Anji County launched China's first Green Rural Housing Loan. China's first "insurance + service + credit" insurance for green building performance was also implemented in Huzhou.

As of the end of 2020, the balance of green building loans in Huzhou was RMB 7.544 billion, an increase of 129.86% throughout the year. The balance of green loans for the construction sector accounted for 7.25% of all green loans.

II. Qingdao Experience

In December 2020, the Ministry of Housing and Urban-Rural Development, the People's Bank of China, and the China Banking and Insurance Regulatory Commission jointly approved Qingdao to carry out the pilot work of green city development. In the initial stage of the pilot, Qingdao promoted green finance to support green urban development from policy implementation, and product innovation & application.

First, the Qingdao Municipal Government issued the *Opinions on Accelerating the Development of Pilot Green Cities*, which divides the pilot work into four categories and 27 specific tasks. The document clarified the task of building a green financial system, which mainly includes spreading the market application model, building a regular electronic platform for financial institutions and enterprises, setting up a green development fund and promoting the development of green bonds, It also aimed to establish a market-oriented resource allocation structure for urban-rural development characterized by green financing, and improve the interconnected development mechanism of green city and green finance.

Second, the supporting mechanism for green finance were explored. We focused on strengthening cooperation with financial institutions and business entities, guided banking institutions to satisfy financing needs in the field of green cities, formed strategic partnership with six financial enterprises (institutions) such as China Construction Bank, and obtained financial support for green cities worth of RMB 350 billion. At the same time, we increased the scale of green credit, rolled out more innovative products, issued the country's first performance insurance policy for ultra-low energy consumption buildings, as well as the "carbon reduction insurance" policy for energy-efficient buildings, offered the province's first 10-million-yuan "carbon neutrality" loan and the first 500-million-yuan "carbon neutrality" bond, and worked hard to harness capital to charter a new course for green city development.

Third, a green insurance pilot was launched. The owner of the passive housing demonstration project (Phase II) in Sino-German Ecological Park insured for ultra-low energy consumption buildings. The insurance company organized a third-party risk control service provider to supervise the construction of the insured buildings from start to finish. If the annual heating consumption, annual cooling consumption and air tightness of the insured project failed to meet the performance requirements of ultra-low energy consumption buildings, the insurance company would pay for the upgrading costs of the project, or offer compensation for the extra energy consumption. The company would also cover the corresponding appraisal costs and legal costs in line with the insurance contract.

IV. Green Finance Facilitating Orderly Garbage Classification

The pilot zones use green financial instruments to control the growth rate of waste and improve the efficiency of waste treatment. Huzhou launched the innovative Park Loan, credit card loading points, and green credit loans. They promoted low-level, small, and scattered enterprises to enter industrial parks for unified pollution treatment. They also inicreased residents' awareness of garbage classification and encouraged them to form a green lifestyle. Guangzhou launched a medicine replacement insurance. Bringing together the power of the government, pharmaceuticals, and insurers, this product provides residents with free replacement of expired medicine, reducing the pollution of expired medicine to the air, soil, and water.

V. Green Finance Supporting the Continuous Advancement of Clean Heating

Financial support for clean heating is an important way to help fighting pollution and making China's skies blue again. On the whole, cross-departmental collaboration, the construction of an information sharing mechanism, the innovation of financial products and services are key to promoting financial support for clean heating. In particular, the improvement of relevant credit standards has further improved the efficiency and accuracy of financial support for clean heating.

(I) Multiple Measures in Changzhi, Shanxi

As one of the "2+26" key cities along the air pollution transmission channel in the Beijing-Tianjin-Hebei region, Changzhi in Shanxi focuses on "joining forces, standard-setting, optimization of services, and data platforms" to steadily promote green finance to support clean heating. From 2017 to 2020, Changzhi's financial institutions issued RMB 798 million in loans to clean heating companies. As of the end of 2020, the loan balance was RMB 373 million, a year-on-year increase of 69.17%, and the credit satisfaction rate was 85.7%. 298,000 households in Changzhi completed clean heating renovation, an increase of 16.41% year-on-year. The coverage rate of clean heating in the central area of the city and established areas of the counties of Changzhi was 100%, and the coverage rate of clean heating in rural areas was 88%.

The main practices of Changzhi are as follows: First, issuing the *Standard for Clean Heating Loans*. It clarifies the conditions of the loan subject, loan application, the issuance process, post-loan management, and penalties, which provides a unified standard for clean heating credit products for banks and enterprises. Second, continuing to optimize financial services through refinancing of small businesses, direct monetary policy tools, and product innovation. Take Changzi Rural Commercial Bank as an example. As of the end of 2020, the bank lent RMB 9.3 million to clean heating companies from the special re-loan limit for small enterprises at an annual interest rate of 4.35%. It used direct tools to renew the loan of RMB 14.4 million without repayment for clean heating enterprises, and refunded the interest of RMB 669,000. It also launched the Thermal Power Loan and the Biogas Loans to help more than 450 rural households achieve clean heating. Third, strengthening the construction of the monitoring platform and the information platform for clean heating. As of the end of 2020, the monitoring platform recorded the basic data of 566,000 clean heating farmer households, an increase of 18.7% year-on-year. These data make reference for financial institutions in credit services and risk prevention and control for clean heating companies. As of the end of 2020, 8 financial institutions and 8 clean heating companies in Changzi were all connected to the information platform, which has promoted the exchange of information between the government, banks, and enterprises and fund issuance.

(II) Xinjiang Making Innovations in Credit Models

As of the end of 2020, the balance of green loans for the clean construction, operation, and transformation of urban central heating systems in Xinjiang was RMB 3.892 billion, accounting for 6.18% of the balance of green loans for the green upgrade of infrastructure. Financial institutions in Xinjiang strengthened the innovation of credit models to effectively solve companies' problems. China Construction Bank Changji Branch provided Wujiaqu Capital Heating Hongda Thermal Power Co., Ltd. with a basic construction loan of RMB 580 million to fill the funding gap in its project through the "PPP+franchise" model. In this way, the bank helped the enterprise realize comprehensive utilization of waste heat from power plants for heat supply. Kunlun Bank developed the Blue Sky Loan. It treats state-owned enterprises and private enterprises indiscriminately in terms of customer access and interest rates, and effectively addresses difficulties in financing and high financing costs for private enterprises. As of the end of 2020, local financial institutions granted loans of RMB 4.169 billion to 20 power generation and heating companies and a cumulative investment of RMB 2.324 billion.

VI. Green Finance Supporting Innovation in Disposal and Recycling of Waste in Livestock and Poultry Breeding

In 2020, Gongqingcheng City in Jiangxi Province and Longyou County in Zhejiang Province' Quzhou City continued carried out pilot programs and explord effective ways to financially support the disposal and recycling of waste in livestock and poultry breeding. Fuzhou City in Jiangxi Province and Rongchang in Chongqing increased financial support for the recycling of livestock and poultry manure based on local actual needs.

(I) The Gongqing Model of Jiangxi Promoted around the Province

Gongqinig in Jiangxi's Ganjiang New Area continued to promote the Clean Breeding Loans. Two livestock and poultry breeding companies in Gongqing received Clean Breeding Loan of RMB 9.8 million, which helped the disposal of 7,855 tons of manure in the year. The dry manure and biogas they produced were used for farming on 4,000 acres of land and domestic power generation of the companies, saving RMB 840,000 in production costs.

The Gongqing Model has been promoted around Jiangxi Province. In 2020, the Jiujiang Central Branch of the People's Bank of China promoted Xiushui County to issue the *Plan of Xiushui County for the Pilot Zone for Livestock and Poultry Breeding and Manure Recycling*. It set up a risk compensation fund of RMB 5 million. It also organized the Bank of Jiujiang and Jiangzhou Rural Commercial Bank to explore for innovating the pledge model of the third-party income right and issuing loans to enterprises for upgrading environmental protection facilities. The Bureau of Animal Husbandry, the Live Pig Association, and other departments of Dongxiang District in Fuzhou jointly launched a three-in-one mortgage loan model for the breeding management right, which integrates the Certificate of Project Registration of the Development and Reform Commission, the Qualification Report of Environmental Assessment, and the Qualification Report of Animal Epidemic Prevention. As of the end of 2020, Dongxiang Rural Commercial Bank issued Smart and Clean Livestock and Poultry Breeding Loans of RMB 49.3 million to 16 pig breeding companies.

(II) The Fiscal-financial Collaboration in Rongchang, Chongqing

The livestock and poultry industry in Rongchang District in Chongqing is well developed. Rongchang Pig is one of the world's eight excellent local pig breeds and among the top three in China. Its brand value ranks first among local pig brands in China. In recent years, as livestock and poultry breeding expand in an organizational manner and at a large scale, the district faces great pressure from the pollution load and land consumption of livestock and poultry breeding. The land carrying capacity and environmental carrying capacity of some towns and sub-districts have reached the limit, and resource and environmental constraints have become tighter. Rongchang District has launched an innovative "fiscal-financial collaboration" model to promote disposal and recycling of waste in livestock and poultry breeding in the district as a whole. In 2020, the balance of loans for livestock and poultry manure as financial support was RMB 114 million, a year-on-year increase of 89.19%. 290 large-scale breeding farms and eligible small and medium-sized breeding farms in 20 towns and sub-districts in Rongchang upgraded their facilities, with a total investment of RMB 91.033 million. The comprehensive recycling rate of livestock and poultry manure was 93.23%. 100% of the large-scale farms were equipped with manure treatment facilities and equipment. The district generated 872,000 tons of manure, and the recycled manure was used in 118,000 mu (7,866.67 ha) of farmland, saving 14,000 tons of chemical fertilizer and generating RMB 28 million in economic benefits.

The main practices of Rongchang District are as follows. First, improving mechanisms and the policy system. Yongchuan Central Branch of the People's Bank of China, together with the Rongchang District Bureau of Finance, the District Bureau of Animal Husbandry, and other departments, issued the *Implementation Plan of Rongchang District for the Financial Support for the Green Development and Recycling of Livestock and Poultry Manure*. Yongchuan Central Branch also promoted the Rongchang District Government to issue the *Guiding Opinions of Rongchang District on the Promotion of Loans for the Pig Industry*, which guides financial institutions to support the pig industry. The second is the fiscal-financial coordinated support. Rongchang District increased direct financial subsidies. In 2020, the financial subsidy reached RMB 49 million. It also increased indirect financial support. The Agricultural Assistance Loan, a risk compensation fund of RMB 10 million, was set up, with 1 : 10 magnification, to play the role of leverage. It also used re-loan funds to support livestock and poultry breeding companies and reduce corporate financing costs. The third is innovating financial products and services. Financial institutions inspected livestock and poultry breeding companies and solved their financing difficulties on a one-on-one basis. The Agricultural Bank of China Rongchang Sub-branch launched the ABC Two-way Guaranteed Payment System based on the Pig Stock Exchange platform, a national live pig trading market of Chongqing (Rongchang). The average daily transaction volume of the system was RMB 15 million-40 million. It also launched the Live Pig E-commerce E-loan with the Pig Stock Exchange. In 2020, the bank issued 82 Live Pig E-commerce E-loans with a total amount of RMB 20.51 million.

VII. Green Finance Supporting the Treatment of Black and Odorous Water Bodies and Other Key Areas of Pollution Prevention and Control

The Ministry of Housing and Urban-Rural Development, the Ministry of Ecology and Environment, the People's Bank of China, and other departments actively support financial institutions to use market mechanisms to increase their efforts in treating black and odorous water bodies. More and more black and odorous water bodies have been eliminated in the established areas of municipalities directly under the Central Government, provincial capitals, and cities under separate state planning. As of the end of 2020, 98.2% of the 2,914 black and odorous water bodies in cities at the prefecture level and above were eliminated. China is committed to eliminating most of the black and odorous water bodies in the established areas of cities at the county level during the 14th Five-Year Plan period.

Column 4-3

Green Finance Supporting the Treatment of Black and Odorous Water Bodies: Guangdong Practice

Guangdong improves its policy framework, enhances the cooperation between the government and banks, strengthens the innovation of green financial products and services, and explores diversified financing models, to continuously increase financial support for the treatment of black and odorous water bodies. As of the end of 2020, the balance of green loans for the treatment of black and odorous water bodies in Guangdong cities was RMB 15.104 billion, a year-on-year increase of 31.23%. Most cities in Guangdong have basically eliminated the black and odorous water bodies.

The first is guiding policy banks to use PSL funds to support the development of black and odorous water treatment projects. Agricultural Development Bank Yunfu Branch used PSL funds to grant RMB 300 million in credit and RMB 229 million in loans to Yunan County's County Domestic Sewage Treatment Package PPP project. Its interest rate was 4.45%, 0.46 percentage points lower than the interest rate of the bank's own funds loans.

The second is strengthen government-bank and government-bank-enterprise cooperation. Ping An Bank Guangzhou Branch signed a memorandum of cooperation with Guangdong Yueke Group and Guangdong Construction Engineering Group for Guangdong Environmental Protection Fund. The three parties jointly initiated the parent fund for Guangdong Environmental Protection Fund of RMB 6.3 billion, leveraging social capital to domestic waste and sewage treatment in the east, west, and north of Guangdong.

The third is exploring diversified financing models. The People's Government of Guangdong

Province issued the province's first local government special green bond, which was also the first in the area of water resources in China. The total amount of issuance was RMB 2.7 billion, which was used for the construction of water resources allocation projects in the Pearl River Delta. China Development Bank Guangdong Branch employed the PPP model to increase investment in infrastructure construction projects such as water environment remediation and sewage treatment. It focused on supporting the construction of the Guangzhou Aquatic Ecological project, the Dongguan Aquatic Ecological project, and the PPP project of domestic sewage treatment in towns and villages in Suixi County and its supporting pipeline network engineering. Guangdong Nanhai Rural Commercial Bank raised funds by issuing green financial bonds and invested RMB 2.797 billion in green industries and projects. It supported the construction of environmental infrastructure projects such as the River Treatment Project in Lishui Town, Nanhai District.

CHAPTER V
In-depth Development of International Cooperation in Green Finance

Green finance is an important area for China to participate in global economic and financial governance. In 2020, China actively promoted green finance to serve the community with a shared future for mankind. The country has carried out extensive cooperation on a global scale, and reached consensuses on green development with many countries and international organizations. The country has achieved significant results in implementing the *Green Investment Principles for the Belt and Road*, environmental information disclosure, and climate and environmental risk assessment. In September 2020, at the general debate of the 75th United Nations General Assembly, President Xi Jinping solemnly declared to the world that China will peak its carbon emissions before 2030, and strive to achieve carbon neutrality before 2060. This is the first time that China has put forward a carbon neutrality timetable on a formal global occasion. The move highlights the responsibility of a major country and is widely recognized by the international community. Later on, at the UN Biodiversity Summit and the Climate Ambition Summit, President Xi Jinping showed China's determination to participate in global environmental governance and made clear the series of measures to reduce carbon emissions by 2030. That is, by 2030, China's carbon emissions per unit of GDP will be reduced by more than 65% compared with that in 2005, the proportion of non-fossil energy in primary energy sources will reach about 25%, the forest stock will increase by 6 billion cubic meters over that in 2005, and the total installed capacity of wind and solar power will reach more than 1.2 billion kilowatts. The international community generally believes that China's proposals and initiatives have played an exemplary role and represent an important step to promote the building of a community with a shared future for mankind.

Section 1 Progress Made in the Green Finance Cooperation under the Belt and Road

The *Green Investment Principles for the Belt and Road* (GIP), as a set of voluntary guidelines, has been more generally recognized by relevant investment and financing entities. As of the end of 2020, 38 large international financial institutions and companies from 14 countries and regions signed the GIP, with total assets exceeding USD 41 trillion. The number of supporting institutions increased to 12, including global and regional financial service providers such as the Big Four accounting firms.

I. GIP Actively Implemented

(I) First Meeting of the GIP Steering Committee

On April 6, 2020, the GIP Steering Committee held its first meeting. The meeting discussed the mid- and long-term plans for the GIP and studied issues such as improving the GIP governance structure and building a professional secretariat. It also made recommendations on further promoting the implementation of the GIP. The suggestions included strengthening the environmental information disclosure of GIP signatories, tracking green investment flowing into the countries along the Belt and Road, and cooperating with other international initiatives and government departments of the countries along the Belt and Road.

(II) Second Plenary Meeting of GIP

On September 24, the second plenary meeting of GIP was held in Beijing. Nearly 140 delegates from more than forty financial institutions and international organizations around the world attended the meeting. It released the *2020 Annual Report of the Green Investment Principles for the Belt and Road*. First, the implementation of GIP was evaluated. Most GIP members announced sustainable development strategies and green transformation goals, and made progress in setting rules and regulations in accordance with international standards. However, from the perspective of best practice requirements, members still had work to do for improvement. Second, the key tasks of GIP in the future were clarified. They include (1) guiding members to further incorporate green development goals into company business and governance structure; (2) improving the sustainability assessment, risk assessment, and management capabilities of members; (3) organizing the compilation of manuals for best practices of green investment and environmental information disclosure; (4) encouraging members to release more green financial products; (5) supporting the construction of the green Belt and Road; and (6) setting information disclosure improvement goals for members in accordance with the requirements of the Task Force on Climate-Related Financial Disclosures (TCFD). Third, the GIP mid- and long-term plans were put forward. GIP's Visions 2023 include five key pillars, namely, self-assessment, information disclosure, green commitment, increased investment, and member development.

II. Deepening the Green Finance Capacity Building of the Belt and Road

(I) Developing Climate and Environmental Risk Assessment Tools for GIP

At the end of 2019, the First Working Group of GIP initiated the development of environmental and climate risk assessment tools for Belt and Road projects. In 2020, ICBC, its secretarial entity PricewaterhouseCoopers, and the GIP Secretariat led 15 members to jointly promote environmental risk analysis. They developed CERAT, a climate and environmental risk assessment tool for GIP, and introduced it to the internal testing and research phase. The tool is capable of measuring the carbon emissions of projects in the energy, transportation, and power industries. At present, CERAT is available to GIP members with the calculation function and to visitors for browsing.

Column 5-1

Overview of CERAT

The Industrial and Commercial Bank of China, Pricewaterhouse Coopers (PwC), and the GIP Secretariat led 15 members to complete the first phase development of the Climate & Environmental Risk Assessment Toolbox (CERAT). Internal tests were carried out among GIP members.

CERAT is a project-based comprehensive accounting tool for carbon emission reduction. Embedded with different project types and technologies, it can calculate carbon emissions for "green" and "brown" projects. CERAT is available in both Chinese and English, with a software interface in the corresponding language. On the surface, there is a user guide, an instruction on the carbon emission calculation logic, and carbon emission standards in different regions (such as the EU and China) for users to fill in and calculate according to actual projects. Users can directly download the report on project carbon emissions.

Next, the First Working Group of GIP will continue to optimize CERAT and add measurement modules, such as pollutant discharge, water risk, and biodiversity, in due course.

(II) Developing a Belt and Road Framework for Environmental and Climate Information Disclosure

In 2020, the Industrial Bank and Cadbury Bank jointly led the GIP Working Group on Environmental and Climate Information Disclosure to develop a reporting framework for members' implementation of GIP principles and environmental information disclosure. The framework is based on the best practices of the market, combined with the recommendations of the Task Force on Climate-Related Financial Disclosures (TCFD) and the actual conditions of GIP members. Under the framework, the GIP Secretariat evaluated the implementation of GIP and information disclosure by members and presented the GIP Best Practice Award to outstanding members. The award is for encouraging the implementation of green investment principles and increasing the breadth and depth of information disclosure.

(III) Cooperation in the Green Finance Capacity Building of the Belt and Road

GIP held five online seminars. The topics covered carbon emission calculation tools; environmental, social and governance (ESG) information disclosure; and the innovation of green financial products. The seminars aimed to strengthen knowledge sharing and experience exchange among financial institutions in the partner countries along the Belt and Road. The Belt and Road Bankers' Roundtable led by the Industrial and Commercial Bank of China has become an important platform for mutual assistance, cooperation, and capacity building among commercial and financial institutions in countries along the Belt and Road. Based on market demand and their advantages, China Development Bank, Export-Import Bank, Agricultural Bank, and Bank of China also delivered training on the sustainable development of the Belt and Road Initiative.

The Research Center for Green Finance Development of Tsinghua University supports Mongolia, Kazakhstan, Pakistan, and other countries along the Belt and Road to set definition standards for green finance and develop environmental benefit assessment tools for green projects. It also initiated the Green Finance Leadership Program (GFLP) with the International Finance Corporation and other institutions. In 2020, GFLP held two large capacity building events themed by "Environmental Information Disclosure of Financial Institutions and Green Bond Issuers" and "Green Recovery in the Post-pandemic Era and Green Finance in Promoting Biodiversity Conservation", respectively. 3,000 financial industry policymakers, executives, professional service agency experts, and people from all sectors from more than 60 countries and regions participated in the events.

(IV) The Classification System for Belt and Road Overseas Projects

In 2019, the Ministry of Ecology and Environment and its Chinese and international partners jointly initiated and established the BRI International Green Development Coalition. In December 2020, the Coalition released the classification system for Belt and Road overseas projects as the guidelines for stakeholders in identifying and responding to the ecological and environmental risks of overseas investment and selecting key projects. The system suggests that investment projects be classified into encouraged cooperation (green), general impact (yellow), and key supervision (red), based on their impacts on environmental pollution prevention and control, climate change mitigation, and biodiversity conservation.

III. Financial Institutions Actively Supporting the Construction of Belt and Road

(I) The Export-Import Bank's Belt and Road Green Investment Practice

First, the Export-Import Bank made renewable energy projects a priority for overseas investment in 2020. It provided credit support for a number of Belt and Road green projects, including the Suki-Knari hydropower station project in Pakistan; the sewage treatment plant project in Ulaanbaatar; the 2400-MW clean coal-fired power station project Hassyan, Dubai. Second, in equity investment for participation and holding, the Export-Import Bank allocated special funds of USD 37 million and RMB 330 million to support the green economy. They included USD 19.50 million in 1 green economy project through the ASEAN Fund; RMB 330 million in 13 projects through the China-Japan Energy Conservation and Environmental Protection Fund, promote the listing of 2 projects; USD 17.5 million in a 250 MW photovoltaic power station in Poland through China-Central and Eastern Europe Investment Cooperation Fund Phase II invested. Third, the Credit Guarantee and Investment Facility (CGIF) supported the development of the green economy with credit enhancement guarantee. It provided guarantees for 3 overseas green bonds in total, with a guarantee liability balance of approximately USD $353 million.

(II) Silk Road Fund's Belt and Road Green Investment Practice

The Silk Road Fund practices the new development concept. It has incorporated the principles of sustainable investment into the company's investment decision-making and management and steadily promoted the high-quality co-construction of the Belt and Road. In August, 2020, as the

Chapter V In-depth Development of International Cooperation in Green Finance

Regional Comprehensive Economic Partnership Agreement (RCEP) was signed, the Silk Road Fund and Kohlberg Kravis Roberts & Co. jointly invested in a waste disposal project in South Korea. Taking this opportunity, the Silk Road Fund learned Korea's leading technical standards and management experience in medical solid waste treatment. Furthermore, it discussed the introduction of these standards and experience to help optimize and upgrade China's solid waste industry. In September, the CSP and new energy platform projects in Dubai, where were invested by the Silk Road Fund, won the Best Green Financing Project of the Year of GIP.

The Silk Road Fund actively promotes the green governance of companies with projects that it has invested in. Among them, SIBUR International GmbH (Russia) has continued its efforts in energy saving and emission reduction. Its assessment ranking in 2020 exceeded the average of European companies and petrochemical companies around the world. With its outstanding achievements in saving fuel and improving efficiency, Orient Overseas (International) Limited won the Hong Kong Awards for Environmental Excellence and the Fuel Efficiency Award in Seatrade Maritime Awards Asia in 2020.

Section 2 Engaging in and Leading Multilateral International Cooperation on Green Finance

I. Playing an Important Role in Governance and Research of Contral Banks and Supervisors Network for Greening the Financial System (NGFS)

The Central Banks and Supervisors Network for Greening the Financial System (NGFS) is an important platform for China to participate in international cooperation on green finance. The People's Bank of China is one of the members of the NGFS Steering Committee and participates in decision-making on important matters bearing on the development of NGFS. By the end of 2020, the full membership of NGFS had increased to 84 central banks and financial institutions as well as 13 observers. On December 15, the Federal Reserve declared to join NGFS, becoming the 84th member.

Since 2018, PBOC has chaired the Micro Prudential Working Group, focusing on issues such as how to incorporate environmental and climate risks into the prudential regulatory framework and the practice of financial institutions in disclosing environmental and climate risks. In September

2020, the Working Group completed the *Overview of Environmental Risk Analysis by Financial Institutions* and *Case Studies of Environmental Risk Analysis Methodologies*, which summarized the key steps of environmental risk analysis, provided methods, tools and application cases for banks, asset managers, and insurance companies to conduct environmental risk analysis, and represented important public goods for the financial sector to improve the level of environmental risk assessment and management.

At the same time, to meet the needs for climate related macro research, NGFS officially established a research working group in September 2020, chaired by the PBOC. The research working group plans to focus on the impact of biodiversity loss on the financial system in 2021 and how to mobilize more funds to protect biodiversity.

Column 5-2

A Brief Introduction to the *Overview of Environmental Risk Analysis by Financial Institutions*

The *Overview of Environmental Risk Analysis by Financial Institutions* (the *Overview*) introduces typical cases where environmental risks evolve into financial risks. It introduces the environmental risk analysis tools and methods commonly used by banks, asset managers and insurance companies in an easy-to-understand manner.

The *Overview* points out that the promotion and application of environmental risk analysis in the financial sector still face many challenges. For example, the sector has not yet fully understood environmental risks nor realized their relevance to financial risks. Public data and methodology for assessing environmental risks are generally lacking. Financial institutions have insufficient investment and capacity in environmental risk analysis. Pollution-related risk analysis and environmental risk analysis of emerging economies are inadequate. Existing environmental risk analysis methods are still incomplete, and data quality is also problematic.

To encourage financial institutions to carry out environmental risk analysis, the *Overview* puts forward the following six recommendations. First, central banks and other financial regulators should take the lead in carrying out macro environmental risk analysis and release clear policy signals to financial institutions to clarify their determination to promote environmental risk analysis. They should also set standards to encourage financial institutions to carry out environmental risk analysis. Second, environmental risk analysis methods should be made

Chapter V In-depth Development of International Cooperation in Green Finance

available to the financial sector as public goods. Third, demonstration research projects in key industries or key regions should be supported. Fourth, an internationally recognized sound environmental disclosure framework should be established. Financial institutions should be encouraged to disclose their risk exposure to environmental and climate factors and the results of environmental risk analysis in accordance with TFCD recommendations. Fifth, Key Risk Indicators (KRI) and relevant statistical databases should be set up to enable financial institutions and regulators to identify, evaluate, and manage environmental and climate risks and improve the comparability of data. Sixth, a classification system for green and brown economic activities should be established.

II. Carrying Forward the G20 Consensus on Green Development

In 2020, spurred by the PBOC and other stakeholders, the G20 continued to focus on sustainable finance issues, and on how to achieve green, low-carbon economic recovery in the post-pandemic era. At the G20 Finance Ministers and Central Bank Governors' video conference hled in October 2020, participants generally believed that we should seize the window of post-pandemic recovery to advance low-carbon economic transformation. Green finance is an important lever to harness private sector funds and can make up for the capital gap in fighting against climate change. All stakeholders call on financial institutions and enterprises to integrate sustainable factors into investment decision-making and business activities, so as to amplify the effect of the government's low-carbon policy.

In November 2020, the G20 Leaders' Summit in Riyadh approved the *Declaration of the G20 Leaders' Summit in Riyadh*. The *Declaration* confirmed the important role of sustainable finance in global economic growth and stability, and clearly stated that "the development of sustainable finance and inclusive finance is vital to global economic growth and stability".

Supported by the PBOC and Europe, Italy became the rotating presidency of the G20 in 2021. It has regarded sustainable finance as the focus area of the G20 work agenda, and planned to restart the Sustainable Finance Research Group led by the PBOC in 2016, which would be co-chaired by the PBOC and the US Treasury Department.

III. Engaging in International Platform on Sustainable Finance (IPSF) Cooperation

IPSF was officially launched by eight members including the European Commission and the PBOC in October 2019. It aims to deepen international coordination and cooperation in the field of green and sustainable finance and mobilize private sector funds to carry out environmental sustainable investment. By the end of 2020, the number of IPSF members had grown to 14, and the member countries accounted for 50% of the national economic volume, total population and carbon emissions.

In October 2020, IPSF held its first anniversary online activity and released its first progress report. The report points out that COVID-19 has highlighted the urgent need for all parties to take concerted action and provide financing support for the sustainable development of the global economy. In recent years, sustainable financial markets have gained momentum in terms of scale and diversification, but they are yet to achieve the *Paris Agreement*. IPSF has basically sorted out the progress of member countries in green finance related fields, and believes that IPSF members are still in their infancy when it comes to green taxonomy, and many IPSF member countries are considering developing their own green taxonomy. To this end, the European Commission and the PBOC have established a Working Group on Green Taxonomy under the IPSF, which focuses on comparing the similarities and differences between China and EU green standards, and on this basis, puts forward a common classification scheme. The goal is to promote the coordinated development of the international green financial market and reduce the cost of green cross-border investment. In terms of sustainable information disclosure, most IPSF members have issued regulatory requirements for sustainable information disclosure and consider the transition to mandatory oversight. In terms of green label standards, more IPSF members are developing standards or labels for sustainable financial products and supporting regulatory standards or guidance documents to improve transparency and accuracy and resolve the risk of green washing.

Column 5-3

The Research on the Consistency between China and Other Countries in Green Finance Taxonomy is Making Progress

Green finance/sustainable finance standards have been established in major economies, and cross-border green capital flows become a more prominent trend globally. Against this backdrop, it is increasingly urgent to promote the compatibility of different green finance standards. In October 2019, the People's Bank of China joined the International Platform on Sustainable Finance (IPSF) on behalf of China to promote international cooperation in green and sustainable finance with European countries and members such as Argentina, Canada, and Morocco. In July 2020, China and the EU took the lead in setting up a working group to carry out a comparative study of the green finance/sustainable finance taxonomies of China and the EU. It sorts out the similarities and differences in the framework, scope of support, and technical standards between the taxonomies of the two sides, with an aim to propose a common standard scheme between China and the EU. The task force maintains an open attitude and recruits other countries for more suggestions. With the participation of technical experts from Canada, Japan, Singapore, and other countries, the task force is increasingly representative and influential.

By now, the technical task force's comparative analysis of green finance standards of China and the EU has achieved preliminary results that are commonly agreed, laying the foundation for the establishment of a consistent standard that is commonly recognized in the future.

I. The Green Finance/sustainable Finance Standards of China and the EU Agree in Environmental Objectives

The *EU Taxonomy* aims to provide policymakers, industries, and investors with a practical tool to identify environmentally sustainable economic activities and investment opportunities. The *Taxonomy* clearly sets six environmental objectives. An economic activity will be regarded as sustainable only if it substantially contributes to at least one of them and does no significant harm to the others. The six environmental objectives include climate change mitigation, climate change adaptation, sustainable use and protection of water and marine resources, transition to a circular economy, pollution prevention and control, and the protection and restoration of biodiversity and ecosystems. The *Catalogue of Projects Backed by Green Bonds (2020)* (Draft for Comments), China's representative green financial standard, shows three dimensions of environmental objectives: environmental improvement, climate change response, and resource conservation and efficient use. Despite the differences in classification and definitions, the actual coverage of the environmental objectives of the two sides basically overlaps and are highly consistent.

Table 5-1   Comparison of the Main Green Finance Objectives of China and the EU

EU's objectives	China's objectives
Climate change mitigation	Climate change response
Climate change adaptation	
Sustainable use and protection of water and marine resources	Environmental improvement
Transition to a circular economy Pollution Prevention and control, and waste recycling	
Pollution prevention and control	
the Protection and restoration of biodiversity and ecosystems	Efficient use of resources: transition to a circular economy, pollution prevention and control, and waste recycling

II. The Scope of Green Economic Activities in the Green Finance Standards of China and the EU is Highly Overlapping and Complementary

Although the two parties have different classification frameworks and methods for green finance standards, the green economic activities they support highly overlap. The *EU Taxonomy* has identified of green economic activities for the environmental objectives of climate change mitigation and climate change adaptation. The identification of green economic activities for other environmental objectives will be completed in the up-coming years. China's *Catalogue of Projects Backed by Green Bonds (2020)* (Draft for Comments) has completed the definition of green economic activities in all environmental objectives. The *EU Taxonomy* has not yet listed green economic activities for the environmental objectives such as the protection of ecosystems and pollution prevention and control. However, it does not mean that economic activities that substantial contribute to the above environmental objectives are opposed or excluded, or the green finance standards of the two parties are significantly different in the above areas. In the definition of green economic activities for the objective of climate change mitigation, which both sides have completed, their specific coverage highly overlaps. Especially in the area of renewable energy, the two sides support basically the same objects. In terms of industrial energy efficiency, the two sides have significant differences in the types of green economic activities. This reflects the differences in the industrial structure of the two parties, as well as the diversity of technological paths for low-carbon industrial transformation. This also suggests that to improve the compatibility of green finance standards, it is necessary to consider the industrial structure and characteristics of different industrial development stages in different countries and economies. While adhering to the consensus of environmental objectives, the assessment should include industries with a significant impact on specific environmental objectives in the local country or economy, from which we identify economic activities that substantially contribute to environmental objectives. This approach will enhance the representativeness and inclusiveness of the green finance standards.

III. China and the EU may Learn from Each Other in Green Finance Standards

By now, in addition to the initiators and leaders of the consistency research on green finance standards, i.e., China and the EU, more and more countries and international organizations have joined the program. This has laid a good foundation for the establishment of internationally recognized green finance standards. China and the EU are leaders in the research on green finance standards. Their green finance standards have their own unique advantages. Nevertheless, they can still learn from each other and improve their standards. For example, the

EU Taxonomy is clearer in terms of technical standards and benchmarks; China's *Catalogue of Projects Backed by Green Bonds* is highly representative in the areas and scope of green economic activities. When advancing the establishment of internationally recognized green finance standards, China should learn from the positive experience of other green finance standards such as the *EU Taxonomy*. The country should also reflect the reality of itself and other countries and economies in the same stage of development, and exert the influence and voice of China's green finance standards.

IV. Joining in the Sustainable Finance Task Force (STF)

In February 2020, the International Organization of Securities Commissions (IOSCO) established a Sustainable Finance Task Force (STF) under its Council to focus on regulatory issues such as issuer sustainable information disclosure and investor protection. China Securities Regulatory Commission joined the STF and actively participated in the work of sustainable disclosure of issuer information. It shared China's regulatory dynamics and business practices by filling in questionnaires and submitting industry seminar reports.

V. Stock Exchanges Actively Participating in International Cooperation on Green Finance

In July 2020, Shenzhen Stock Exchange joined the Special Advisory Working Group on climate information disclosure of the United Nations Sustainable Stock Exchange Initiative (UNSSE). The Working Group, jointly led by the London Stock Exchange and the Johannesburg Stock Exchange, aims to encourage global exchanges to disclose climate related information and provide issuers with workflow guidance and relevant comprehensive disclosure guidance in accordance with the TCFD framework. In August, with the consent of China Securities Regulatory Commission, Shanghai Stock Exchange joined the UNSSE Climate Information Disclosure Advisory Group. On June 29, 2021, UNSSE officially released the *Guidelines for Climate Information Disclosure* and the *Action Plan to Prepare the Market for Climate Change*. The relevant feedback offered by Shanghai Stock Exchange was adopted, and five green finance cases of Shanghai Stock Exchange were selected into the *Action Plan*. In September, Shanghai Stock Exchange was elected as vice chairman of the World Federation of Exchanges (WFE) Sustainability Working Group and continued to participate in the green finance work of international organizations. First, it participated in ESG database construction project and fed back index information such as green bonds and green ETF. Second, it participated in the sustainability research of global exchanges, shared powerful measures to practice sustainable development initiatives, and implemented the United Nations Sustainable

Development Goals (SDGs). Third, it participated in the formulation of global ESG standards. In November, in response to the *Advisory Opinions on Sustainable Development Reports* issued by the International Financial Reporting Standards (IFRS), Shanghai Stock Exchange, as vice chairman of WFE Sustainable Working Group, organized many meetings to listen to the opinions of auditing institutions, international asset managers, and other market organizations. Together with the chairman of the Working Group, the member exchanges were convened for discussion, and finally drafted WFE's supportive opinions for IFRS to develop a set of global unified sustainable development reporting standards.

VI. Some Financial Institutions Actively Joining International Platforms on Green Finance

The *Sustainable Blue Economy Finance Principles*, managed by the United Nations Environment Programme, aims to use the power of blue finance to rebuild marine prosperity and restore marine health and biodiversity. It is the world's first global guidance framework that provides sustainable blue economy financing for banks, insurance companies and investors. By the end of 2020, Industrial Bank and Bank of Qingdao had voluntarily signed the *Sustainable Blue Economy Finance Principles*.

Column 5-4

Sustainable Blue Economy Finance Principles

In 2018, the European Commission, WWF, the World Resources Institute (WRI) and the European Investment Bank (EIB) jointly developed the *Sustainable Blue Economy Finance Principles*.

1. Protective

We will support investments, activities and projects that take all possible measures to restore, protect or maintain the diversity, productivity, resilience, core functions, value and the overall health of marine ecosystems, as well as the livelihoods and communities dependent upon them.

2. Compliant

We will support investments, activities and projects that are compliant with international, regional, national legal and other relevant frameworks which underpin sustainable development and ocean health.

3. Risk-aware

We will endeavour to base our investment decisions on holistic and long-term assessments that account for economic, social and environmental values, quantified risks and systemic impacts and will adapt our decision-making processes and activities to reflect new knowledge of the potential risks, cumulative impacts and opportunities associated with our business activities.

4. Systemic

We will endeavour to identify the systemic and cumulative impacts of our investments, activities and projects across value chains.

5. Inclusive

We will support investments, activities and projects that include, support and enhance local livelihoods, and engage effectively with relevant stakeholders, identifying, responding to, and mitigating any issues arising from affected parties.

6. Cooperative

We will cooperate with other financial institutions and relevant stakeholders to promote and implement these principles through sharing of knowledge about the ocean, best practices for a sustainable Blue Economy, lessons learned, perspectives and ideas.

7. Transparent

We will make information available on our investment / banking / insurance actives and projects and their social, environmental and economic impacts (positive and negative), with due respect to confidentiality. We will endeavour to report on progress in terms of implementation of these Principles.

8. Purposeful

We will endeavour to direct investment / banking / insurance to projects and activities that contribute directly to the achievement of Sustainable Development Goal 14 ("Conserve and sustainably use the oceans, seas and marine resources for sustainable development") and other Sustainable Development Goals especially those which contribute to good governance of the ocean.

9. Impactful

We will support investments, projects and activities that go beyond the avoidance of harm to provide social, environmental and economic benefits from our ocean for both current and future generations.

10. Precautionary

We will support investments, activities and projects in our ocean that have assessed the environmental and social risks and impacts of their activities based on sound scientific evidence. The precautionary principle will prevail, especially when scientific data is not available.

11. Diversified

Recognising the importance of small and medium enterprises in the Blue Economy, we will endeavour to diversify our investment / banking / insurance instruments to reach a wider range of sustainable development projects, for example in traditional and non-traditional maritime sectors, and in small and large-scale projects.

12. Solution-driven

We will endeavour to direct investment / banking / insurance to innovative commercial solutions to maritime issues (both land- and ocean-based), that have a positive impact on marine ecosystems and ocean-dependent livelihoods. We will work to identify and to foster the business case for such projects, and to encourage the spread of best practice thus developed.

13. Partnering

We will partner with public, private and nongovernment sector entities to accelerate progress towards a sustainable Blue Economy, including in the establishment and implementation of coastal and maritime spatial planning approaches.

14. Science-led

We will actively seek to develop knowledge and data on the potential risks and impacts associated with our investment / banking / insurance activities, as well as encouraging sustainable finance opportunities in the Blue Economy. More broadly, we will endeavour to share scientific information and data on the marine environment.

Moreover, in 2020, Chongqing Rural Commercial Bank, Mianyang City Commercial Bank, and Bank of Guizhou formally adopted the *Equator Principles*, becoming another batch of Equator Banks in China following Industrial Bank (2008), Bank of Jiangsu (2017), and Bank of Huzhou (2019). Bank of Jiujiang joined the Principles of Responsible Bank (PRB), becoming the fourth Chinese bank to join after Industrial and Commercial Bank of China, Industrial Bank, and Hua Xia Bank.

Section 3 New Progress Made in Biliteral Cooperation on Green Finance

I. UK-China Climate and Environmental Information Disclosure Pilot going Deeper

In 2020, the UK-China Climate and Environmental Information Disclosure Pilot of Financial Institutions continued to advance.

First, the pilot institutions cover all types of financial institutions. Following the joining of Ping An Group, AVIC Trust, and PICC P&C in 2019, in 2020, Haitong Securities, Chongqing Rural Commercial Bank, and the leading group of the Huzhou Pilot Zone for Green Finance Reform and Innovation joined the pilot program. Bank of China, Bank of Jiangxi, and Bank of Jiujiang beceme observers. The Chinese pilot institutions expanded from the original 6 (ICBC, Industrial Bank, Bank of Jiangsu, Bank of Huzhou, China Asset Management, and E Fund) to 15 (including observers), covering industries of banking, asset management, insurance, and securities. The total assets managed by participating institutions amounted to more than RMB 90 trillion.

Second, the environmental information disclosure of pilot institutions has improved. China and the UK jointly released the second *Progress Report on UK-China Climate and Environmental Information Disclosure Pilot*. In terms of institutions, Industrial and Commercial Bank of China issued special reports for two consecutive years and benchmarked and indexed the reports with the TCFD framework in their appendices. Ping An Bank released an annual *Climate Change Report* in accordance with the TCFD framework. Bank of Huzhou issued also special reports. Furthermore, some insurers and trusts set up columns in their social responsibility reports or annual reports to disclose environmental information.

Third, the replication and promotion of pilot experience speeded up. On December 21, the Seminar on Environmental Information Disclosure of Financial Institutions and the 8th Meeting of the Working Group on UK-China Environmental Information Disclosure Pilot of Financial Institutions was held in Beijing. At the meeting, the Chinese Working Group released the UK-China Environmental Information Disclosure Framework for Financial Institutions (Chinese). On this basis, Industrial and Commercial Bank of China took the lead in the development of the *Guidelines for Environmental Information Disclosure of Financial Institutions*. The *Guidelines* were first tried out in pilot zones for green finance reform and innovation. They guided Zhejiang's Huzhou to achieve full disclosure of environmental information of financial institutions within its jurisdiction. In addition, the four pilot institutions, namely, Bank of Jiangxi, Industrial Bank, Bank of Jiangsu, and Haitong International, released the latest results and reports on environmental information disclosure. Among them, Industrial Bank and Bank of Jiangsu disclosed the results of stress tests in the green building and pharmaceutical and chemical industries; Haitong International announced the group's goal of carbon neutrality before 2025 and the path to achieve it.

II. Strenghening China-EU Cooperation on Green Finance and Building a Partnership for Green Development

On June 22, President Xi Jinping met with Charles Michel, President of the European Council and Ursula von der Leyen, President of the European Commission in Beijing via video link. They reached consensus in a wide range of fields such as green, low-carbon, and digital economy.

On July 28, Vice Premier Liu He and Valdis Dombrovskis, Executive Vice President of the European Commission, co-chaired the 8th China-EU High-level Economic and Trade Dialogue via video link. The two sides had in-depth, candid, pragmatic, and efficient discussions under the theme of "opening a new phase of China-EU cooperation in the post-pandemic era and leading the steady recovery and growth of the global economy". Content about green finance was listed as the 14th outcome of the dialogue. In the future, the two parties will strengthen information sharing and exchanges and cooperation in digital currency, sustainable finance, and financial technology, and explore and promote the convergence of green finance standards of China and the EU.

III. The 7th China-France High Level Economic and Financial Dialogue Strengthening Cooperation on Green Finance

On July 21, Vice Premier Hu Chunhua and Bruno Le Maire, Minister of the Economy, Finance and Recovery of France, co-chaired the 7th China-France High Level Economic and Financial Dialogue. The two sides had in-depth discussions on China-France cooperation on the battle against COVID-19 and international macroeconomic policy coordination, as well as China- France bilateral cooperation in key areas and major projects. Content about green finance was listed as the 21st outcome of the dialogue. The two sides agreed to continue to promote cooperation between the financial regulators of the two countries, including on sustainable finance. China welcomes eligible French institutional investors to invest in the Chinese bond market. China is willing to maintain communication with France on issues related to investment and bond issuance in the inter-bank bond market, and provide necessary support and convenience. China welcomes French banks and financial market infrastructure to apply for the access to the Cross-border Interbank Payment System (CIPSX). China and France jointly initiated and committed to promoting the work of the Network of Central Banks and Supervisors for Greening the Financial System (NGFS). The two parties will continue to strengthen cooperation in green finance, including ESG information disclosure, green asset risk weighting, and green finance to support biodiversity, for the purpose to jointly promote sustainable financial development.

IV. The Second China-Italy Finance Dialogue Strengthening Bilateral Cooperation on Green Finance

On November 11, Minister of Finance Liu Kun and Roberto Gualtieri, Minister of Economy and Finance of Italy, co-chaired the second China-Italy Finance Dialogue. To deepen China-Italy economic and financial cooperation, the two sides had in-depth discussions on the battle against COVID-19, macroeconomic policy coordination, global economic governance cooperation, and financial cooperation. They reached consensuses on many issues. Content about green finance was listed as the 14th outcome of the dialogue. The two sides will continue to strengthen cooperation in green finance, including cooperation under the NGFS framework. The two sides will encourage financial institutions from the two countries to sign the *Green Investment Principles for the Belt and Road*.

Section 4 More International Cooperation Practices of Market Institutions

I. Green Areas Supported by International Cooperation Expanding

In 2020, the green industries supported by Chinese financial authorities and international financial organizations expanded to energy-saving and environmental protection industries such as power generation by cement waste heat, new energy vehicles, comprehensive river management, and air pollution prevention and control; clean production industries such as medical solid waste treatment; clean energy industries such as hydropower, photovoltaic power generation, clean coal utilization, and renewable energy; green upgrade of infrastructure such as green smart public transport; and green finance research.

With the support of CSRC, China Institute of Finance and Capital Markets applied for and got the knowledge service and technical assistance project from the Asian Development Bank, i.e. "Sustainable development of green investment and financing and research on the construction of environmental disclosure index system for enterprises". The project would contribute to the continuous optimization of green financial market ecology.

Column 5-5

Leveraging the Advantages of On-lending to Promote International Sustainability

China continues to carry out on-lending cooperation with international financial institutions such as the New Development Bank, the European Investment Bank, and the KfW Bankengruppe, to promote the sustainable development of energy conservation and emission reduction.

In 2020, the Export-Import Bank obtained a special loan of USD 1 billion from the New Development Bank for key industries and areas hit hard by the COVID-19 pandemic and in urgent need to resume work, such as energy conservation and environmental protection, new and renewable energy, and public health construction. It also obtained the exclusive on-lending bank qualification for a EUR-500-million loan under the Sino-Austrian financial cooperation, with the OeKB as the upstream lender. The fund was dedicated to the construction of environmentally friendly infrastructure, climate and environmental protection, and environmentally friendly transportation. The Export-Import Bank used the on-lending to support the second phase of the comprehensive treatment of river water environment of the Huangxiaohe Airport, with an investment of RMB 3.9 billion. It is a major project integrating water quality purification, drainage improvement, and wetland landscape. It is also part of the comprehensive water governance project (to prevent flooding, drain flooded lands, treat sewage, and ensure water supply), which is vigorously promoted for the overall goal of coordinated conservation of the Yangtze River. It also leveraged on-lending to support the environmental protection upgrade and relocation project of Tangshan Steel Jiahua Coke Oven. The project can realize the efficient conversion and utilization of coal resources, and the dust removal rate of the adopted process is 99.9%, which has significant economic benefits and contributions to energy saving and emission reduction.

Hua Xia Bank issued an on-loan of EUR 10.63 million to Anhui Conch New Energy Co., Ltd. with a maturity of 11 years. The funds were used for the construction of the 12-MWh energy storage power station project of Huai'an Conch New Energy Co., Ltd. and the 32-MWh energy storage power station project of Zhangjiagang Conch New Energy Co., Ltd. The two energy storage projects are operated in the way of peak load shifting, and all electric energy is sold to Huai'an Conch Cement and Zhangjiagang Conch Cement at fair prices for use. At present, the two energy storage power stations are operating stably. This successful model is expected to be replicated and promoted in other cement plants.

II. Sharing China Experience and Strengthening International Green Investment Education

(I) Actively Promoting the Green and ESG Investment Practices of China

The first is to display the progress of ESG and other non-financial information disclosure of Chinese listed companies. In the World Investor Week of the International Organization of Securities Commissions (IOSCO), under the guidance of the Investor Protection Bureau of the China Securities Regulatory Commission, the Shanghai Stock Exchange launched a special program themed by "Social Responsibility of Listed Companies on the SSE STAR Market". It released the *Panorama on Investor Relations of Shanghai A-Share Companies from the Perspective of Big Data*, introducing useful practices in China's green financial investor education. Securities regulators, stock exchanges, 8 global or regional organizations, and investor associations from nearly 90 countries and regions participated in the World Investor Week. The Shenzhen Stock Exchange participated in the special roadshow for ESG of the Bank of America Merrill Lynch and the United Nations Principles for Responsible Investment Forum. In these events, it focused on topics of concern to foreign investors such as ESG and made introduction to Shenzhen listed companies.

The second is to strengthen international investors' understanding of ESG information disclosure with Chinese characteristics. On October 27–29, the Shanghai Stock Exchange held the Global Investor Conference 2020. The conference set up a special panel on ESG, and invited the People's Bank of China, the United Nations Conference on Trade and Development (UNCTAD), the World Federation of Exchanges (WFE), and the Luxembourg Stock Exchange to participate in the discussion on promoting the green recovery of the world economy after the pandemic to raise awareness of green development. At the roundtable of "Promoting High-Quality Development: ESG Practices of Chinese Companies", large domestic and foreign institutional investors, companies listed on the Shanghai Stock Exchange, and index companies at home and abroad were invited to talk about ESG opportunities and challenges from different perspectives.

The third is to organically integrate the international promotion of green finance with the ESG capacity building of listed companies, and promote listed companies to attach importance to ESG in strategic development. On September 25, the Shanghai Stock Exchange held an online workshop on "Dialogue with International Investors: How ESG Empowers Listed Companies". This session explained the importance of ESG information disclosure to listed companies from the perspectives of company quality and investment value, and spread ESG best practices of listed companies to global investors. Nearly 120 international investors and delegates from listed companies participated in the discussion.

(II) Sharing China's Experience in Promoting Post-pandemic Sustainable Recovery

In 2020, the COVID-19 pandemic raged all over the world. Shanghai Stock Exchange provided WFE and its member exchanges with pandemic response measures and business continuity plans to fulfill the social responsibility in international cooperation against COVID-19. Shanghai Stock Exchange, together with Luxembourg Stock Exchange, donated medical supplies to local hospitals in Luxembourg in the name of two exchanges, and worked with China Financial Futures Exchange to give away pandemic control supplies to Pakistan Stock Exchange. The actions indicated its willingness to join hands with global peers to fight the pandemic and tide over current difficulties. WFE, in its official magazine *Focus*, featured in May an English article on non-stop IPO in Shanghai Stock Exchange during the pandemic and its concrete actions to support the pandemic-hit areas.

In June 2020, Industrial and Commercial Bank of China participated the Global Investors for Sustainable Development (GISD) Leaders Extraordinary Meeting on COVID-19: Response and Recovery via video link. It promoted and introduced China's experience in pandemic prevention and control and restarting the economy. It also offered constructive opinions on promoting the recovery of the world economy and accelerating the implementation of the *2030 Agenda for Sustainable Development*. The meeting issued a GISD action statement, calling on global businesses to integrate the Sustainable Development Goals (SDGs) into their core business models and guide investment behaviors to promote a sustainable and resilient recovery of the world economy in the post-pandemic era.

CHAPTER VI
Green Finance Remains an Arduous Task

In the past few years, the global discussion on climate change has undergone fundamental changes. Countries have reached a broad consensus on the occurring of climate change. They have begun to focus on more constructive discussions and practices on how to deal with it. 126 countries and regions have formally declared or are considering proposing net-zero emission targets by the end of 2020, accounting for 51%[①] of total global greenhouse gas emissions. Net-zero emissions and carbon neutrality targets will greatly change the structure of the global economy, industries and investments. The existing financial system will need to go along with the historical trend and make structural adjustments for climate change adaptation and mitigation. Therefore, green finance has a long way to go and huge room for development.

From a domestic perspective, supporting green and low-carbon high-quality development in finance is an honorable and important mission given to the financial system by the CPC Central Committee and the State Council. The financial sector should focus on the goals of carbon peaking and carbon neutrality, continue to make top-level design of green finance, and make full use of the three major support functions of finance to support green development. First, through monetary policy, credit policy, regulatory policy, mandatory disclosure, green rating, industry self-regulation, and product innovation, financial resources will be guided and leveraged to low-carbon projects, green transformation projects, carbon capture and sequestration and other green innovation projects. Second, enhance the financial system's capability to manage climate and environmental risks through such means as stress testing of climate risk analysis, as well as environmental and climate risk analysis. Third, build a national carbon emission rights market, and develop carbon finance in an prudential and orderly manner, so as to contribute to the goals of peaking carbon emissions and

---

① Source: United Nations Environment Programme, Emissions Gap Report 2020. If the U.S. follows the Biden-Harris climate plan to achieve net zero greenhouse gas emissions by 2050, that percentage would increase to 63 percent.

carbon neutrality.

In order to achieve the above three functions and continuously enhance the financial system's ability to support economic recovery, green transformation and carbon reduction, in 2021 and the near future, we should accurately understand the connotations of the national policies on carbon emission reduction and economic green and low-carbon transition, grasp the rhythm and intensity of financial support for peak carbon dioxide emissions and carbon neutrality, and focus on improving the five pillars of green finance.

First, build a long-term mechanism, improve the top-level design of financial support for green and low-carbon transformation, and reduce the economic dependence on high-carbon industries, thus achieving sustainable economic development. We should study and introduce policies and measures to support carbon peaking and carbon neutrality, and make systematic arrangements for financial support to green and low-carbon development and climate change in the 14th Five-Year Plan and other top-level institutional designs. We should improve incentives and regulations and study the impact of climatic and environmental factors on monetary policy and financial stability. We should give full play to the fundamental role of the financial market in allocating resources, prevent short-term behavior of blindly pursuing growth without regard to the capacity of resources and environment, accelerate the transformation or orderly withdrawal of high-carbon industries, and focus on cultivating green industry segments such as green buildings, clean transportation and renewable energy. We should also support the R&D and promotion of green technologies, promote clean production, develop green and environmental industries, and accelerate the green and digital transformation of the industrial sector, thus gradually incorporating green consumption into the scope of green financial support and promoting green lifestyles.

Second, improve policy standards and promote the high-quality and sustainable development of green finance itself. On one hand, we need to further enrich the green finance policy toolbox. We should study and launch green finance regulations and other regulatory documents, and promote the establishment of a mandatory, market-oriented and law-based climate and environmental information disclosure system for financial institutions. The information disclosure template shall be gradually completed to help financial institutions calculate and disclose carbon emission information of their assets. The green finance performance evaluation mechanism of financial institutions shall be adjusted regularly and the application scenarios of green finance evaluation results shall be expanded, so as to provide effective incentives and regulations for green financial business. Besides, carbon emission reduction support tools will be created and preferential refinancing will be used to encourage financial institutions to increase preferential loan investment related to carbon emission reduction. We should also make climate and environmental risk analysis and stress tests to prevent and resolve regional or industry-specific financial risks that may arise from economic and industrial restructuring. On the other hand, we should take carbon neutrality as a constraint and further improve the green financial standard system. A unified new version of *Green Bonds Endorsed Projects Catalogue* shall be issued as soon as possible. According to the principle of "demand-oriented, urgent use first", a new list of green financial standards will be formulated, and implementation of mature standards shall be first tried in pilot zones. We will also deeply participate in the study of sustainable finance standards under ISO/TC 322 and continue to promote the convergence of green financial standards between China and Europe.

Third, innovate product services and enrich the multi-level green finance market system that directly reaches business entities. We need to innovate and develop products like ABS and ABN and study and promote cross-border trading of green financial assets and improve the liquidity of domestic green financial products. In developing digital green finance, we will strengthen the application of digital technology and financial technology in environmental information disclosure and sharing, and reduce the information asymmetry between financial institutions and green subjects. We will develop carbon financial products and instruments such as carbon funds and carbon bonds, and encourage futures exchanges to launch a greater variety of carbon futures, so as to expand the scope of participants in carbon market transactions. We will also encourage the private sector to set up low-carbon transition funds, while enriching green insurance products and encouraging insurance funds to invest in green areas. We should guide financial institutions to fully consider China's actual economic and social development and the stage of development and difficulty in transformation of various industries, and closely follow the carbon emission reduction policies of competent departments. On the one hand, while ensuring the sustainability of their own business, financial institutions should actively support the green and low-carbon transformation of relevant enterprises. On the other hand, they should adjust their asset structure steadily and orderly and avoid simply and rashly demanding early repayment from traditional high-carbon industries.

Fourth, promote local pilot projects and accelerate the replication of the beneficial experience of the green finance reform and innovation pilot zone. We will encourage the government of the pilot zone to raise funds and come up with new support approaches, and continue to enrich the innovation and development of the pilot zones for green finance reform and innovation under the new requirements of carbon peaking and carbon neutral. On the basis of the joint meeting mechanism for self-evaluation of the pilot zones, we will summarize and promote best practices of the pilot and make full use of their role as pilot demonstrations. We will also support pilot zones with outstanding performance to be upgraded into demonstration zones for green finance and start the expansion of the pilot zone in time to encourage more areas that are equipped and willing to make green finance reform and innovations.

Fifth, deepen international cooperation, and participate in and lead global financial governance with green finance. Adhering to the principle of "mutual benefit, win-win outcomes and common development", we will give full play to China's advantages in the huge scale of green finance market and mature policy system and continue to promote China's green finance policies, standards and best practices through multilateral and bilateral platforms such as the G20, Financial Stability Board (FSB), NGFS, IPSF, Bank for International Settlements (BIS), Basel Committee on Banking Supervision (BCBS), and Sustainable Banking Network (SBN). By telling China's story and contributing Chinese wisdom, we will integrate China's successful experience and advantageous resources with the "South-South Cooperation" and "Belt and Road" initiatives, and build our image as a responsible major country.

Marked by General Secretary Xi Jinping's solemn commitment at the United Nations General Assembly in September 2020, China's ecological civilization construction has entered a new stage with peaking carbon dioxide emissions and carbon neutrality as the key strategic direction. History has given us new missions and arduous tasks. Carbon control and emission reduction are of great benefit for this generation and the next. Supporting green low-carbon transformation and high-quality development, and helping to cultivate green industries with international competitiveness are the key tasks of China's financial work in the coming years. Upholding the concept of "lucid waters and lush mountains are invaluable assets", the financial industry should move forward with a broader vision and continue to fight for this cause of man and nature, striving for the best outcome of the Chinese nation for the Party, the country, and the people of the world.

APPENDIX I
Chronicle of Green Finance Events in 2020

On January 11, Beijing Environment Exchange held the 2020 Beijing Green Finance Seminar and Green Project Library Launch Ceremony. At the meeting, the green project library was officially launched, and the nationwide green project registration project was initiated.

On January 15–16, the Research Bureau of the People's Bank of China held the second Joint Meeting of the Pilot Zones for Green Finance Reform and Innovation in Huadu District, Guangzhou. The meeting deliberated the *2019 Evaluation Report on the Pilot Zones for Green Finance Reform and Innovation* and the *2019 Duplication and Promotion Plan for the Experience of Green Finance Reform and Innovation*.

On February 14, the People's Bank of China, the China Banking and Insurance Regulatory Commission, the China Securities Regulatory Commission, the State Administration of Foreign Exchange, and the Shanghai Municipal People's Government jointly issued the *Opinions on Further Accelerating the Construction of Shanghai as an International Financial Center and Providing Financial Support for the Integrated Development of the Yangtze River Delta Region* (PBOC [2020] No. 46).

On February 22, the General Office of the CPC Central Committee and the General Office of the State Council issued the *Guiding Opinions on Building a Modern Environmental Governance System*.

On February 27, Chongqing Rural Commercial Bank officially announced the adoption of the Equator Principles and became the fourth Equator Bank in China.

In February, the China Securities Regulatory Commission joined the Special Working Group on Sustainable Finance (STF) at the board level established by the International Organization of

Securities Commissions (IOSCO) and participated in tasks such as issuers' sustainable information disclosure.

On March 10, the Ministry of Housing and Urban-Rural Development, the People's Bank of China, and the China Banking and Insurance Regulatory Commission jointly issued the *Approval on Supporting Huzhou Municipality in Zhejiang Province to Promote the Coordinated Development of Green Buildings and Green Finance*. Huzhou became China's first pilot city for the coordinated development of green buildings and green finance.

On April 6, the *Green Investment Principles (GIP) for the Belt and Road* Steering Committee held its first meeting in 2020.

On May 15, Bank of Jiujiang officially became the fourth Chinese bank to sign the *Principles for Responsible Banking*.

On May 27, Shenzhen Stock Exchange participated in Merrill Lynch-Bank of America Securities ESG Forum, discussed ESG dynamics with Hong Kong Stock Exchange, Japan Stock Exchange and National Stock Exchange of India, and introduced ESG developments in the Shenzhen market to overseas investors.

On June 15, Shenzhen Stock Exchange was invited by the United Nations Principles for Responsible Investment (PRI) as a keynote speaker to introduce its ESG products at the PRI Forum.

On June 22, President Xi Jinping met with Charles Michel, President of the European Council, and Ursula von der Leyen, President of the European Commission, in Beijing via video link. They reached consensus in a wide range of fields such as green, low-carbon, and digital economy.

On July 14, approved by the State Council, the Ministry of Finance, the Ministry of Ecology and Environment, and the Shanghai Municipal Government jointly established the National Green Development Fund, with a registered capital of RMB 88.5 billion.

On July 20, Mianyang City Commercial Bank officially announced to adopt the *Equator Principles*, becoming the fifth Equator Bank in China.

On July 21, China and France held the 7th High Level Economic and Financial Dialogue. Content about green finance was listed as the 21st outcome of the dialogue.

On July 28, China and the EU held the 8th High-level Economic and Trade Dialogue. Content about green finance was listed as the 14th outcome of the dialogue.

In July, the Shenzhen Stock Exchange joined the United Nations Sustainable Stock Exchanges Initiative (UNSSE) Advisory Group on Climate Disclosure led by the London Stock Exchange.

On August 20–21, the Research Bureau of the People's Bank of China held the second Joint Meeting of the Pilot Zones for Green Finance Reform and Innovation in Gui'an New Area. The meeting deliberated the *Self-evaluation Report of the Pilot Zones for Green Finance Reform and Innovation* and the *Duplication and Promotion Plan for the Experience of Green Finance Reform and Innovation.*

In August, the Shanghai Stock Exchange joined the UNSSE Advisory Group on Climate Disclosure and participated in the first group conference call.

On September 4, 2020, under the guidance of the Green Finance Committee of China Society for Finance and Banking, the Green Finance Committee of Shenzhen Society for Finance and Banking, the Green Finance Committee of Guangdong Society for Finance and Banking, the Hong Kong Green Finance Association, and the Macau Association of Banks jointly established the Guangdong-Hong Kong-Macao Greater Bay Area Green Finance Alliance. The Green Finance Committee of Shenzhen Society for Finance and Banking serves as the secretariat.

On September 10, the Network of Central Banks and Supervisors for Greening the Financial System (NGFS) released the *Overview of Environmental Risk Analysis by Financial Institutions* and *Case Studies of Environmental Risk Analysis Methodologies.*

On September 19, the Annual Meeting of the Green Finance Committee of China Society for Finance and Banking and China Green Finance Forum was held in Beijing.

On September 24, the second plenary meeting of the *Green Investment Principles (GIP) for the Belt and Road* was held in Beijing.

On September 25, the Shanghai Stock Exchange held an online training session on "Dialogue with International Investors: How ESG Empowers Listed Companies" for companies listed on the SHSE and global investors.

In September, the Shanghai Stock Exchange was elected as the Vice Chair of the World Federation of Exchanges (WFE) Sustainability Working Group.

Appendix I Chronicle of Green Finance Events in 2020

In October, MSCI launched an exchange meeting with Shenzhen Stock Exchange on ESG investment and growth trends both at home and abroad.

On October 16, Yi Gang, Governor of the People's Bank of China, was invited to attend the online event for the first anniversary of the IPSF. He and Valdis Dombrovskis, Executive Vice President of the European Commission, jointly announced the establishment of a working group on taxonomies led by China and the EU.

On October 26, the Ministry of Ecology and Environment, the Development and Reform Commission, the People's Bank of China, China Banking and Insurance Regulatory Commission, and China Securities Regulatory Commission jointly issued the *Guiding Opinions on Promoting the Investment and Financing in Response to Climate Change*.

On October 27–29, the Shanghai Stock Exchange held the Global Investor Conference 2020. The Conference set up a special panel on ESG, where international organizations and institutional investors in China and beyond participated in the discussion on "Promoting the Green Recovery of the World Economy after the Pandemic" and "Promoting High-quality Development: ESG Practices of Chinese Companies".

On November 11, China and Italy held the second Finance Dialogue. Content about green finance was listed as the 14th outcome of the dialogue.

On November 13, Industrial Bank officially became the 27th signatory and 49th member of the United Nations *Sustainable Blue Economy Finance Initiative* in the world, and also the first Chinese signatory and member.

On November 15, the International Finance Forum (IFF) announced the winners of the Global Green Finance Innovation Award 2020. China Emissions Exchange won the award for its project of "Helping Shenzhen Special Economic Zone to Build a Green Financial System and Achieve Green Financial Legislation".

On November 16, Bank of Qingdao was approved by the United Nations Environment Programme (UNEP) and formally became the 50th member of the *Sustainable Blue Economy Finance Initiative* in the world.

On November 28, the Annual Meeting of China Society for Finance and Banking was held in Beijing. The theme of the meeting was "Finance Supporting the Dual-Circular New Development Pattern". Participating experts had special discussions on "Green Finance and 2030 and 2060 Goals".

On November 30, Bank of Guizhou officially announced to adopt the *Equator Principles* and became the sixth Equator Bank in China.

On December 10, the Seminar on China Green Finance Reform and Innovation Led by the Two Mountain Theory was held in Huzhou.

On December 12, President Xi Jinping delivered an important speech entitled *Building on Past Achievements and Launching a New Journey for Global Climate Actions* at the UN Climate Ambition Summit via video link. He announced a series of new measures of China.

On December 16–18, the Central Economic Work Conference was held in Beijing. The meeting outlined policy priorities in eight specific area in 2021, including to conduct work to peak carbon dioxide emissions by 2030 and achieve carbon neutrality by 2060. It required to formulate an action plan for peaking carbon dioxide emissions before 2030, support areas with favorable conditions to peak the emissions ahead of the schedule, and speed up the construction of national trading markets for carbon emissions.

In December, the EU-China Green Finance Forum 2020: ESG Special Session was successfully held in Beijing.

On December 21, the Seminar on Environmental Information Disclosure of Financial Institutions and the 8th Meeting of the Working Group on UK-China Environmental Information Disclosure Pilot of Financial Institutions was held in Beijing.

APPENDIX II
List of 2020 Green Finance Policies and Regulations

Notice on the Trial Implementation of Some Green Finance Standards in Green Finance Reform and Innovation Pilot Zones (PBOC [2020] No. 15), February 2020.

Opinions on Further Accelerating the Construction of Shanghai as an International Financial Center and Providing Financial Support for the Integrated Development of the Yangtze River Delta Region (PBOC [2020] No. 46), February 2020.

Guidelines of the Shenzhen Stock Exchange for Standardized Operation of Listed Companies (Revised in 2020) (SZSE [2020] No. 125), February 2020.

Guiding Opinions on Building a Modern Environmental Governance System, February 2020.

Special Provisions on Shareholding Reduction by Venture Capital Fund Shareholders of Listed Companies (Announcement of the China Securities Regulatory Commission [2020] No. 17), March 2020.

Notice on Issuing No. 2 Guidelines of Shanghai Stock Exchange for the Approval of Corporate Bond Issuance and Listing: Specific Types of Corporate Bonds (SHSE [2020] No. 87), March 2020.

Notice on Issuing Issuing the Interim Provisions of the Shanghai Stock Exchange on Application and Recommendation for Issuance and Listing of Enterprises on the STAR Market (Revised in April 2020) (SHSE [2021] No. 238), April 2020.

Notice on Issuing the Catalogue of Projects Backed by Green Bonds (Consultation Paper), July 2020.

Opinions on Financial Support for the Development of the Guangdong-Hong Kong-Macao Greater Bay Area (PBC [2020] No. 95), May 2020.

Implementation Opinions to Support the Healthy Development of Private Energy-Saving and Environmental Protection Enterprises (NDRC [2020] No. 790), May 2020.

Notice on the Work Concerning the Green Financing Statistical Rules (CBIRC [2020] No. 739), June 2020.

Guidelines of the Shenzhen Stock Exchange for Standardized Operation of Companies Listed on the Growth Enterprise Board (Revised in 2020) (SZSE No. [2020] No. 499), June 2020.

No. 2 Guidelines of the Shanghai Stock Exchange for the Implementation of the Self-Regulatory Rules for STAR Listed Companies: Voluntary Information Disclosure (SHSE [2020] No. 70), September 2020.

Guiding Opinions on Promoting the Investment and Financing in Response to Climate Change (MEE [2020] No. 57), October 2020.

Notice on Issuing No. 1 – 5 *Guidelines of Shenzhen Stock Exchange for Innovations of Corporate Bonds* (SZSE [2020] No. 1173), November 2020.

Measures for the Administration of Carbon Emissions Trading (for Trial Implementation) (Order of the Ministry of Ecology and Environment No. 19), December 2020.

Notice on Issuing the Implementation Plan for Quota Setting and Allocation for the National Carbon Emissions Trading 2019 – 2020 (Power Generation Industry), the List of Key Emissions Entities in the Quota Management of National Carbon Emission Trading 2019 – 2020, and Effectively Completing the Pre-allocation of Quotas for the Power Generation Industry (MEE [2020] No. 3), December 2020.

The Reform Plan of the Law-Based Environmental Information Disclosure System, December 2020.

Appendix III
List of Achievements in Building the System of Green Finance Standards in 2020

Serial Number	Name of Policy Document	Issuance Unit	Issuance Date
1	*Notice from the General Office of China Banking and Insurance Regulatory Commission on Relevant Work of Green Financing Statistical System*	CBIRC [2020] No.739	June 2020
2	*Notice on Issuing the Guidelines for the Application of the Review Rules for Issuance and Listing of Corporate Bonds of Shanghai Stock Exchange No. 2: On Specific Types of Corporate Bonds*	SHSE [2020] No. 87	November 2020
3	*Business Guidelines for Innovative Varieties of Corporate Bonds of Shenzhen Stock Exchange No. 1: On Green Corporate Bonds*	SZSE [2020] No. 1173	November 2020